Solutions to Social Problems

Lessons from Other Societies

Solutions to Social Problems

Lessons from Other Societies

FOURTH EDITION

D. STANLEY EITZEN

Boston • New York • San Francisco
Mexico City • Montreal • Toronto • London • Madrid • Munich • Paris
Hong Kong • Singapore • Tokyo • Cape Town • Sydney

Senior Series Editor: *Jeff Lasser*
Series Editorial Assistant: *Erikka Adams*
Senior Marketing Manager: *Kelly May*
Editorial-Production Service: *Omegatype Typography, Inc.*
Composition Buyer: *Linda Cox*
Manufacturing Buyer: *JoAnne Sweeney*
Electronic Composition: *Omegatype Typography, Inc.*
Cover Administrator: *Elena Sidorova*

For related titles and support materials, visit our online catalog at www.ablongman.com.

Between the time website information is gathered and then published, it is not unusual for some sites to have closed. Also, the transcription of URLs can result in typographical errors. The publisher would appreciate notification where these errors occur so that they may be corrected in subsequent editions.

Library of Congress Cataloging-in-Publication Data

Solutions to social problems : lessons from other societies / [edited by] D. Stanley
     Eitzen—4th ed.
         p.   cm.
     Includes bibliographical references.
     ISBN 0-205-48243-0 (pbk.)
         1. Social problems   2. Social problems—United States   3. Social policy.
     4. United States—Social policy.   I. Eitzen, D. Stanley.

HN17.5.S653 2007
361.10973—dc22

                                                                    2005056459

Printed in the United States of America

10   9   8   7   6   5   4   3   2   11   10   09   08   07   06

CONTENTS

Part Three:
Institutional Problems   89

Part Four:
Problems of People, Resources, and Place   167

Part Five:
Individual Deviance   197

PREFACE

This collection of readings is intended to supplement traditional textbooks for courses dealing with U.S. social problems. It fills a void because social problems textbooks, generally, have two fundamental shortcomings: (1) they focus too much on U.S. society, and (2) they are long on the descriptions of social problems and short on the policies to alleviate them. The readings included in this text present situations from other societies and demonstrate successful alternatives for overcoming the social problems that plague the United States.

This unique approach is timely and important for at least four reasons. First, social problems in the United States are worsening. To illustrate: the numbers of the poor and the near poor are increasing; the income and wealth inequality gaps are widening; incidents of racial discord are increasing; health care is rationed according to one's ability to pay; the inner cities continue to crumble from an inadequate tax base and shortage of jobs; and the degradation of the environment accelerates. These and other social problems require solutions or the United States will continue in a downward spiral.

Second, contemporary students must be prepared to live in a global environment. As parents, workers, and consumers, they are vitally affected by the global economy and other elements of globalization. In our interdependent world the political and economic events from around the globe impinge on the United States and its residents, affecting expenditures, taxes, public policies, and military strategies. Expanding our knowledge and our appreciation of other societies is important as we adjust to being responsible citizens of the world, as well as citizens of the United States.

Third, since the presidency of Ronald Reagan, the U.S. government has been dismantling the welfare state, which began under President Franklin Roosevelt. This process has accelerated since the terrorist attacks on the World Trade Center and the Pentagon on September 11, 2001. Declaring a war on terrorism, the Bush administration, with the support of Congress, invaded Afghanistan to rid that country of al-Qaeda terrorists and the Taliban. This was followed by a preemptive war against Iraq. To fight these wars and the scourge of terrorism, the president asked for and received much higher budgets for the military and homeland security. Simultaneously, President Bush and Congress passed a series of tax cuts to, it was argued, stimulate the moribund economy. Higher military expenditures combined with lower tax revenues resulted in huge government deficits. Any attempt to reduce these deficits resulted in cutting expenditures for social programs and thus a further weakening of the social safety net. This raises key questions: Is the reduction or the elimination of the welfare state a good idea? What will be the likely consequences? Will it solve or intensify social problems? Comparing the United States with more generous welfare states will help to answer these important questions.

Finally, a comparative examination of public policies regarding social problems will demonstrate what works under what social conditions. This is a crucial precondition for the formation of creative and workable social policies that will reduce or eliminate social problems in the United States.

The book is divided into five parts. Part One focuses on two important foundational issues: first, a comparison of the United States with other advanced industrial societies on a number of dimensions; and second, a consideration of why the United States fails to adopt social policies that appear to solve social problems in other industrial societies. Part Two examines inequality (poverty, income inequality, gender, sexual orientation, and age). Part Three looks at institutional problems (families, schools, work, and health care delivery). Part Four concentrates on problems of people, resources, and place (cities and environment). Part Five addresses the attempts by societies to control individual deviance (crime and drugs).

For each of the social problems considered, several articles have been selected. These either describe the situation in a single country or in multiple countries, or expressly contrast the situation of a country or countries with the United States. We have limited the sample of countries to the major industrial nations (Canada, the nations of Scandinavia and Western Europe, Australia and New Zealand, and Japan). In each instance, we invite the reader to assess *critically* the situation in the United States and in the nation or nations under examination, considering such questions as, Will the successful public policies used elsewhere work in the United States? If not, why not? If possible here, how might they be implemented?

While engaged in this comparative exercise, we must guard against the tendency to be either overly defensive about the United States or, at the other extreme, too accepting of the social policies of other societies. Regarding the first instance, we must acknowledge the magnitude of our social problems as a precursor to finding appropriate solutions. Regarding the second possibility, we must recognize that we cannot simply import the social policies of other societies without some modification. A sociologist, William Julius Wilson, has said:

> The approaches [used in Japan and the Western European nations] are embedded in their own cultures and have their own flaws and deficiencies as well as strengths. We should . . . learn from the approaches used in other countries and adapt the best aspects into our own homegrown solutions.[1]

ACKNOWLEDGMENTS

The first three editions were co-edited by Craig S. Leedham. Because of prior commitments Craig was unable to work on this edition. I am indebted to Craig for his valuable contributions to this project and for his friendship. I would also like to thank the reviewers of this edition for their comments and suggestions: James Crone, Hanover College, and F. Kurt Cylke, SUNY Geneseo.

[1]William Julius Wilson, *When Work Disappears: The World of the New Urban Poor.* New York: Alfred A. Knopf, 1996, p. 220.

Solutions to Social Problems

Lessons from Other Societies

PART ONE

Introduction

Section 1: The Comparative Approach to Social Problems

U.S. Social Problems in Comparative Perspective

D. STANLEY EITZEN

Social problems in the United States are worsening. Since 1970 two social scientists, Marc and Marque-Luisa Miringoff of Fordham University, have compiled an "Index of Social Health" for U.S. society (Fordham Institute for Innovation in Social Policy, 2003). This index includes measurements on sixteen major social problems, among them unemployment, percent of children in poverty, the gap between the rich and the poor, levels of child abuse, and health insurance coverage. This barometer of social problems, which is kind of a Dow Jones (stock market) average (the higher the score, the better), has declined from a composite score of 78 (out of 100) in 1973 to 46 in 2001. The trend is downward, despite reductions in infant mortality, high school dropouts, poverty among the elderly, homicides, and alcohol-related traffic fatalities. Among the declining indicators are child abuse, child poverty, teenage drug abuse, average weekly earnings, health insurance coverage, food stamp coverage, access to affordable housing, and the gap between the rich and the poor.

Not only are social problems in this country deteriorating for the most part, the United States does not compare favorably with other modern, advanced nations. This introductory essay addresses three fundamental questions. First, how does the United States compare to the other advanced industrial countries on a number of social problems? Second, what are the consequences of U.S. social policies regarding social problems? And third, why doesn't the United States adopt public policies that other countries have found successful in reducing or eliminating certain social problems?

WE'RE NUMBER ONE: THE UNITED STATES COMPARED TO ITS PEERS ON SOCIAL PROBLEMS

Americans are extremely competitive. We want to be the best in all things: Olympic victories, world records, getting to the moon first, harnessing the atom, finding a cure for AIDS, or whatever. So far, we have done remarkably well in these and other competitions. But there is one area where we outrank the other modern nations that is not a source of pride—*we are number one, or nearly number one, in the magnitude of social problems.*

Comparing the United States with the other major industrial nations, it ranks Number One in real wealth, number of billionaires, the amount of space in homes, defense spending and military capability, executive salaries, physicians' salaries, ethnic diversity, percentage of the population with access to safe drinking water, and the percentage of residents enrolled in higher education.

At the same time, however, the United States ranks first (i.e., worst) among its peers on a number of social problems indicators: murder rate, reported rapes, robbery rate, incarceration rate, the number of drunken driving fatalities, cocaine use, greenhouse gas emissions, contributions to acid rain, forest depletion, hazardous waste per capita, garbage per capita, the number of cars per capita (and the use of cars rather than public transportation), the number of children and elderly in poverty, homelessness, inequality of wealth distribution, bank failures, military aid to developing countries, divorce, single-parent families, reported cases of AIDS, infant mortality, the death of children younger than five, and teenage pregnancy.

Some additional facts underscore the depth of social problems in the United States relative to its peers: First, compared to its industrialized counterparts, the United States had the highest incidence of poverty (12.5 percent in 2003, U.S. Census Bureau, 2004). Among the industrialized nations, the United States has the highest rate of child poverty (17.6 percent). In 2003, 8.4 million children (11.4 percent of all children) were not covered by health insurance. Compared to its peers, the poor in the United States experience the longest periods in poverty. And, compared with Canada and the nations of Western Europe and Scandinavia, the United States eliminates much less poverty through welfare subsidies than any of the other 14 nations (Solow, 2000). Moreover, the United States ranks first in the percent of its children under 6 in poverty (at 18.5 percent in 2003); this rate is three to five times the rate of Western European nations.

Second, the United States is the only industrialized nation without some form of universal health care. As a result, in 2003 about 45 million people, or 15.6 percent of U.S. residents, lacked health coverage for the year. A 2002 study estimates that 18,000 adults in the United States die each year because they are uninsured and cannot get proper health care (Sternberg, 2002). The United States, however, has the most advanced health care system in the world and it spends 35 to 40 percent more for health care than the other industrialized countries. But because health care in the United States depends on ability to pay, the overall indicators of health are low with the poor disproportionately disadvantaged.

Third, the United States has the most unfair distribution of wealth and income in the industrialized world. There are several indications of this inequality gap in the United States.

• The gap between the chief executive officers and the average blue-collar workers who make the products is enormous—around 475 times as much in 2004. This measure of income inequality is much higher in the United States than in the other industrialized nations and is getting wider—up from 120-to-1 in 1990. Another indicator of this gap increasing is that between 1990 and 2000, average CEO pay rose 571 percent, while the pay of the average worker increased only 37 percent (Huffington, 2002). Actually the gap is even wider because the executives in the other countries pay higher taxes on their relatively lower incomes than do U.S. executives. Moreover, the workers in the other countries receive much more in nonmonetary compensation (e.g., universal medical care, subsidized child care), than do U.S. workers (Fischer et al., 1996:102, 122).

• Wealth inequality is also much more skewed in the United States than among its peers. The richest 13,000 families possess a net worth equivalent to the assets owned by the country's 20 million poorest families (Lapham, 2003). This wealth gap is greater than that of any other advanced nation.

• In 2001 the median net worth for families of color was $17,100, while it was $120,400 for white families (United For a Fair Economy, 2004). In terms of income: in 2003 whites averaged $46,119 compared to $29,692 for minorities (U.S. Census Bureau, 2004).

The historical evidence suggests that in the early part of this century (the 1920s are the earliest period for which data are available), wealth inequality was much lower in the United States than in the United Kingdom, and U.S. figures were comparable to Sweden. America appeared to be the land of opportunity, whereas Europe was a place where an entrenched upper class controlled the bulk of wealth. By the late 1980s, the situation appears to have completely reversed, with much higher concentration of wealth in the United States than in Europe. Europe now appears to be the land of equality (Wolff, 1995:21).

Fourth, as for cities: "None of the other industrialized democracies has allowed its city centers to deteriorate as has the United States" (Wilson, 1996:218). "No European city has experienced the level of concentrated poverty and racial and ethnic segregation that is typical of American metropolises. Nor does any European city include areas that are as physically isolated, deteriorated, and prone to violence as the inner-city ghettos of urban America" (Wilson, 1996:149). Many U.S. cities have child poverty rates higher than 35 percent and black child poverty rates of more than 50 percent.

Fifth, compared to its peers, the United States ranks first on a number of crime and criminal justice dimensions: the percentage of population who have been the victim of a crime; the murder rate (e.g., it is 6 times greater than the rate in Great Britain, 5 times that of Japan and Spain, and 22 times that of Austria) (Wellstone and Dauster, 2002); the murder rate of children; reported rapes (the U.S. rate was nearly three times higher than found in Sweden, the industrialized country with the second highest rate); and the rate of imprisonment (greater than any other industrialized nation). U.S. citizens constitute less than 5 percent of the world's population, yet the number of U.S. prison inmates amount to 25 percent of the world's prisoners. The United States incarcerates its citizens at a rate six times higher than Canada, England, and France, seven times higher than Switzerland and Holland, and ten times Sweden and Finland (Street, 2001).

Sixth, a comparative study of child supports for families (e.g., housing, health, education, welfare allowances, and tax benefits) found in fifteen nations ranked Luxembourg, Norway, France, and Belgium among the most generous countries; Denmark, Germany, the United Kingdom, Australia, and the Netherlands among those with middle range provisions; and Portugal, Italy, Ireland, Spain, Greece, and the United States as the nations with the least generous child benefit packages (Bradshaw et al., 1993). Since that study in 1993 the amount of government spending in the United States for social supports for families has declined further.

The litany of U.S. social problems could go on but the point has been made: *the United States has more serious social problems than those found in the countries most similar to it.* These other societies, like the United States, are modern, affluent, industrialized, democratic, and capitalist. Why, then, are the social problems in the United States of such greater magnitude?

THE CONSEQUENCES OF U.S. SOCIAL POLICIES REGARDING SOCIAL PROBLEMS IN THE UNITED STATES

Let's begin by describing the differences between the United States and the other developed nations on the dimensions that might affect the severity of social problems within societies. Most significant, the nations comparable to the United States devote a greater percentage of their Gross Domestic Product to social expenditures. The United States chooses to spend a smaller proportion of its budget on social security and welfare programs (housing, food, health, family allowance to single parents) than other advanced industrialized nations.

In contrast to the United States, the advanced industrial societies provide excellent, publicly funded health care for all of their citizens. In the United States, workers who do not have health insurance (about one-fourth) are not eligible for Medicaid, which is reserved for the poor. Those who do receive Medicaid often find the health services provided them insufficient for their needs. The situation is especially dire in difficult economic times such as the recession of 2001–2002, when states have reduced their funding of Medicaid. Moreover, because Medicaid does not compensate doctors as much as private health insurance, many doctors refuse to take Medicaid patients.

The other industrialized countries also provide much more support for parents than the United States does in such areas as family allowances, housing subsidies, publicly subsidized child care, and paid family leaves from work. In the United States, child care for working parents is tax deductible, which expands the benefits as income increases, thus providing the working poor with little benefit. The other developed countries have programs that provide maternity (and sometimes paternity) leaves with pay, whereas United States law requires that companies employing more than fifty workers must allow *unpaid* maternity leave. Workers in smaller enterprises may or may not receive family leaves depending on the whims of their employers.

The United States differs from the other developed countries in the way public education is organized. Education in the United States is decentralized with each of the 15,000 school districts responsible for much of the financing and curriculum decisions for the local schools. This is in sharp contrast to the other countries where national standards are set and schools are financed much more equally. As a result of its emphasis on financing education through a heavy reliance on local property taxes, the U.S. school system is rigged in favor of the already privileged, with lower class children tracked by race and income into the most deficient and demoralizing schools and classrooms (Sklar, 1997).

Prekindergarten programs are universal in the other developed countries, while dependent on parents' resources in the United States. Compensatory preschool programs for the disadvantaged are underfunded in the United States, with only about one-fourth of those eligible actually receiving programs such as Head Start. Contrast this with the almost 100 percent of four-year-old French children and 98 percent of Belgian and Dutch children enrolled in preprimary programs. As a result of these differences, American students graduating from high school are more varied in their skills and aptitudes (and this is correlated with parents' income and with the wealth of school districts) than are their counterparts in other industrialized countries.

Public education is taken more seriously elsewhere. In contrast to the United States, teacher salaries are higher, more resources are spent on public education, the school year is longer, and, for those eligible, higher education through graduate school is subsidized.

The differences in worker benefits are considerable when comparing the United States to its more generous peers. Take wages, for example, where total compensation (wages, health benefits, vacations) for the typical U.S. worker in manufacturing has either remained flat or declined since the mid-1970s while it has increased by 40 percent for a European worker in a comparable job. In most of these societies, national law requires that workers receive such benefits as strong job security, four-week paid vacations, an ample minimum wage, and generous unemployment benefits (in some of these societies this is $1,000 a month indefinitely). In the United States, in contrast, job security is weak, paid vacations are not universal but depend, rather, on seniority and job status, and unemployment benefits are meager and short in duration. Moreover, more than twelve million workers labor for poverty wages, usually without health coverage or pension plans and about one-fourth of the entire workforce are temporary workers, part-timers, and "independent contractors," working for low wages, no health and pension benefits, and few, if any, basic legal protections for their health and safety on the job.

As we have seen, policies in the United States are much different in regard to its citizens than are the policies the other developed nations. The other societies are much more generous to their citizens, providing social supports that encourage equal opportunity and provide for the basic needs of income maintenance, housing, job security, and health care. To reiterate, the other developed societies have much more comprehensive programs that minimize economic deprivation and insecurity. The few supports found in the United States are now under severe attack. During the 1990s, even with a Democratic president, and in the 2000s, with President Bush and a Republican-controlled Congress, the federal government eliminated the Aid to Families with Dependent Children, reduced welfare benefits, and let the states devise and administer the program. Food stamps, legal services to the poor, housing subsidies, vaccination for children, school lunch programs, and the like have been reduced and remain under the threat of further reductions or elimination.

The prevailing ideology has two postulates. First, the unequal distribution of economic rewards is none of the government's business. Americans value individualism and the market economy. The obvious result is inequality and that is good because it motivates people to compete and it weeds out the weak. Whatever suffering that occurs is not the fault of society but lies, rather, in the actions of society's losers.

The second postulate of the current conservative creed is that government efforts to reduce poverty and class inequality actually cause those very problems. Welfare dependency, in this view, is the source of poverty, illegitimacy, laziness, crime, unemployment, and other social pathologies. They agree with Charles Murray that only when poor people are confronted with a "sink or swim" world will they ever really develop the will and the skill to stay afloat (Murray, 1984).

Acceptance of these two postulates leads to the obvious solution—do away with the welfare state and the quicker the better. This leads to these related questions: Will dismantling the welfare state be beneficial or will it create chaos? Will society be safer or more dangerous? Will crime rates increase or decrease? Will more or fewer people be on the economic margins?

I believe that the answers to these questions are self-evident. Society will be worse off rather than better off. The number on the economic margins will rise. Hunger and homelessness will increase. Crime rates will swell. Public safety will become much more problematic.

One result will be the exacerbation of the already high degree of income and wealth inequality. This phenomenon has serious implications for society. As one sociologist has concluded, "Growing inequality erodes social solidarity" (Gitlin, 1995:225).

Criminologists have shown that poverty, unemployment, and economic inequality are powerful determinants of street crime (DeKeseredy and Schwartz, 1996). As shown earlier, crime rates (e.g., homicide, robbery, and rape) are much higher in the United States than in the more generous welfare states. As a consequence, not only is society more dangerous but so is the economic cost of imprisoning so many.

The generous benefits in the social democracies are costly with income, inheritance, and sales taxes considerably higher than in the United States. The trade-off is that these other countries have comprehensive, universal health care systems; pensions and nursing home care are provided for the elderly; families are supported with paid parental leaves; jobs are well paid and relatively secure; and poverty, hunger, and homelessness are relatively rare. In short, the people in the high tax, industrial societies feel relatively safe from insecurities over income, illness, and old age.

The United States, in sharp contrast, has the highest poverty rate by far among the industrialized societies, a withering bond among those of different social classes, a growing racial divide, and an alarming move toward a two-tiered society.

The United States is experiencing a dramatic rise in private schooling, home schooling, private recreational clubs, and in the number of walled and gated affluent neighborhood enclaves on the one hand, and ever greater segregation of the poor and especially poor racial minorities in segregated and deteriorating neighborhoods and inferior schools, on the other. Personal safety is more and more problematic as violent crime rates increase among the young. Finally, democracy is on the wane as more and more people opt out of the electoral process (e.g., in the 2000 election when George W. Bush was elected president 51 percent of those who could have voted *did not,* which meant that Bush became president with 24 percent of the votes of the electorate). The United States consistently has the lowest voter turnout among the industrialized nations, presumably the consequence of so many potential voters being alienated by their issues being trumped by big money contributions to candidates and political parties.

In sum, the comparison of U.S. policies with those of the generous welfare states leads to the following conclusion: we ignore the problems of poverty, wealth inequality, and a rationed health care system at our own peril. If the United States continues on the present path of ignoring these and other social problems or reducing or eliminating programs to deal with them, Americans will be less secure and there will be more problem people that require greater control at an ever greater social and economic cost.

BARRIERS TO THE ADOPTION OF MORE GENEROUS WELFARE STATE POLICIES IN THE UNITED STATES

If the social policies of the other developed societies minimize social problems, why doesn't the United States adopt them or at least try to modify them to fit our situation? There are significant barriers that make such social changes very difficult.

First, there is the fundamental American belief in competitive individualism. Americans celebrate and support individual rights. Seymour Martin Lipset puts it this way:

> *Citizens have been expected to demand and protect their rights on a personal basis. The exceptional focus on law here as compared to Europe, derived from the Constitution and the Bill of Rights, has stressed rights against the state and other powers. America began and continues as the most anti-statist, legalistic, and rights-oriented nation. (Lipset, 1996:20)*

The high value Americans place on individualism has several implications, all of which work against efforts for the collective good. First, the individual is exalted, which makes working for group goals difficult. Americans, typically, do not want to pay taxes for the good of others. Opinion surveys taken in various developed countries, for example, reveal that Americans are much less prone than Europeans and Canadians to favor measures to help the underprivileged (Lipset, 1996:145). Second, government intrusions into personal lives or into local schools or communities are opposed. Third, there is a resistance against efforts to establish preferential rights for disadvantaged groups (e.g., affirmative action based on race or gender). Fourth, Americans combat government handouts to those they deem undeserving. And finally, the strong emphasis on competitive meritocracy means that individuals are believed to be advantaged or disadvantaged because of their skills, effort, and motivation or the lack thereof. Thus, the affluent are venerated and the poor vilified.

A second barrier to the adoption of welfare state policies is political. To begin, the majorities in the federal and state legislatures are political conservatives, which means they will opt for reducing or eliminating the welfare state rather than expanding these government programs. The political debate in these assemblies is from the right to the political center, with little, if any, voice from the political left. As the U.S. population ages (the leading edge of the baby boomers are now in their late 50s), and the sunbelt states continue to attract population disproportionately, this tendency to elect centrist and right-of-center politicians will increase. Another political barrier is the two-party system, where both parties market their appeals to those categories most likely to vote: the affluent, the successful, and suburbanites—all categories interested in low taxes and the status quo. Moreover, the major parties are financed by big business and wealthy individuals, both of which favor low taxes and reduced social programs (Green, 2002). Also, the two-party system that has evolved in the United States makes it structurally difficult for third parties to emerge as viable alternatives.

The current political climate obstructs spending for social programs by reducing the amount available in two ways. First, there is the prevailing notion that to stimulate the economy, the government should provide tax breaks to the wealthy, who will invest it, and companies, who will then hire more workers. President Bush and a conservative Congress have applied this "trickle down" strategy in passing huge tax cuts through 2011. About 40 percent of this tax relief is targeted to the wealthiest 1 percent of the taxpayers, while the poorest 20 percent receive about 1 percent of the total relief (Tyson, 2002). Moreover, there is a push to make these tax cuts permanent and to eliminate the estate tax (a tax that falls only on the wealthiest 2 percent of the population).

A second way to limit social spending is by increasing government spending for defense. The 2006 fiscal budget for military spending was $420 billion (not counting the cost of the wars in Afghanistan and Iraq). Taking all military related expenditures into account, the United States outspends the combined budgets all other nations on defense.

When the federal government cuts its tax income while increasing its budget for defense, the shortfall is made up by reducing or eliminating social programs. Theoretically, the difference should be made up by the states but their fiscal budgets have been reduced by the economic downturn. For example, in 2002 some 41 states cut their Medicaid programs. If states can't match federal grants for child care, they lose out and, of course, so do the children from low-wage families in those states, as occurred in Alabama, Louisiana, Mississippi, Oklahoma, Texas, Utah, and Wyoming in 2001 (Dionne, 2002). Jesse Jackson put it this way, speaking just of defense:

> *War abroad drowns out desperation at home. We can read about the conditions of every faction, ethnic group or tribe in Iraq. But we read nothing about the growing desperation of poor people in this country. The president and the Congress have agreed to an unprecedented increase in our military budget. . . . There is money to erect missile defenses against countries that have no missiles. It always pays to be prepared. But there is no money to ensure heat in the winter for the poorest families in America (Jackson, 2003:15).*

And, we would add, no money to provide adequate inoculations, school lunches, Head Start, subsidized child care, legal services, unemployment compensation, health care, and the like as do the democracies in western Europe, Scandinavia, and Canada.

One of the necessary ingredients for a generous welfare state is the existence of a heavily unionized workforce. Strong unions use their collective clout to support issues favorable to the working class, as evidenced in Canada and the welfare states of Europe. The labor movement in the United States has fought for Social Security, Medicare, Medicaid, FHA mortgages, the GI Bill, civil rights legislation, voting rights legislation, student loans, and increasing the minimum wage. In the past, U.S. unions were a powerful force for economic security and social justice. But that was forty years ago when unions were strong. In the mid-1950s, 35 percent of all U.S. workers belonged to unions, 80 to 90 percent in major industries such as auto, steel, and coal mining. This percentage slipped to 28 percent in the mid-1970s and now is about 13 percent. Weak unions do not present a countervailing force against powerful business interests. The result is that efforts to expand the welfare state in the United States have no powerful ally.

CONCLUSION

The political-social-economic system of a society does not just evolve from random events and aimless choices. The powerful in societies craft policies to accomplish certain ends, within the context of historical events, budgetary constraints, and the like. Addressing the issue of inequality, Fischer and his colleagues say:

> *The answer to the question of why societies vary in their structure of rewards is more political. In significant measure, societies choose the height and breadth of their "ladders." By loosening markets or regulating them, by providing services to all citizens or rationing them according to income, by subsidizing some groups more than others, societies, through their politics, build their ladders. To be sure, historical and external constraints deny full freedom of action, but a substantial freedom of action remains. . . . In a democracy, this means that the inequality Americans have is, in significant measure, the historical result of policy choices Americans—or, at least, Americans' representatives—have made. In the United States, the result is a society that is distinctly unequal. Our ladder is, by the standards of affluent democracies and even by*

the standards of recent American history, unusually extended and narrow—and becoming more so (Fischer et al., 1996:8).

In other words, America's level of inequality *is by design* (Fischer et al., 1996:125).

Social policy is about design, setting goals and determining the means to achieve them. Do we want to regulate and protect more as the well-developed welfare states do or should we do less? Should we create and invest in policies and programs that protect citizens from poverty, unemployment, and the high cost of health care, or should the market economy sort people into winners, players, and losers based on their abilities and efforts? Decision makers in the United States have opted to reduce the welfare state. Are they on the right track or are there policies that the generous welfare states have adopted that might, with modification, reduce America's social problems? If societies are designed, should the United States change its design?

REFERENCES_____

Bradshaw, J., J. Ditch, H. Holmes, and P. Whiteford. 1993. "A Comparative Study of Child Support in Fifteen Countries." *Journal of European Social Policy* 3(4):255–271.

DeKeseredy, W. S., and M. D. Schwartz. 1996. *Contemporary Criminology.* Belmont, CA: Wadsworth.

Dionne, E. J., Jr. 2002. "America's Poor: War Wounded." *Washington Post National Weekly Edition.* (September 30/October 6):26.

Fischer, Claude S., Michael Hout, Martin Sanchez Jankowski, Samuel R. Lucas, Ann Swidler, and Kim Voss. 1996. *Inequality by Design: Cracking the Bell Curve Myth.* Princeton, NJ: Princeton University Press.

Fordham Institute for Innovation in Social Policy. 2003. *2003 Index of Social Health: Monitoring the Social Well-Being of the Nation.* Tarrytown, NY: Fordham University Graduate Center.

Gitlin, Todd. 1995. *The Twilight of Common Dreams.* New York: Henry Holt.

Green, Mark. 2002. *Selling Out: How Big Corporate Money Buys Elections, Rams Through Legislation, and Betrays Our Democracy.* New York: Regan Books.

Huffington, Arianna. 2002. "Upstairs/Downstairs." *Progressive Populist.* (November 15):14.

Jackson, Jesse. 2003. "Bush, GOP Give Cold Shoulder to Nation's Poor." *Progressive Populist* (January 1–15):15.

Lapham, Lewis H. 2003. "When in Rome." *Harper's* 306 (January):9–11.

Lipset, Seymour Martin. 1996. *American Exceptionalism: A Double-Edged Sword.* New York: W. W. Norton.

Murray, Charles. 1984. *Losing Ground: American Social Policy 1950–1980.* New York: Basic Books.

Sklar, Holly. 1997. "Imagine a Country." *Z Magazine* (July/August). www.deanza.edu/faculty/yuen/poli5/sklar.htm.

Solow, Robert M. 2000. "Welfare: The Cheapest Country." *New York Review of Books.* (March 23):20–24.

Sternberg, Steve. 2002. "Study Blames 18,000 Deaths in USA on Lack of Insurance." *USA Today* (May 22):1A.

Street, Paul. 2001. "Race, Prison, and Poverty," *Z Magazine. 14* (May):25–31.

Tyson, Laura D'Andrea. 2002. "Tax Cuts for the Rich are Even More Wrong Today." *Business Week.* (July 8):26.

United For a Fair Economy. 2004. "Wealth Inequality by the Numbers." *Dollars and Sense, 251* (January/February):20–21.

U.S. Census Bureau. 2004. "Poverty in the United States: 2003." *Current Population Reports*: 60–226.

Wilson, William Julius. 1996. *When Work Disappears: The World of the New Urban Poor.* New York: Alfred A. Knopf.

Wolff, Edward N. 1995. *Top Heavy: A Study of the Increasing Inequality of Wealth in America.* New York: The Twentieth Century Fund Press.

2

The European Social Model

T. R. REID

The following is from a chapter in T. R. Reid's The United States of Europe *devoted to describing the European social model. The essence of this model is that there is a shared commitment to a welfare state with cradle to grave benefits for all.*

Access to the generous benefits of the social model is seen as a basic right of every European—and the word *every* is crucial here, because the social model is relentlessly egalitarian. At the same time, paying for the social model is seen as a basic responsibility of every European. And this widely shared sense of the government's social responsibility to everybody is another unifying force that makes Europeans feel they all belong to a single place—a place, they believe, that is definitely not American.

The responsibility for all to help pay is reflected in the tax structure that supports the continent's extensive welfare programs. European nations have the same panoply of corporate and personal income taxes, inheritance taxes, property taxes, and so forth as the United States, with the same type of exemptions that essentially exclude the poorest citizens from paying these wealth-based taxes. But the European countries rely much more heavily than most of the world on sales taxes—the Europeans call them value-added taxes—which are paid by just about anybody who buys anything. This system was created deliberately to make sure that lower-income people help pay for the social system. . . .

But if the burden is spread fairly equally, the benefits of the public welfare programs in the European social model are also distributed with a fairly even hand. To Americans, it is simply a matter of common sense that rich families get better medical care and better education than the poor; the rich can afford the doctors at the fancy clinics and the tutors to get their kids into Harvard. But this piece of common sense does not apply in most of Europe. The corporate executive in the back seat of the limo, her chauffeur up front, and the guy who pumps the gas for them all go to the same doctor and the same hospitals and send their children to the same (largely free) universities. It's not that the truly rich are resented, or hated, in Europe. People who have made billions in business—people like Stelios Haji-Ioannou, the budget-airline wizard from Cyprus, or Britain's Richard Branson, or Austria's

Source: Excerpts from T. R. Reid, *The United States of Europe.* New York: Penguin Press, 2004, pp. 146–159.

Dietrich Mateschitz—are treated like heroes in their native countries. But no European would agree that a Stelios or a Mateschitz should get better health care or education just because they're rich.

This zeal for spreading the wealth fairly equally is reflected most dramatically in poverty rates. European nations certainly do have families living below the established poverty line (according to the definition preferred by the Organization for Economic Cooperation and Development, "poverty" means a family income at least 50 percent below the mean personal income in the nation as a whole). But they have a lot fewer poor families than the United States does. In America, about 20 percent of adults are living in poverty at any given time. In France, the comparable figure is 7.5 percent; it is 7.6 percent for Germany and 6.5 percent in Italy. Britain, with a somewhat leaner benefit system than its continental neighbors, has about 14.6 percent of its adults in poverty.

The helping hand of the social model is particularly evident when a worker becomes unemployed. Americans on the unemployment rolls tend to get a monthly government check, together with help in buying food and paying heat and light bills. At some level, when his savings fall low enough, an unemployed American worker may also apply for free government-supplied health care through Medicaid. In Europe, by contrast, a worker who is "made redundant"—that's the brutal British term for being laid off—will get a housing benefit, a heat and light benefit, a food benefit, a child care benefit, and a monthly unemployment payment that is almost always higher than the American standard. The European, of course, will have the same access as everybody else to the public health-care system. The American system, in which you lose your health insurance when you lose your job, strikes the Europeans as exactly backward. "I don't understand your approach to health care," a junior minister in Sweden's health department told me once. "It seems to me that your country takes away the insurance when people most need it.". . .

Of course, the welfare state also forces Europeans to pay sky-high taxes. And the plush arrangements provided for people who are out of work may explain why Europeans who are laid off tend to accept their fate as a fairly permanent condition, rather than getting up and looking for a new job. But these problems tend to be ignored, except by a few marginal voices on the right, because Europe in general assumes the social model is preferable to what's going on in other parts of the world. "The reason why Europe compares so favorably with the U.S. in respect of social and income mobility," Will Hutton says, "is that every European state sets out to offer equality of opportunity to all its people; the American neglect of the bottom 50 percent in the name of individualism is not reproduced in Europe."

The European social model involves a much bigger role for the public sector in daily life than Americans are comfortable with. The Public Broadcasting System (PBS) in the United States fills a fairly small niche in a TV and radio world dominated by giant private companies. In most European countries, by contrast, the public broadcaster tends to be largest and the most prestigious by far. Britain's BBC, funded by a tax of $170 per year paid by every home and office that has a television set, operates six TV and five radio stations. France's TF1, Germany's ARD, and Italy's RAI are more popular and more respected than any private network. Public transit systems are much more pervasive in Europe than in the United States, as are public art, public universities, and public medical systems. Public housing is so common in major European cities that it can't all be stuck away in a few big complexes. Instead, government-owned homes and apartment buildings are found in every neighborhood of every city and town. The inhabitants include not just the poor but a good proportion of the middle class as well. . . .

Europe's welfare state begins at birth, with government payments to each newborn citizen and generous support for parents. In essence, the European governments pay new parents to leave their jobs temporarily and stay home. "We have made a fairly basic decision," Valgard Haugland, the leader of Norway's Christian Democratic Party and the cabinet minister for children and family affairs, told me. "We have decided that raising a child is real work. And that this work provides value for the whole society. And that the society as a whole should pay for this valuable service. Americans like to talk about family values. We have decided to do more than talk; we use our tax revenues to pay for family values."

In a small but comfortable two-bedroom apartment on a leafy green hill high above the ice blue Oslofjord, I came face-to-face with Norwegian family values. When a beaming blue-eyed girl with golden hair was born to Martin Aenstad and his wife Suranhild, Suranhild decided to leave her job as a secretary in downtown Oslo and stay home to raise her daughter, Serine. This cost her nothing. Suranhild was "hired" by the Norwegian government to be the mother of her baby. The state paid her a yearly salary equivalent to $18,800, or 80 percent of what she made as a secretary. With the savings on clothes and commuting, Suranhild came out slightly ahead.

Shortly after Serine's first birthday, Suranhild went back to her office job; her employers were required by law to take her back, in the same position. At that point, Martin took over the parental slot, taking a year's leave from his job as a junior engineer and drawing his paycheck as a father for Serine's second year of life. Sitting in his cozy apartment here, with eighteen-month-old Serine bouncing happily on his knee, Martin Aenstad told me that he felt no qualms about being a stay-at-home father. "I've had jobs, and now I'm raising my daughter. And I can tell you that being a house-father is hard work. At least when I was on the job, they gave me a lunch break. If Serine is hungry or crying or has a full diaper—well, you try telling her that Daddy needs a lunch break." Martin's pay was considerably lower than his wife had received, because the second year of parenting only draws a third of the worker's normal salary. But Martin knew that his old job was waiting for him when his year as full-time daddy came to an end. For her third year, Serine would go to a state-run child-care facility called a Kindergarten.

The United States pays a small percentage of its mothers a monthly stipend to help them raise and feed their children. The recipients are known as "welfare moms," and are generally stigmatized as women who can't find a real job. Norway, in contrast—like most other European countries—treats the monthly payment to parents as a salary. Income and social security taxes are withheld, just as with any paycheck. The payment is specifically designed for working parents, to encourage them to leave their jobs for a while and raise their children. Parents who don't have a job outside the home also get a monthly benefit for raising children, but it is considerably less than the "surrogate salary" provided those who leave a job to be full-time parents. In America, the White House and state governors routinely boast about how much their welfare rolls are being reduced. In Norway, the government takes pride in statistics showing that the number of recipients has been growing rapidly. . . .

Once a European is educated, she moves on to the labor market and the broad array of employment rights that are considered a basic element of the social model. Wages are often not left to market mechanisms. They are set, either by unions or by government formulas, generally on a regional or sectoral basis, so that all auto companies, for example, pay all workers about the same weekly amount. As we have seen, mandatory programs of sick leave and family leave are far more expansive in Europe than the United States. Working hours tend to be restricted by law or union agreement. Italy and France have both made the thirty-five-hour week de rigueur. This doesn't mean that no worker can stay on for the thirty-sixth hour in a given week; rather, thirty-five hours is the point at which an employer is required to start paying overtime rates. This is supposed to encourage companies to hire more people—on the grounds that it is cheaper to pay a second man at the basic rate than to keep the first one on at overtime—but the economists don't agree on whether the laws have achieved that purpose. Holidays and paid vacations are generous; in much of Europe, a worker can expect five weeks of vacation from the first year on the job. British law mandates at least twenty-three days of paid holidays per year; France requires twenty-five days or more; Sweden, at least thirty. In contrast, the wretched overworked Americans have to get by with a meager four to ten mandatory paid holidays, depending on the state. . . .

In the United States, more and more employers are responding to the sharp increase in health-care expenses by dropping medical insurance altogether for their employees (or at least for their blue-collar employees). In the spring of 2004, some 45 million Americans had no health insurance whatsoever. That option is simply unthinkable in Europe. The notion that everybody must have equal access to health care is a basic and incontestable fact of European life. Universal medical care is one of the things Europeans always mention, with pride, when they talk about the differences between the EU and the United States.

For these reasons, public health systems are entrenched in Europe and cannot be replaced by private medical care. Even if a conservative government swept into power somewhere, the "socialized medicine" system would be untouchable.

3

The Swedish Welfare State

D. STANLEY EITZEN

The Swedish welfare state provides extensive public support for families and individuals, including universal health insurance, family supports for parents and children, programs to reduce the hardships of unemployment, elderly care, and subsidized housing. Swedish taxes are high to pay for these programs, but an important benefit of this investment has been to level extremes in wealth and poverty

Sweden is a prosperous and productive nation of 9 million (the facts on Sweden throughout this essay come from the "Fact Sheets on Sweden" series, 2001–2005). For a long time Sweden's population was ethnically homogeneous, but this has changed with immigration after World War II, resulting in some 20 percent of Sweden's current population being either foreign-born or having at least one parent born outside the country. Contrary to common belief, it has a capitalist economy; that is, most businesses producing goods and services are owned by private enterprises. The government does own the railroads, mineral resources, a bank, and liquor and tobacco operations. Sweden does have high taxes, which are used to provide for numerous generous cradle-to-grave public supports for its population, leveling extremes in wealth and poverty.

COMPONENTS OF THE SWEDISH WELFARE STATE

The Swedish welfare state began with legislation passed in 1891 that provided some health insurance. Ten years later the legislature instituted compulsory employer responsibility in the event of occupational injury. In 1913 a general pension system began and in 1931 a system for sickness benefits was put into place. From 1932 the welfare state was further developed and expanded as the Swedish Social Democratic Party controlled the government with only brief interruptions for the next 60 years. "The social democratic government . . . developed one of the world's best social welfare systems. It implemented a broad range of people-oriented social service programs, supported by taxes on larger incomes, landed

Source: This essay was written expressly for the fourth edition of *Solutions to Social Problems: Lessons from Other Societies.*

estates, and the profits of corporations, to protect all Swedish citizens from poor housing, poor health care, poverty incomes, and lack of jobs" (Feagin and Feagin, 1997:468). In 1991, however, there was an economic crisis that resulted in relatively high unemployment and reduced government revenues. As a consequence the services and subsidies of the welfare state were reduced, including periods when no benefits were paid for certain welfare plans. In the late 1990s the economy recovered and the benefits of the welfare state were partially restored. The description that follows is of the current welfare system as it has evolved through good times and bad, expansions and constrictions.

The Swedish welfare state is based on the principle that the government is responsible to provide basic services for the entire population. In broad outline, the present welfare system includes the following provisions:

- *A national health insurance program.* In this plan patients choose their own physicians and health services are subsidized for all residents of Sweden (the fees charged to patients in 2005 U.S. dollars were $11.21 per day for hospital stays, $21.02 for consultation with a doctor). Once a patient has paid $126, he or she is entitled to free medical care for the rest of the year. After a person has spent $252 for medicines, the remainder of pharmaceutical costs are free for the rest of the year.

- *A family support program for parents and children.* Prenatal care, delivery, and postnatal care are free. All children under the age of 20 receive free medical and dental care. Family planning services and advice on contraception are provided throughout the country. Working parents may take a leave from work to care for their infant for a total for both parents of 480 days (divided as they choose), while being compensated at 80 percent of their wages. Either parent may also take time off for the care of a sick children (60 days a year per child) with compensation for loss of earnings. Parents receive a cash bonus of $133 per month per child up to the age of 16. Each child is guaranteed a place in child care programs (there is a sliding scale for this service, with no one paying more than $137 a month). All children ages 4 and 5 are provided three hours of free preschooling a day.

- *Employment programs to reduce unemployment.* A laid-off worker has access to a state-run employment agency where employers must by law list their job openings. If no job is available, job-retraining and unemployment insurance benefits are provided (at 80 percent of previous income). During difficult economic cycles, the government often expands public employment programs (e.g., building infrastructure such as roads, public buildings, pipelines) to reduce unemployment.

- *Care of the elderly.* Everyone who has lived in Sweden for at least three years is entitled to at least a minimum pension. Full pension is for those who have lived in Sweden for 40 years between the ages of 16 and 64. There are also pension programs for those incapable of working, and for widows and other survivors. The elderly receive a housing subsidy (means tested but not to exceed 90 percent of the rent). Institutionalized care is provided where needed but the preference is for the elderly to receive nursing care in their homes, which is subsidized, whenever possible. The cost for all of the programs for the elderly is about 20 percent of the nation's GNP.

- *Subsidized housing.* The goal of Sweden's housing policy is to give everyone the chance for a good home, at a reasonable price. The means to achieve these ends include planning for housing, nonprofit municipal housing, establishing rent ceilings, subsidized financing, and housing allowances. The latter allows lower-income families to afford decent housing. The government's goal is for every family to have a housing arrangement that at a minimum has a bedroom for each child, a bedroom for the parents, plus a kitchen and living room.

PAYING FOR THE WELFARE STATE: TAXATION

To provide these many and expensive services of the welfare state, Swedish taxes are relatively high. Direct taxes include an income tax on employment, income from capital (e.g., dividends and capital gains from the sale of stocks, real estate, or other property), business income, a national property tax on real estate, and an inheritance tax. Indirectly, there is a state sales tax (value-added tax) and consumption taxes used as a means to curb the consumption of energy (oil and gas, electrical power, motor vehicles), tobacco, gaming, and alcohol. As a result the total tax revenue for Sweden as a percentage of Gross Domestic Product in 2000 was 54.2 percent (compared to 29.6 percent for the United States, 37.9 percent in Germany, 37.4 percent in the United Kingdom, and 35.8 percent for Canada) (Organization of Economic Cooperation and Development Report, cited in Francis, 2003).

WHY DOES SWEDEN CHOOSE TO HAVE AN EXPENSIVE WELFARE STATE?

Sweden has a high-tax/high benefit welfare state. There are at least four major reasons for the welfare state in Sweden. First, the Swedes have accepted the overarching goal of the Social Democrats that provides the basis for Sweden's expansive and expensive welfare state.

> The ambition is for financial security and social rights to be guaranteed to all citizens—not by being focused on certain hard-pressed groups in society, but by being given to all, without any application procedure or means-testing. . . . The basis of this policy is a tax system in which all taxpayers contribute, for the good of all, according to capacity, and in which funds are distributed with the objective of leveling out differences in people's living conditions, according to the principle of an egalitarian society. ("Disability Policies in Sweden," 2000:1)

While there are complaints about the high taxes opinion surveys reveal that the "majority of Swedes . . . are willing to pay higher taxes in order not to have such problems as chronic unemployment, homelessness, and health care rationed by income" (Feagin and Feagin, 1997:469). Further evidence of the general support of the welfare state in Sweden is the longtime support of the Social Democratic Party. Even when this party is out of power, there is little retrenchment in the welfare policies.

Second, the Swedes receive a lot of benefits. Directly, they receive health care, early childhood education, and various subsidies. In other societies, where these are not provided by society, the cost of these services is up to individuals and families, which means, in effect, there is unequal access to these services. Indirectly, if poverty, hunger, homelessness, and other social problems are minimized, then so, too, is street crime.

Third, Sweden has strong labor unions, which represent the middle and lower social classes. Through pressure these unions have received considerable concessions from the capitalist class. In effect, "labor and capital worked out a cooperative agreement whereby labor got a welfare state and capitalists got labor peace" (Feagin and Feagin, 1997:468).

And, the fourth reason for the support of the welfare state is that all citizens of Sweden are represented in the decision-making. Sweden has a parliamentary democracy with one assembly of 349 seats. Seats in parliament are distributed proportionately between those parties that poll at least 4 percent of the national vote or at least 12 percent in any one constituency. Unlike the United States, which has a two-party system and a winner-take-all policy, minorities and groups with different agendas are represented in the Swedish legislature, guaranteeing a voice and the possibility of coalitions with other groups. This democratic tradition promotes citizen participation, with high voter turnout, and subsequent attention by politicians to all citizens. Most important, it reduces the power of wealth in the decision-making.

REFERENCES_____

"Fact Sheets on Sweden" series, 2001–2005, The Swedish Institute. Stockholm, Sweden. Internet: www.swedeninfo.com.
  "Taxes in Sweden" (November 2001).
  "The Swedish Population" (June 2003).
  "The Health Care System in Sweden" (September 2003).
  "Social Insurance in Sweden" (January 2004).
  "Childcare in Sweden" (September 2004).
  "Financial Circumstances of Swedish Households" (March 2004).
  "Sweden in Brief" (April 2005).
Feagin, Joe R., and Clairece Booher Feagin. 1997. *Social Problems: A Critical-Conflict Perspective,* 5th ed. Englewood Cliffs, NJ: Prentice-Hall.
Francis, David R. 2003. "Tax Cuts as 'Stimulus'—a Global Reality Check." *Christian Science Monitor* (January 10):3.

PART TWO

Problems of Inequality

Section 2

Poverty

THE UNITED STATES CONTEXT

Using the official statistics on poverty (which understate the magnitude of this social problem), 12.5 percent of the United States population (35.9 million people) were poor in 2003 (the statistics throughout are from U.S. Bureau of the Census, 2004). The likelihood of being poor is heightened for some categories: (1) *racial minorities* (24.3 percent of all African Americans, 22.5 percent of all Latinos); (2) *women* (22.6 percent of single women; two-thirds of impoverished adults are women); *children* (17.6 percent of all those under age eighteen); (4) *elderly women* (one in five women 75 and over is poor compared to only one in ten men); and (5) those *living in certain places* (in central cities compared to the suburbs, and those living in four rural regions—the Mississippi Delta, which is primarily African American; the Rio Grand/U.S.–Mexico border, which is largely Latino; the Native American reservations of the Southwest and Plains; and Appalachia, which is predominantly white).

The U.S. poverty rate is the highest in the industrialized world. Child poverty has worsened over time. Among those under 18, poverty has increased by more than 30 percent from 1970. Two experts on comparative poverty rates, Lee Rainwater and Timothy M. Smeeding, state that "Coincidentally, around the end of the twentieth century there were roughly the same number of children in the United States and the twelve European countries—around seventy-two million. But we find that as many as fourteen million American children are poor compared with some seven million poor children in our comparison European countries" (2003:17).

The safety net for the poor and their parents in the United States (e.g., Head Start, health care, housing subsidy) has declined steadily since the Reagan administration, and this decline has increased dramatically as the Bush administration and Congress have enacted tax cuts while increasing the budget allotments to Homeland Security and defense/war. The fiscal year 2006 federal budget, for example, decreased the allocation to Medicaid (health services to the poor) by $10 billion while giving $131 billion in tax cuts (primarily going to the affluent). The poor in Europe, in contrast, have generous supports including universal health care, paid maternity leave, child care subsidies, and housing allowances.

REFERENCES

Rainwater, Lee, and Timothy M. Smeeding. 2003. *Poor Kids in a Rich Country.* New York: Russell Sage Foundation.

U.S. Bureau of the Census. 2004. "Poverty in the United States: 2003," *Current Population Reports,* (August):60–226.

4

The State of Welfare at Home and Abroad

AUSTRALIAN FINANCIAL REVIEW

Competing models of welfare capitalism are outlined in this article. Researchers found that the United States, which is described as having a welfare system consisting of a "rather patchy safety net and unregulated labor market," had the least amount of social mobility of the countries studied. This fact runs counter to popular rhetoric about the United States as a land of equal opportunity.

There are worse places to be poor than Australia—but fewer than you think.

In 1989, the "short 20th century," which had begun with the outbreak of the Great War in 1914, ended with the defeat of communism and, at least by default, the victory of capitalism. For American observers like Francis Fukuyama, this victory was sufficient grounds to proclaim "the end of history" and the dawning of "the second American century." Much the same conclusion was expressed in postmodernist claims about the passing of the era of "grand narratives" of which Marxism was the preeminent example.

With the end of the Cold War, however, the big historical question was not "Communism or capitalism," but "what kind of capitalism?". At least until 1996, when Bill Clinton announced "the end of welfare as we know it," the choice could be posed more narrowly, as one between different forms of "welfare capitalism," in which the exigencies of the free market were softened by a welfare system designed to eliminate or minimise poverty.

In comparing different models of welfare capitalism, the United States stands alone at one pole, with a welfare system confined to a rather patchy "safety net" and a largely unregulated labour market. The other English-speaking countries form a group with more generous, but still relatively restricted, welfare systems. Most other developed countries (with the enigmatic exception of Japan) can be regarded as "welfare states" of different kinds, but different analytical frameworks give rise to different classifications.

One of the most detailed and sophisticated comparisons of competing models of welfare capitalism has recently been presented by two Australian and two Dutch researchers, including philosopher Robert Goodin, political scientist Bruce Heady, labour market researcher Ruud Muffels and statistician Henk-Jan Dirven (GHMD for short). GHMD used

Source: Australian Financial Review. 2001 (September 14), p. 8. Reprinted by permission.

comparative data for the US, Germany and the Netherlands, which they classed as respectively "liberal," "corporatist" and "social democratic."

For those who dislike suspense, the back cover reveals that the contest resulted in an easy win for the "home team," the Netherlands. Not surprisingly, the Netherlands performed best on social-democratic criteria such as maximising equality and minimising poverty. More interestingly, the Netherlands outperformed the United States on the key liberal criterion of maximising income growth and Germany on the key corporatist criterion of minimising family breakdown (GHMD take for granted the idea that the United States is a liberal society in which high rates of family breakdown are to be expected. The notion, popular in English-speaking countries, that free market radicalism can be married to "family values" conservatism is not even addressed).

The core of the analysis is the use of large-scale panel data sets, in which individuals are interviewed at annual intervals over a period of a decade or more. This approach has big advantages over the more common "snapshot" offered by once-off surveys. For example, in considering a society in which surveys consistently show that 10 percent of the population are poor (by some definition), it makes a big difference whether the same 10 percent of the population are always poor or whether, over a given decade, everybody in the population experiences poverty at least one year in 10. In the latter case, if income is averaged over the entire decade, no-one will be poor. Not surprisingly, panel data analysis reveals a picture intermediate between these two extremes. The longer the period over which income is averaged, the smaller the proportion of the population who turn out to be poor. The international comparisons might surprise those used to thinking of free markets as bastions of equal opportunity.

About 6 percent of Dutch people experience poverty (defined as a disposable income less than 50 percent of the national median) in any given year, but, when income is averaged over a decade, the proportion of poor people falls to 1 percent. In the United States, about 18 percent of households are poor in any given year, and averaging over a decade only reduces the proportion to 13 percent. The finding that the United States has less social mobility than other advanced countries is well-established in the social science literature, but not reflected in popular rhetoric.

It is also possible to test how many people are consistently poor in each of the 10 years. Almost no-one in the Netherlands experiences a decade of consistent poverty, compared to 3 percent of Germans and 10 percent of Americans. Not surprisingly, the failure of the US welfare system to combat poverty contributes to poor outcomes on other measures, such as equality of access to educational opportunities.

One difficulty with the GHMD is that, despite a sophisticated discussion of concepts of poverty, the statistical analysis focuses exclusively on a relative measure of poverty, setting the poverty line at 50 percent of median income. Since the US is generally regarded as the world's richest country, it might be, for example, that the standard of living of Americans classed as poor is higher than that of Europeans living above their national poverty lines.

Because exchange rates fluctuate widely, the best way of assessing this question relies on the notion of Purchasing Power Parity. The basic idea is to convert one currency into another in such a way that the cost of buying a representative basket of goods and services is the same in both nations. (The idea of a "representative basket," like the associated mythical "average consumer" raise plenty of problems, but this is not the place to explore them.)

In its Human Development Report, the United Nations Development Program estimates the proportion of the population in different countries whose purchasing power was less than $US11 a day in 1994–95. The results are more favourable to the US than those of GMHD, but not much more so. An estimated 13.6 percent of the US population fell below this absolute poverty line compared to 7.1 percent in the Netherlands and 7.3 percent in Germany.

Australia, by the way, was among the worst performers in the developed world, with 17.6 percent of the population falling below the $US11 a day level, putting us 14th out of 17 OECD countries in the Human Poverty Index. On the other hand high life expectancy and participation in education put us near the top of the league table, second only to Norway, for the UNDP's Human Development Index.

Another problem is that the comparisons were made for a period ending in the mid-1990s before the passage of the Welfare Reform Act, which led to "the end of welfare as we know it" in the US. Although the Welfare Reform Act has indeed been followed by drastic reductions in the number of welfare beneficiaries, announcements of victory are premature for two reasons. First, the passage of the act coincided with the beginning of one of the most spectacular, and unsustainable, booms of the 20th century. Second, the act provided a transitional mechanism, in the form of a five-year lifetime limit on access to welfare, beginning at the end of 1996. The five-year limit will begin to bite at the beginning of 2002, in what looks certain to be a deeply depressed economy.

As GHMD observe, no matter how comprehensive and representative, statistics are an abstraction from reality. It is easy to point to statistics showing that the US has a large number of "working poor" people, but harder to say what this means in terms of lived experience.

Barbara Ehrenreich's recent book *Nickel and Dimed: On (Not) Getting by in America* represents the revival of a tradition of investigation that predates the regular collection of official statistics. Ehrenreich sought to answer the question "how can you make a living on the minimum wage" by direct experience. Over a period of two years, she took a series of low-wage service-sector jobs in different American cities.

The jobs included waitressing, nursing-home care and retail sales, but the most memorable was that with the "Merry Maids" housecleaning service (names were changed to protect co-workers). Ehrenreich has written in the past of her unwillingness, unusual now in the middle class, to have others do her housework and her stint with the Merry Maids seemed to confirm her worst fears. Despite backbreaking work (the Maids' motto is "We clean houses the old-fashioned way—on our hands and knees!"), the cleaning system required by the company focused exclusively on superficial gleam, with no regard to whether houses were actually cleaned or not.

Despite holding down two jobs and working 50 hours a week in a number of stints, Ehrenreich's experimental attempt ended in failure. The big problem was rent. As she observes, the jobs for the poor are mostly close to where the rich live. In Key West, a half-size trailer (i.e., a caravan) rented for $US625 per month, prompting Ehrenreich's observation that "trailer trash" had become an aspirational category for her.

Ehrenreich's coworkers, or at least those without an employed partner, dealt with the housing problem in various mostly unsatisfactory ways—living in trucks, sharing motel rooms in the off-season and so on.

For them, the real problem was health care. US workers rely on their employers for health insurance, but minimum wage jobs provide little or nothing in the way of health benefits. The various, and fairly desperate, safety net options provided through schemes such as Medicaid are often not available to the working poor. Minimum-wage workers simply have to put up with bad teeth, work-related injuries and so on.

How much is all this specific to the US? It might be useful to compare the jobs undertaken by Ehrenreich with comparable jobs in Australia. The big problem is to estimate the purchasing power of US wages in Australian terms. For the mythical average consumer, the average bundle of goods bought for $1 in Australia could be obtained for around 75 cents in the United States, suggesting that the $US6–$US7 an hour earned by Ehrenreich in most of her jobs corresponds to around $8 to $9 an hour in Australia. At 50 hours per week or 2,500 per year, this would be around $20,000, which is about equal to the minimum wage in Australia for a work year of around 1,750 hours.

Rents in our own "global city" of Sydney are high, but don't appear to be quite as crippling as Ehrenreich found them. Equally importantly, whatever the problems of Australian public hospitals and pharmaceutical benefits, they are far better than the desperate options available to uninsured workers in the United States.

Taking the results of these studies as a whole, there is little cause for complacency. The United States may be the worst country in the developed world in which to be poor, but Australia is not very far behind it.

REFERENCES_____

The Real Worlds of Welfare Capitalism. Robert E Goodin, Bruce Heady, Ruud Muffels and Henk-Jan Dirven. 358pp. Cambridge University Press.
Nickel and Dimed. Barbara Ehrenreich. 221pp. US: Metropolitan Books.

5

Is There Hope for America's Low-Income Children?

LEE RAINWATER AND TIMOTHY M. SMEEDING

Lee Rainwater and Timothy M. Smeeding have chronicled the differences among the industrialized societies on a number of dimensions. In this excerpt from their recent book they examine childhood poverty and what the United States might learn from the more generous welfare state policies in Canada, Western Europe, and Scandinavia.

Despite high rates of economic growth and improvements in the standard of living in industrialized nations throughout the twentieth century, a significant percentage of American children are still living in families so poor that normal health and growth are at risk (Duncan et al. 1998; Duncan and Brooks-Gunn 1997a, b). The previous chapters have shown that it does not have to be this way: in many other countries child poverty afflicts only one-half to one-quarter as many children as in the United States.

These numbers are startling and worrisome. For more affluent nations, child poverty is not a matter of affordability—it is a matter of priority. This country made a commitment nearly sixty years ago to deal with old-age poverty, and that effort has been fairly successful (Burtless and Smeeding 2001). When we found ourselves discussing the large federal and state budget surpluses at the beginning of the twenty-first century, that was a period when we could have made a serious commitment to reduce child poverty in the United States. This opportunity was missed. Even today, with the economy in a brief recession, making a commitment to spend the modest amount of money it would take to bring about a large reduction in child poverty is well within our grasp. Of course, such a policy would need to conform to American values (market work and self-reliance), utilize American social institutions (such as the income tax system), and continue the successful antipoverty efforts of the 1990s, such as the Earned Income Tax Credit.

Consider tax policy for a moment. There are progressive substitutes for the recent 2001–2002 regressive federal income tax reductions that would shore up income support for the working poor. For instance, as part of an expanded tax reduction plan, we could

Source: Rainwater, Lee, and Timothy M. Smeeding. 2003. "Is There Hope for America's Low-Income Children?" In *Poor Kids in a Rich Country: America's Children in Comparative Perspective* (pp. 132–141). © Russell Sage Foundation, 112 East 64th Street, New York, NY 10021. Reprinted with permission.

make the child tax credit refundable for working families with no federal income tax obligations; these families do pay Social Security and Medicare taxes, of course. Similarly, we could expand the Earned Income Tax Credit and link it to the child tax credit (Sawicky and Cherry 2001). These modest measures would be relatively inexpensive and effective first steps in the process of further reducing child poverty for the working poor.

While such changes are meant to be suggestive, our study underlines the need for a comprehensive policy to reduce child poverty rates and improve the well-being of children. Policymakers committed to reducing child poverty must address each of the six problem areas (employment, parental leave, child care, child-related tax policy, child support, and education) identified in this chapter. And they must also consider the much smaller number of children living in families with no parent who can work.

EMPLOYMENT

The most important step in reducing poverty among children is to ensure that at least one parent is employed. In particular, the labor market position of mothers needs to be improved, as their earnings are crucial for maintaining an adequate standard of living in a society where two-income families dominate. Obviously, this is doubly true for single parents, where subsidized child care is an absolute necessity for employment.

In low-wage, high-employment societies such as the United States, employment is both a virtue and a challenge. Working mothers feel better about themselves when they are employed, and children feel better about their parents when they are employed (Chase-Lansdale et al. 2003). However, low-skill employment is almost always low-paying, sometimes requires working nonstandard hours, can involve long commutes, and is vulnerable to lay-offs when the economy turns down. Thus, while employment is important, it needs to be supported by flexibility in work schedules and other public support services (Haveman 2003). For two-parent families, some mixture of these policies will suffice. For single parents who must act as both provider and caretaker, employment must be coordinated with their children's needs. To be successfully employed, parents, especially mothers, need state support to facilitate that employment. The evidence is that low-income American single mothers work more hours than single mothers in any other nation (Osberg 2002). The evidence is also clear that American single mothers receive the least income support of any nation's low-income mothers (Smeeding 2003). American policymakers therefore must find a better mix of income support and work that makes all working single parents nonpoor (see also Gornick and Meyers 2003).

PARENTAL LEAVE, CHILD CARE SUBSIDY, AND CHILD SUPPORT

In many cases, parents—particularly mothers—need state support to enable them to work and to adequately take care of their children. The development of parental leave programs, guarantees for child support not paid by absent parents, and affordable child care are important conditions for keeping mothers in the full-time work-force and preventing poverty among their children. Child support enforcement measures are important and have become more successful over the past decade. But their potential for reducing child poverty is limited, since many of the parents who fail to pay child support are low earners themselves.

The policy design issue is to find a public way to ensure child support, while not reducing the efforts that absent parents make to support their children.

The United States has lagged in these areas in all dimensions: our family leave is not universal and is, in fact, relatively short and unsubsidized; we have no child support insurance to protect single mothers from absent fathers who do not pay their obligated child support; and our child care support system helps the rich more than it helps the poor, despite many recent welfare reform-related efforts to expand child care subsidies for low-income parents (Ross 1999; Gornick and Meyers 2003).

According to the evidence presented earlier, Sweden has low child poverty rates not only because of unique cultural characteristics but because as a society it has integrated women—mothers in general and single mothers in particular—into its labor force. In its configuration of welfare state policies, Sweden has traditionally stressed the importance of women's continued attachment to the labor market and supported them as wage earners by providing child care, a good parental leave program, and a comprehensive system of child care support.

Adequate parental leave programs and child care provisions are clearly important conditions for keeping mothers in full-time employment. For instance, the increased availability in the United Kingdom of child care, maternity leave, and more family-friendly corporate policies has increased the employment continuity of British women around the time of childbirth and thus reduced the indirect cost of children to their parents (Davies and Joshi 2001). It is also reported that British women can increasingly afford to make use of child care services. However, the direct cost of child care services still proves to be too high for women with smaller earnings potential. This is one of the main reasons why British women with low earnings potential, as well as those with middle earnings potential and more than one child, are more likely to stay home (see, for example, Meyers et al. 2001).

Child Care

Clearly, the introduction of comprehensive child care provisions should be complemented by measures that would make it possible for women with lower earnings potential to make use of these services. The greater the cost of child care services relative to the mother's wage potential, the less likely it is that she will seek employment. It is therefore important to expand public support for child care services that reduces the direct cost of those services, with direct subsidies and also with indirect support through refundable child care tax credits, which would (partially) compensate low-income families' remaining expenditures for this type of service.

In 1989 the European Commission published a "Communication from the Commission on Family Policies" that underlined the importance of affordable, accessible, and high-quality child care arrangements to member states' efforts to increase the labor participation of women (European Commission 1989; Kamerman and Kahn 2001). The British government's 1998 green paper "Meeting the Childcare Challenge" (United Kingdom 1998) contains several proposals for improving access to child care in Britain that are now being implemented. Clearly, the lack of affordable child care support is not a uniquely American problem, but it does cripple efforts by single parents in this country to find steady employment and make work economically viable.

Many governments seem to have understood the need for such measures. According to Sheila Kamerman and Alfred Kahn (2001), child care services continued to increase in supply during the 1990s in most nations, including the United States. Many governments have extended existing parental leave policies, and these policies were even introduced for the first time in a few other countries. In 1998 President Clinton pushed an initiative to improve child care for working families that would have made child care more affordable in various ways and doubled the number of children receiving child care subsidies to more than two million by the year 2003. Unfortunately, most elements of the proposal were not enacted into law. The expansion of affordable child care services was still on the political agenda in 2003, but the recession from 2001 to 2003 forced many state governments to cut back on child care services and subsidies in the face of rising state government deficits. While child care subsidies continued, even during the recession, for many single parents who were leaving welfare, support was more generally needed for parents in families who had already left welfare and become independent of the welfare system.

Parental Leave

Parental leave policy is another area where much could be done. In 2000, Canada instituted paid family leave as a national policy, and Australia did the same in 2003. In the United States, where unpaid family leave is very short and still unpaid, California has made a first step by instituting a paid family leave policy for some workers. Other states are likely to follow suit. The actions of these states may pave the way toward a more effective and expansive federal policy in the near future (Ross 1999; Gornick and Meyers 2003).

Parental leave programs and comprehensive and affordable child care services represent, of course, only some of the policy measures needed to integrate mothers into the workforce. Improving the skills of low-skilled workers (often women), job counseling, the removal of various structural obstacles (such as unemployment traps), and transportation assistance are also important initiatives that would make it easier for mothers to work full-time.

Child Support

The provision of steady, reliable child support is another important element of the semi-private safety net in the United States and elsewhere. It is a widely held value that parents should support their children. The problem in doing so is often that absent fathers cannot or do not pay, owing to weak enforcement of child care laws or low earnings capacity. While significant progress has been made in upgrading child support enforcement for divorced mothers, much still remains to be accomplished for unmarried mothers (Ellwood and Blank 2001). Enforcement is uneven across states, paternity establishment by unwed mothers varies greatly across states, and often the fathers of the children of unwed mothers do not earn enough to support themselves, much less their children.

In Europe a different set of values prevails. The well-being of the child and the mother is usually the foremost value, and the absent father's willingness and ability to pay are of secondary concern. In these countries full child support is guaranteed by governments when absent fathers cannot or will not pay (Skevik 1998). While universal guaranteed child support on the European level would not fit American values, a more modest system might be achievable. When the custodial mother has established paternity and the absent father is deemed unable to pay (owing to imprisonment, unemployment, or low wages), a modest level of guaranteed child support—say, $2,000 per year for a first child and $1,500 for a second—could be a very important source of steady support for a single mother who is not otherwise receiving such aid. Similarly, states could increase the dollar amount of child support allowed to "pass through" to mothers receiving Temporary Assistance to Needy Families (TANF) without penalty, a measure that would increase the monthly amount received by the mother to $150 or $250, rather than only the first $50, which is the norm.

CHILD-RELATED INCOME TAX POLICY

The minimum wage is insufficient to meet the income needs of working families with children. Full-time work at the current minimum wage leaves a family of three far below the poverty line, and the Earned Income Tax Credit does not fully close the gap. If we continue to pursue this policy line, additional child-related tax benefits are necessary to ensure that working families with children are not poor. Making families headed by parents with low earnings potential more dependent on market income is not sufficient to end child poverty in a period of increased earnings inequality and slack labor markets (Haveman 2003). Earnings are often not sufficient to protect households with children from poverty, and although children living in two-parent dual-earner families are far less likely to be poor, poverty rates among children living in working single-parent families remain very high in the United States.

In recent years several countries have introduced or increased minimum wages, but these often remain insufficient to keep households with children out of poverty. Governments are reluctant to further increase the minimum-wage levels in their countries because they risk aggravating the unemployment problem faced by low-skilled workers. The "living wage" laws, which pay hourly wages of seven to nine dollars per hour to governmental contractors in some parts of the United States, are rarely applied to the private sector for this same reason—many fewer employees will be hired at this level of labor cost. Since the expansion of low-wage work might improve the job prospects of less-educated workers and make it easier for single-earner households to acquire a second income, we do not advocate significantly higher minimum wages, and certainly not "living wages" for all U.S. workers. It is clear, however, that many governments should do more to support the working poor when wages are insufficient to keep a family from becoming poor. The United States EITC is one important way to supplement earnings and help working families meet their financial responsibilities. However, it does not always guarantee that a family will avoid poverty (Moffitt 2002).

There is evidence of an increasing role for refundable tax credits in the support given to low-income working-age households in other nations as well. Many OECD countries offer social tax breaks and allowances to replace cash benefits, although they tend to be less important in countries with relatively high direct tax levies, such as Denmark, Finland, the Netherlands, and Sweden. In Germany, the value of tax allowances for the cost incurred in raising children alone amounted to almost 0.6 percent of the German GDP in 1993 (Adema and Einerhand 1998). Both the Netherlands and the United Kingdom have specific tax subsidies for single-parent families, and, as we mentioned before, many countries also use tax credits to compensate these families for expenditures such as child care costs. Yet we must emphasize that such measures have less effect on the incomes of families with earnings that are too low to fully benefit from them. It is therefore important that tax credits for child care and similar measures aimed at families with low earnings be made refundable.

In addition to the EITC, the American income tax system contains a set of tax credits that are partially refundable, but not to low-income parents who do not make enough to pay federal income tax. The several plans that have been proposed to integrate these two programs would produce a single family tax credit with more benefit adequacy and lower work disincentives than in the phase-down regime of the EITC (Cherry and Sawicky 2000; Sawicky and Cherry 2001). Adoption of these programs would give a well-targeted boost to the incomes of working poor parents.

INVESTMENT IN A SOCIALLY ORIENTED EDUCATION POLICY

Central to the promotion of employment in a knowledge-based society is quality education for all children, regardless of their financial situation or their health. Such policies could reduce the likelihood that child poverty is passed on from generation to generation (Gregg and Machin 2001; Büchel et al. 2001). A special effort needs to be made to target education resources to the areas where they can do the most good for poor children in bad schools and to prepare low-income children for elementary school more generally.

It is the responsibility of every democracy to provide an equal opportunity from birth for every child. We sorely need to give increased attention to the quality of schooling in low-income areas and develop better and more widespread preschool programs in low-income areas if we are to increase the chances of reducing adult poverty among the next generation of children. Making schools more accountable may be a partial answer to this need, but the legislation entitled "Leave No Child Behind" is insufficient by itself to reach this goal (Smeeding 2002).

AN AMERICAN INCOME SUPPORT PACKAGE
FOR FAMILIES WITH CHILDREN

The previous six policy arenas can be drawn together into a benefit or "income" package that includes a role for the state, for the family, and for work, and a package that conforms to American values. Clearly, work alone is not enough to guarantee escape from poverty for low-income working families, especially single parents (Haveman 2003). The EITC is a good step, but it is not enough by itself to reach the goal. Additional refundable tax credits, subsidized child care, guaranteed child support (for those who meet specified criteria), and paid family leave must also be woven into the policy mix. This combination of work and benefits should increase the incomes and well-being of children whose mothers work. And both low-income students and their schools need to be better prepared to advance and thrive.

Policy efforts must be redoubled to meet the needs of mothers who cannot work and of households with no workers. Perhaps the answer lies in disability policy—for example, through the Supplemental Security Income (SSI) program. We will not delve into these issues here, except to say that the remaining TANF caseload (about two million households as of early 2003) is a manageable issue that could be tackled by a reauthorization of welfare reform targeted not only at removing these last welfare recipients from the rolls but at meeting their divergent and serious human needs.

FINDING THE WILL IS FINDING THE WAY

The findings in this book underline the need for a comprehensive policy to reduce child poverty rates and improve the well-being of children. Human capital concerns in industrialized countries offer an overwhelming and very practical case for adequate investment in succeeding generations. Especially in the affluent economies of the industrialized world, there are no valid economic excuses for high child poverty rates. We can all afford low child poverty rates.

But no two countries can fight poverty in exactly the same way. Each nation's policies must fit its own national culture and values. Thus, the policy suggestions made here must be hewn together into a system of child poverty reduction that will work in the United States. Moreover, these policies cannot simply be taken off the shelf and plugged in. It takes political leadership to make such policies national priorities and to make programs mesh in a supportive fashion.

In recent years Prime Minister Tony Blair of the United Kingdom has shown that when a nation makes a commitment to reduce child poverty, much can be accomplished (see, for example, Bradshaw 2001; Walker and Wiseman 2001). Since 1997 the Blair government has spent an additional 0.9 percent of GDP (about $1,900 per family) on poor families with children (Hills 2002). An equivalent degree of effort in the United States would cost $90 billion. The high poverty rates of the late 1990s in the United Kingdom are now being gradually reduced (Bradshaw 2001; Hills 2002). Unfortunately, not all countries share this priority, particularly not the United States (Danziger 2001; Smeeding 2002).

The American social assistance system has now achieved a primary goal: increasing work and reducing welfare dependence for low-income mothers. Fewer than five million persons (two million cases) remain dependent on TANF benefits. The "welfare problem" is no longer. However, as welfare rolls have been trimmed, corresponding decreases in child poverty have not been achieved because market income alone is not enough to bring about serious reductions in child poverty. The United States needs to make this goal a top priority for its political agenda. Even a commitment of $45 billion—half the effort of the Blair government—could at least partially fund most of the policy options listed in this chapter. The integrity of our democratic values will be ensured and the cultural and economic fabric of our society enriched when we can say that many fewer children grow up poor in America.

REFERENCES_____

Adema, William, and Marcel Einerhand. 1998. "The Growing Role of Private Social Benefits." Labor Market and Social Policy occasional paper 32. Paris: Organization for Economic Cooperation and Development (April 17).

Bradshaw, Jonathan. 2001. "Child Poverty Under Labour." In *An End in Sight?: Tackling Child Poverty in the United Kingdom,* edited by Geoff Fimister. London: Child Poverty Action Group.

Büchel, Felix, Joachim R. Frick, Peter Krause, and Gerg G. Wagner. 2001. "The Impact of Poverty on Children's School Attendance: Evidence from West Germany." In *Child Well-Being, Child*

Poverty, and Child Policy in Modern Nations: What Do We Know?, edited by Koen Vleminckx and Timothy M. Smeeding. Bristol, Eng.: Policy Press.

Burtless, Gary, and Timothy M. Smeeding. 2001. "The Level, Trend, and Composition of Poverty." In *Understanding Poverty,* edited by Sheldon H. Danziger and Robert H. Haveman. New York and Cambridge, Mass.: Russell Sage Foundation and Harvard University Press.

Chase-Lansdale, P. Lindsay, Robert A. Moffitt, Brenda J. Lohman, Andrew J. Cherlin, Rebekah Levine Coley, Laura D. Pittman, Jennifer Roff, and Elizabeth Votruba-Drzal. 2003. "Mothers' Transitions from Welfare to Work and the Well-being of Preschoolers and Adolescents." *Science* 299(March): 1548–52.

Cherry, Robert, and Max B. Sawicky. 2000. "Giving Tax Credit Where Credit Is Due: A 'Universal Unified Child Credit' That Expands the EITC and Cuts Taxes for Working Families." Briefing paper. Washington, D.C.: Economic Policy Institute (April). Available at: www.cpinet.org/briefingpapers/EITC_BP.pdf.

Danziger, Sheldon H. 2001. "After Welfare Reform and an Economic Boom: Why Is Child Poverty Still So Much Higher in the United States Than in Europe?" Paper presented to the Eighth Foundation for International Studies on Social Security (FISS) Conference on Support for Children and Their Parents: Why's Ways, Effects, and Policy. Sigtuna, Sweden (June).

Davies, Hugh, and Heather Joshi. 2001. "Who Has Borne the Cost of Britain's Children in the 1990s?" In *Child Well-being, Child Poverty, and Child Policy in Modern Nations: What Do We Know?*, edited by Koen Vleminckx and Timothy M. Smeeding. Bristol, Eng.: Policy Press.

Duncan, Greg J., and Jeanne Brooks-Gunn, eds. 1997a. *The Consequences of Growing up Poor.* New York: Russell Sage Foundation.

———. 1997b. "Income Effects Across the Life Span: Integration and Interpretation." In *The Consequences of Growing up Poor,* edited by Greg J. Duncan and Jeanne Brooks-Gunn. New York: Russell Sage Foundation.

Duncan, Greg J., Wei-Jun J. Yeung, Jeanne Brooks-Gunn, and Judith Smith. 1998. "How Much Does Childhood Poverty Affect the Life Chances of Children?" *American Sociological Review* 63(3, June): 406–23.

Ellwood, David, and Rebecca Blank. 2001. "The Clinton Legacy for America's Poor." Research working paper RWP01–028. Cambridge, Mass.: Harvard University, Kennedy School of Government (July).

European Commission. 1989. "Communication from the Commission on Family Policies (COM [89]363 final)." *Social Europe: Official Journal of the European Communities* 1(94, October 31): 121–29.

Gornick, Janet, and Marcia K. Meyers. 2003. *Families That Work: Policies for Reconciling Parenthood and Employment.* New York: Russell Sage Foundation.

Gregg, Paul, and Stephen Machin. 2001. "Child Experiences, Educational Attainment, and Adult Labor Market Performance." In *Child Well-being, Child Poverty, and Child Policy in Modern Nations: What Do We Know?*, edited by Koen Vleminckx and Timothy M. Smeeding. Bristol, Eng.: Policy Press.

Haveman, Robert. 2003. "When Work Alone Is Not Enough." *LaFollette Policy Report* 13(2): 1–15.

Hills, John. 2002. "The Blair Government and Child Poverty: An Extra One Percent for Children in the United Kingdom." Unpublished paper. London School of Economics.

Kamerman, Sheila B., and Alfred J. Kahn. 2001. "Child and Family Policies in an Era of Social Policy Retrenchment and Restructuring." In *Child Well-Being, Child Poverty, and Child Policy in Modern Nations: What Do We Know?*, edited by Koen Vleminckx and Timothy M. Smeeding. Bristol, Eng.: Policy Press.

Meyers, Marcia K., Janet C. Gornick, Laura R. Peck, and Amanda J. Lockshin. 2001. "Public Policies That Support Families with Young Children: Variation Across U.S. States." In *Child Well-Being, Child Poverty, and Child Policy in Modern Nations: What Do We Know?*, edited by Koen Vleminckx and Timothy M. Smeeding. Bristol, Eng.: Policy Press.

Moffitt, Robert. 2002. "From Welfare to Work: What the Evidence Shows." Welfare Reform and Beyond 13. Washington, D.C.: Brookings Institution (January).

Osberg, Lars. 2002. "Time, Money, and Inequality in International Perspective." Luxembourg Income Study working paper 334. Syracuse, N.Y.: Syracuse University, Maxwell School of Citizenship and Public Affairs, Center for Policy Research (November).

Ross, Katherin. 1999. "Labor Pains: Maternity Leave Policy and the Labor Supply and Economic Vulnerability of Recent Mothers." Ph.D. diss., Syracuse University.

Sawicky, Max B., and Robert Cherry. 2001. "Making Work Pay with Tax Reform." Issue brief 173. Washington, D.C.: Economic Policy Institute (December 21). Available at: www.epinet.org/ Issuebriefs/ibl73/ ib173.pdf.

Skevik, Anne. 1998. "The State-Parent-Child Relationship After Family Break-ups: Child Maintenance in Norway and Great Britain." In *The State of Social Welfare, 1997: International Studies on Social Insurance and Retirement, Employment, Family Policy, and Health Care,* edited by Peter Flora, Philip R. de Jong, Julian Le Grand, and Jun-Young Kim. London: Ashgate.

Smeeding, Timothy M. 2002. "No Child Left Behind?" *Indicators* 1(3): 6–30.-67.

———. 2003. "Real Standards of Living and Public Support for Children: United Kingdom. Department for Education and Skills. 1998. "Meeting the Child Care Challenge." National Child Care Strategy Green Paper. London: Department for Education and Skills (May). Available at: www .dfes.gov.uk/childcare.

Walker, Robert, and Michael Wiseman. 2001. "The House That Jack Built." *Milken Institute Review* (fourth quarter): 52–62.

Section 3

Income and Wealth Inequality

Income and wealth inequality refers to the gap between the rich and the poor on these related dimensions. The United States has the greatest inequality gap in the industrialized world. Moreover, the rate of growth in inequality is faster than in any other industrialized country. Some of the facts concerning income and wealth inequality in the United States include:

- The top 1 percent now own 38 percent of the nation's wealth, while the bottom 40 percent own 1 percent. In short, the combined wealth of the richest 3 million Americans is nearly 40 times that of the 113 million at the bottom (Packer, 2003).
- Among the 252 of the largest U.S. companies, average CEO pay was up 5.2 percent in 2003, to $7.8 million (Lavelle and Brady, 2004). That same year, more than 28 million people, about a quarter of the workforce, earned less than $9.04 an hour (about $18,000 a year) (Sklar, 2005).
- Over the past 20 years the income of the top 1 percent of Americans rose 157 percent, that of middle-income families rose 10 percent, and that of people in the bottom fifth fell slightly (*Christian Century,* 2002).
- The 13,000 wealthiest families in the United States earn more income than the bottom twenty million families (Sanders, 2004).
- In 1992 it took the combined wages of 287,400 retail clerks to equal the pay of the top 400 individuals. In 2000 it required the combined pay of 504,600 retail clerks to match the pay of the top 400 (Barlett and Steele, 2004).
- In 2003 there were 3.8 million millionaires in the U.S. (up 15 percent from the previous year). In 2003 there were 35.9 million people living below the poverty line (up 9.6 percent from 2002).
- The Bush administration and Congress enacted massive tax cuts totaling $1.7 trillion in 2001 and 2003. The richest 1 percent of Americans reaped 54 percent of the total of these two tax breaks (Children's Defense Fund, 2004:xxviii).

This rising inequality gap in the United States has enormous consequences. If the trend continues, the number of people on the economic margin will rise. Homelessness and hunger will increase. Family disruption will escalate. Crime rates will swell. Public safety will become much more problematic. More generally, this phenomenon of economic inequality has implications for democracy, crime, and civil unrest. Economist Lester Thurow, wondering about this move toward a two-tiered society asks: "How much inequality can a democracy take? The income gap in America is eroding the social contract. If the promise of a higher standard of living is limited to a few at the top, the rest of the citizenry, as history shows, is likely to grow disaffected, or worse" (Thurow, 1995:78).

REFERENCES

Barlett, Donald L., and James B. Steele. 2004. "Has Your Life Become a Game of Chance?" *Time* (February 2):42–44.

Children's Defense Fund. 2004. *The State of America's Children 2004.* Washington, D.C.: Author.

Christian Century. 2002. "Is It Fair?" (December 4–17):5.

Lavelle, Louis, and Diane Brady. 2004. "The Gravy Train May Be Drying Up." *Business Week* (April 5):52–53.

Packer, George. 2003. "The End of Equality." *Mother Jones* 28 (November/December):30–33.

Sanders, Bernie. 2004. "We Are the Majority." *The Progressive* 68 (February):26–29.

Sklar, Holly. 2005. "King's Dream Included Decent Wages." Knight Ridder/Tribune Services (January 12).

Thurow, Lester. 1995. "Why Their World Might Crumble." *New York Times Magazine* (November 19):78–79.

6

Inequality: USA vs. Other Industrial Nations

AMERICANS FOR DEMOCRATIC ACTION

Income inequality is far greater in the United States than in other industrialized countries. This excerpt provides data to support that assertion.

Income inequality in America is far greater than in other major industrial nations. Numerous studies have documented this situation. One frequently cited study is the Luxembourg Income Study that compared the Income gap between the rich and the poor in the United States with that of ten industrial European countries, Canada and Australia.

The study also contains a series of other income figures. One set compares the median income of the poorest 10% of families with the overall median income in that country. Here are some key findings:

- The poorest 10% of families in the U.S. had income equal to 36% of median income. At the other end of the income ladder, the wealthiest 10% of families had income equal to 208% of the median.
- The statistics in the other countries showed that income for the poorest 10% of families averaged 51% of the median, and for the richest 10% percent, 186%. In other words, the poorest American lived on income only about one third of the income of the average family; in other countries, families in similar economic conditions lived on income of about half of the income of the average family.
- In Sweden, the Netherlands, and Finland, the poorest families had incomes equal to 57% of the median income in those countries. The country with the highest percentage was Belgium with a 58% figure; the United Kingdom had the lowest figure of 44%. These figures are for the early 1990s.

More recent data compiled by the Organization for Economic Cooperation and Development (OECD) shows that, from 1991 to 1995, earning inequality in the U.S. continued to rise more rapidly than in other countries. As the OECD staff wrote,

"United Kingdom and the United States stand out as the only countries where there has been a pronounced rise in earnings inequality."[1]

Source: Americans for Democratic Action (ADA), *Income and Inequality: Millions Left Behind,* 3rd ed. Washington, DC, 2004, pp. 9–10.

The table below with the accompanying text was presented by the Public Broadcasting System on May 17, 2003 and provides the evidence to support that statement. The OECD and the World Bank found the gap between the income of the wealthiest and poorest 30% of families was greater in the U.S. than in 11 other industrialized nations.

The table shows that the wealthiest in America held 52.5% of disposable income while the poorest 30% held only 11.8%—a 4.5 to 1 ratio. In contrast, in Finland the ratio was 2.7 to 1. Details of inequality in other industrialized countries show similar smaller gaps between their wealthiest and poorest citizens than in the U.S.

NOTE_____

1. Cited by David R. Howell of the Center for Economic Policy Analyses, New School University in October 1999.

LOSING GROUND—GLOBAL INEQUALITY	WEALTHIEST 30%	POOREST 30%
Denmark: Total disposable income held by the wealthiest and poorest:	48.3%	13.8%
Sweden: Total disposable income held by the wealthiest and poorest:	45.8%	15.8%
Finland: Total disposable income held by the wealthiest and poorest:	45.6%	17.0%
Norway: Total disposable income held by the wealthiest and poorest:	46.1%	16.3%
Netherlands: Total disposable income held by the wealthiest and poorest:	46.3%	15.8%
Germany: Total disposable income held by the wealthiest and poorest:	48.9%	14.7%
Canada: Total disposable income held by the wealthiest and poorest:	49.2%	14.3%
France: Total disposable income held by the wealthiest and poorest:	49.0%	15.6%
Belgium: Total disposable income held by the wealthiest and poorest:	48.3%	15.5%
Australia: Total disposable income held by the wealthiest and poorest:	49.3%	13.8%
Italy: Total disposable income held by the wealthiest and poorest:	53.2%	12.0%
United States: Total disposable income held by the wealthiest and poorest:	52.5%	11.8%

Source for statistics: OECD Reports: Income Distribution and Poverty in 13 OECD Countries: 2000.
Other sources: The World Bank; The Economist.

7

Inequality Here and There

CLAUDE S. FISCHER, MICHAEL HOUT, MARTIN SANCHEZ JANKOWSKI,
SAMUEL R. LUCAS, ANN SWIDLER, AND KIM VOSS

The authors argue that inequality is not due to the distribution of talent in society nor to the natural workings of the market. Inequality in the United States is the result of societal choices based on the cultural support for rewarding difference and the resulting supply-side policies. In effect, inequality in the United States is by design. As the authors point out, other nations have designed systems that are less unequal than that of the United States.

A glance behind us to American history shows that our pattern of inequality is far from fixed or naturally determined. A glance sideways to other wealthy nations makes the same point. The United States has the greatest degree of economic inequality of any developed country. It is a level of inequality that is not fated by Americans' talents nor necessitated by economic conditions but is the result of policy choices. The nations with which we will compare the United States are also modern, affluent, democratic, and capitalist—they are our competitors in the global market—and yet they have ways to reduce inequality and remain competitive.

The best and latest evidence on how nations compare in levels of inequality comes from the Luxembourg Income Study (so named because the project is headquartered in Luxembourg). Social scientists affiliated with the study have collected detailed, comparable data on earnings and income from over a dozen nations. Our first use of their research appears in Figure 7.1, which speaks to the question of inequality in *earnings,* specifically earnings of men, aged 25–54, who worked full-time, all year during the mid- to late 1980s. (Comparable data on earnings were available for only five nations. We are looking just at men here, because the situation of women in the labor force was in such flux and varied so much among nations.) The vertical line in the figure serves as an anchor for looking at inequality in each nation. It represents the earnings of the average (median) worker. The horizontal bars to the left of the median line display the ratio of the earnings that men near, but not at the top of, the earnings ladder received—those at the 90th percentile in

Source: Fischer, Claude, et al. *Inequality by Design.* © 1996 Princeton University Press. Reprinted by permission of Princeton University Press.

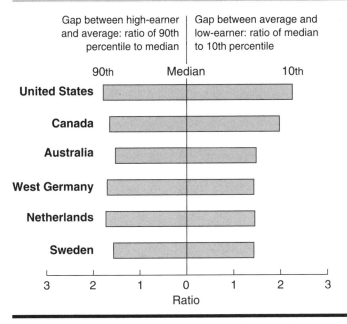

The gap between the highest- and the average-earning men was widest in the United States—as was the gap between the average- and the lowest-earning men.

Gap between high-earner and average: ratio of 90th percentile to median | Gap between average and low-earner: ratio of median to 10th percentile

90th   Median   10th

United States

Canada

Australia

West Germany

Netherlands

Sweden

3   2   1   0   1   2   3
Ratio

FIGURE 7.1   Ratios of Earnings for High-, Median-, and Low-Earners in Six Nations

Source: Adapted from Peter Gottschalk and Timothy Smeeding, 1995. "Cross-National Comparisons of Levels and Trends in Inequality." Working Paper no. 126, Luxembourg Income Study. Syracuse, NY: Maxwell School of Citizenship and Public Affairs, July.

earnings—to the earnings of men at the median. In 1986 the 90th percentile American male worker earned 1.8 times what the median worker earned. The bars stretching to the right represent the same comparison between the median earner and a low-paid worker, one at the 10th percentile of earnings. In the United States, the median worker brought home 2.8 times the amount the 10th percentile worker did. The left-hand bars, therefore, display inequality of earnings between the high-earners and the average; the right-hand bars display inequality between the average and the low-earners. Together, they display total inequality. In the United States, the 90th percentile worker earned five times that of the 10th percentile worker.

These numbers are highest in the United States. That is, the gap in earnings between the rich and the average worker is greater here than elsewhere, as is the gap between the average and the low-paid worker. The contrast between the United States and Europe sharpens further when non-monetary compensation is added to the picture. In most European nations, national law requires that virtually all workers have the kinds of benefits such as strong job security and four-week vacations that in the United States only workers with seniority in major firms have.

These national differences expanded in the 1980s, when inequality increased globally. International economic forces widened the gaps between what the better- and the worse-educated earned in most industrialized nations, but this chasm opened up farthest and fastest in the United States and the United Kingdom. (These were the years of Thatcherite reforms that reduced the role of government in the United Kingdom.) Elsewhere, the gap in earnings between the better- and worse-educated widened less, barely at all, or even narrowed. There seems no clear connection between these differences and other economic trends such as growth rates. The reasons lie in government policies, notably the relative power of unions and the expansions of higher education in the other Western countries.

The biggest contrast in income inequality between the United States and the rest of the developed world, however, appears *after* taking into account how government deals with the results of the market. That means accounting for taxes, tax deductions, transfer payments, housing subsidies, and the like. (Again, we note that this before- and after-government distinction underestimates the role of government. Where, for example, governments require employers to provide certain benefits, there is more market equality.)

To look at international differences in *household income,* we turn again to the Luxembourg Income Study. Peter Gottschalk and Timothy Smeeding compiled comparable data on households' disposable incomes—income after taxes and government support, adjusted for household size—in seventeen nations. In Figure 7.2, we use just the figures for nations with over ten million residents in 1980; our conclusions about the United States would be virtually the same if we showed the smaller nations, too. As in Figure 7.1, the bars to the left of the median display the ratio of a rich household's income (at the 90th percentile) to an average one's income, while the right-hand bars show the ratio of an average household's income to that of a poor one (10th percentile). The rich-to-average ratio is greatest in the United States, 2.1, as is the average-to-poor ratio, 2.9, and so the rich-to-poor ratio, 5.9 (not shown) is much higher than that of the next most unequal nations (4.0 for Italy, Canada, and Australia). In short, the United States has the greatest degree of income inequality in the West whether one focuses on the gap between the poor and the middle or the gap between the middle and the rich. Even these numbers underestimate America's distinctiveness, because they do not count the sorts of "in-kind" help that middle- and lower-income families receive in most other nations, such as free health care, child care, and subsidized housing and transportation. They also underestimate inequality in America by not displaying the concentration of income at the very top of the income ladder.

Western nations generally take two routes to reducing inequality. . . . Some intervene in the market to ensure relatively equal distributions of *earnings* by, for example, brokering nationwide wage agreements, assisting unions, or providing free child care. Others use taxes and government benefits to reduce inequality of *income* after the market. A few do both seriously, such as the Scandinavian countries. The United States does the least of either. If one sets aside older people, who benefit a great deal from government action in the United States, the net effect of taxes and transfers here is to leave the degree of inequality virtually unchanged from the way it was determined by market earnings.

When everything is accounted for, the Western nation with the most income inequality is the United States. But the United States is also exceptionally unequal in terms of *wealth*.

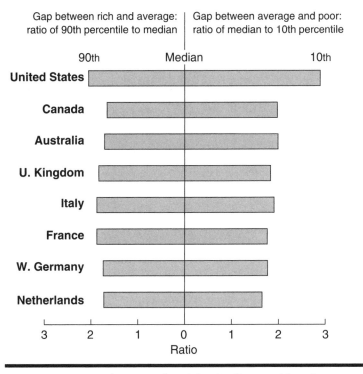

The income gap between the richest and the average household and the gap between the average household and the poorest are both wider in the United States than elsewhere.

FIGURE 7.2   Ratios of Incomes for High-, Median-, and Low-Income
Households in Eight Nations

Source: Adapted from Peter Gottschalk and Timothy Smeeding, "Cross-National Comparisons of Levels and Trends in Inequality." Working Paper no. 126, Luxembourg Income Study. Syracuse, NY: Maxwell School of Citizenship and Public Affairs, July.

At the end of the 1980s, the richest 1 percent of families owned about 40 percent of household wealth here, more than in any other advanced nation; the richest 1 percent owned only 25 percent of the wealth in Canada and 18 percent of the wealth in Great Britain, for example. Add the less tangible features of "wealth," such as vacations and security of medical care, and the conclusion is reinforced that Americans are remarkably unequal.

(Some critics of crossnational comparisons contend that one ought not to contrast the United States to other nations, because the United States is distinct in certain ways. We have so many single-parent families, for example. But even looking only at two-parent families, the United States is still unusually unequal. America also seems exceptionally diverse racially and ethnically. But other Western nations also have ethnic diversity, if not the racial caste system we do. And poverty among American whites *only* still exceeds that among white or majority populations elsewhere. Such reservations do not challenge the conclusion that the United States is unusually unequal.)

America's level of inequality is by design. It is not given by nature, nor by the distribution of its people's talents, nor by the demands of a "natural" market. Other Western nations face the same global competition that we do and are about as affluent as we are and yet have managed to develop patterns of inequality less divisive than ours. Ironically, it was not so long ago that Americans were proud of comparing their relatively egalitarian society to the class-riven, hierarchical, decadent societies of Europe. In the last couple of decades, America has become the more class-riven and hierarchical society.

The United States is unusually unequal and Americans are unusually supportive of this inequality. Surveys show that Americans back moves toward expanding *opportunity* but oppose moves toward equalizing *outcomes.* They endorse wage differences among jobs that are pretty similar to the wage differences that they believe exist today (although the real differences are greater than Americans imagine), and they do not approve of government programs to narrow those differences. In a survey of people in six nations, only 28 percent of Americans agreed that government should reduce income differences. The next lowest percentage was 42 percent (Australians), while in the other countries majorities supported reducing income differences. Whether we have as much opportunity as Americans want is debatable but we seem to have a rough match between the desired and the perceived level of outcome inequality. That may be because Americans think that considerable inequality is needed for stimulating productivity and a high standard of living. Is it?

Some commentators straightforwardly defend our current level of inequality. A congressional report in 1995 conceded that the recent trends toward inequality were real but argued, "All societies have unequal wealth and income dispersion, and there is no positive basis for criticizing any degree of market determined [*sic*] inequality." Disparities in income and wealth, some analysts argue, encourage hard work and saving. The rich, in particular, can invest their capital in production and thus create jobs for all. This was the argument of "supply-side" economics in the 1980s, that rewarding the wealthy—for example, by reducing income taxes on returns from their investments—would stimulate growth to the benefit of all. The 1980s did not work out that way, as we have seen, but the theory is still influential. We *could* force more equal outcomes, these analysts say, but doing so would reduce living standards for all Americans.

Must we have so much inequality for overall growth? The latest economic research concludes *not;* it even suggests that inequality may *retard* economic growth. In a detailed statistical analysis, economists Torsten Persson and Guido Tabellini reported finding that, historically, societies that had more inequality of earnings tended to have lower, not higher, subsequent economic growth. Replications by other scholars substantiated the finding: More unequal nations grew less quickly than did more equal societies. . . .

Close examination of detailed policies also suggests that greater equality helps, or at least does not harm, productivity. Researchers affiliated with the National Bureau of Economic Research closely examined the effects on economic flexibility (that is, the ability to shift resources to more productive uses) of several redistributive policies used by Western nations—job security laws, homeowner subsidies, health plans, public child care, and so on. They found that such programs did *not* inhibit the functioning of those economies. Indeed, a study of over one hundred U.S. businesses found that the smaller the wage gap between managers and workers, the higher the business's product quality.

This recent research has not demonstrated precisely how greater equality helps economic growth, but we can consider a few possibilities. Increasing resources for those of lower income might, by raising health, educational attainment, and hope, increase people's abilities to be productive and entrepreneurial. Reducing the income of those at the top might reduce unproductive and speculative spending. Take, as a concrete example, the way American corporations are run compared with German and Japanese ones. The American companies are run by largely autonomous managers whose main responsibility is to return short-term profits and high stock prices to shareholders and—because they are often paid in stock options—to themselves as well. Japanese and German managers are more like top employees whose goals largely focus on keeping the company a thriving enterprise. The latter is more conducive to reinvesting profits and thus to long-term growth. Whatever the mechanisms may be, inequality appears to undermine growth. Americans certainly need not feel that they must accept the high levels of inequality we currently endure in order to have a robust economy.

A related concern for Americans is whether "leveling" stifles the drive to get ahead. Americans prefer to encourage Horatio Alger striving and to provide opportunities for everyone. Lincoln once said "that some would be rich shows that others may become rich." Many, if not most, Americans believe that inequality is needed to encourage people to work hard. But, if so, *how much* inequality is needed?

For decades, sociologists have been comparing the patterns of social mobility across societies, asking: In which countries are people most likely to overcome the disadvantages of birth and move up the ladder? In particular, does more or less equality encourage such an "open" society? The answer is that Western societies vary little in the degree to which children's economic successes are constrained by their parents' class positions. America, the most unequal Western society, has somewhat more fluid, intergenerational mobility than do other nations, but so does Sweden, the most equal Western society. There is no case for encouraging inequality in this evidence, either.

In sum, the assumption that considerable inequality is needed for, or even encourages, economic growth appears to be false. We do not need to make a morally wrenching choice between more affluence and more equality; we can have both. But even if such a choice were necessary, both sides of the debate, the "altruists" who favor intervention for equalizing and the supposed "realists" who resist it, agree that inequality can be shaped by policy decisions: wittingly or unwittingly, we choose our level of inequality.

8

The Coming Era of Wealth Taxation

GAR ALPEROVITZ

Taxing wealth is a sure way to address the growing wealth gap: it provides revenue to meet pressing social needs and at the same time slows or reverses the trend toward wealth concentration. Current government policies, however, are aimed at eliminating the estate tax. Contrary to this thinking, political economist Gar Alperovitz explains why he is optimistic about the prospects for a new program of taxing large concentrations of wealth.

Americans concerned with inequality commonly point to huge disparities in the distribution of income, but the ownership of wealth is far, far more concentrated. This fact is certain to bring the question of wealth taxation to the top of the nation's political agenda as the country's fiscal crisis deepens and, with it, the deterioration of public institutions and the pain of all those who rely on them.

Broadly, in any one year the top 20% garners for itself roughly 50% of all income, while the bottom 80% must make [do] with the rest. The top 1% regularly takes home more income than the bottom 100 million Americans combined.

When it comes to wealth, these numbers appear almost egalitarian. The richest 1% of households owns half of all outstanding stock, financial securities, trust equity, and business equity! A mere 5% at the very top owns more than two-thirds of the wealth in America's gigantic corporate economy, known as financial wealth—mainly stocks and bonds.

This is a medieval concentration of economic power. The only real question is when its scale and implications will surface as a powerful political issue. A wealth tax is "by definition, the most progressive way to raise revenue, since it hits only the very pinnacle of the income distribution," notes economist Robert Kuttner. But conventional wisdom says that it is impossible to deal with wealth head-on. The battle over repeal of the estate tax, in this view, demonstrated that even the most traditional of "wealth taxes" are no longer politically feasible.

Perhaps. However, a longer perspective reminds us that times can change—as, indeed, they often have when economic circumstances demanded it.

Source: Gar Alperovitz, "The Coming Era of Wealth Taxation," pp. 162–167 in *The Wealth Inequality Reader*, edited by *Dollars & Sense* and United for a Fair Economy. Cambridge, MA: Economic Affairs Bureau, 2004. Reprinted by permssion of *Dollars & Sense,* a progressive economics magazine, www.dollarsandsense.org

EMERGING SIGNS OF CHANGE

Indeed, times are already beginning to change. One sign: Although many Democrats were nervous about challenging George W. Bush in the first year after he took office, by early 2004 all the Democrats running for president had come to demand a repeal in some form of his tax giveaways to the elite.

It is instructive to trace the process of change. At the outset, only a few liberals challenged the president. The late Paul Wellstone, for instance, proposed freezing future income tax reductions for the top 1% and retaining the corporate Alternative Minimum Tax (AMT), for an estimated $134 billion in additional revenue over 10 years. Ted Kennedy proposed delaying tax cuts for families with incomes over $130,000 and keeping the estate tax (while gradually raising the value of exempted estates from a then-current $1 million to $4 million by 2010). Kennedy estimated this would generate $350 billion over 10 years.

By May 2002, even centrist Democrat Joseph Lieberman urged postponing both the full repeal of the estate tax and reductions in the top income-tax rates. Lieberman estimated his plan would save a trillion dollars over 20 years. The Bush tax cuts were simply unfair, he said, "giving the biggest benefit to those who needed it the least."

The Democrats failed to stop Bush's 2001 and 2003 rounds of tax cuts. But there are reasons to believe that politicians will ultimately come to accept the validity of maintaining and raising taxes on the wealthiest Americans. Just as many Democrats changed their stand on the Bush tax cuts, a similar progression is likely with regard to wealth taxation more generally over the next few years—and for two very good reasons. First, there is an extraordinary fiscal crisis brewing; and second, wealth taxes—like taxes on very high-income recipients—put 95% to 98% of the people on one side of the line and only 2% to 5% or so on the other.

Reasons
For This
- Fiscal
crisis

GO WHERE THE MONEY IS

The hard truth is that it is now all but impossible to significantly raise taxes on the middle class. This reality flows in part from the ongoing decline of organized labor's political power, and in part from the Republicans' take-over of the South—another long and unpleasant political story. At any rate, it means that the only place to look for significant resources is where the remaining real money is—in the holdings of corporations and the elites who overwhelmingly own them. Put another way: Raising taxes first on the income and ultimately on the wealth of the very top groups is likely to become all but inevitable as, over time, it becomes clear that there is no way to get much more in taxes from the middle-class suburbs.

Moreover, as Democratic politicians have come increasingly to realize, the "logic of small versus large numbers" could potentially neutralize a good part of the suburbs politically, painting conservatives into a corner where they're forced to defend the very unreasonable privileges of the very rich.

The knee-jerk reaction that taxing wealth is impossible is based upon the kind of thinking about politics that "remembers the future"—in other words, thinking that assumes the future is likely to be just like the past, whether accurately remembered or not. Since wealth has not been taxed, it cannot be taxed now, goes the argument (or rather, assumption).

Of course, taxation of wealth has long been central to the American tax system for the kind of wealth most Americans own—their homes. Real estate taxes, moreover, are based on the market value of the home—not the value of a homeowner's equity: An owner of a $200,000 home will be taxed on the full value of the asset, even if her actual ownership position, with a mortgage debt of, say, $190,000, is only a small fraction of this amount. A new, more equitable form of wealth taxation would simply extend this very well established tradition and—at long last!—bring the elites who own most of the nation's financial wealth into the picture.

Many Americans once thought it impossible to tax even income—until the 1913 passage, after long debate and political agitation, of the 16th Amendment to the U.S. Constitution. Note, however, that for many years, the amendment in practice meant targeting elites: Significant income taxation was largely restricted to roughly the top 2% to 4% until World War II.

Even more important is a rarely discussed truth at the heart of the modern history of taxation. For a very long time now the federal income tax has, in fact, targeted elites—even in the Bush era, and even in a society preoccupied with terrorism and war. In 2000, the top 1% of households paid 36.5% of federal income taxes. The top 5% paid 56.2%. Although detailed calculations are not yet available, the massive Bush tax cuts are not expected to alter the order of magnitude of these figures. Estimates suggest that, ultimately, the tax reductions may modify the figures by no more than two or perhaps three percentage points.

In significant part this results from the rapidly growing incomes of the wealthiest: even at lower rates, they'll still be paying nearly the same share of total income tax. The simple fact is, however, that the record demonstrates it is not impossible to target elites. We need to take this political point seriously and act on it aggressively in the coming period.

FISCAL CRUNCH AHEAD

What makes wealth taxes even more likely in the coming period is the extraordinary dimension of the fiscal crisis, which will force government at all levels to adopt new strategies for producing additional resources. Projections for the coming decade alone suggest a combined federal fiscal deficit of more than $5 trillion—$7.5 trillion if Social Security Trust Fund reserves are left aside.

A worsening fiscal squeeze is coming—and it is not likely to be reversed any time soon. Critically, spending on Social Security benefits and Medicare will continue to rise as the baby-boom generation retires. So will spending on Medicaid. Recent studies project that by 2080 these three programs alone will consume a larger share of GDP than all of the money the federal government collects in taxes. And, of course, the ongoing occupation of Iraq will continue to demand large-scale financial support.

Nor are the trends likely to be altered without dramatic change: The truth is that the Bush tax and spending strategies, though particularly egregious, are by no means unique. Long before the Bush-era reductions, domestic discretionary spending by the federal government was trending down—from 4.7% of GDP a quarter century ago to 3.5% now, a drop during this period alone of roughly 25%.

A radically new context is thus taking shape which will force very difficult choices. Either there will be no solution to many of the nation's problems, or politicians and the public will have to try something new. Suburban middle-class voters, who rely on good schools, affordable health care, assistance for elderly parents, and public infrastructure of all kinds, will begin to feel the effects if the "beast" of government is truly starved. This pain is likely to redirect their politics back toward support for a strong public sector—one which is underwritten by taxes on the wealthiest. Quite simply, it is the only place to go.

TIME TO TAX WEALTH

Ideological conservatives like to argue that all Americans want to get rich and so oppose higher taxes on the upper-income groups they hope to join. In his recent history of taxation, *New York Times* reporter Steven Weisman has shown that this may or may not be so in normal times, but that when social and economic pain increase, politicians and the public have repeatedly moved to tax those who can afford it most. Bill Clinton, for one, raised rates on the top groups when necessity dictated. So did the current president's father! Now, several states—including even conservative Virginia—have seen pragmatic Republicans take the lead in proposing new elite taxation as the local fiscal crisis has deepened.

The likelihood of a political shift on this issue is also suggested by the growing number of people who have proposed direct wealth taxation. A large group of multimillionaires has launched a campaign opposing elimination of taxes on inherited wealth—paid only by the top 2%—as "bad for our democracy, our economy, and our society." Yale law professors Bruce Ackerman and Anne Alstott in their book *The Stakeholder Society* have proposed an annual 2% wealth tax (after exempting the first $80,000). Colgate economist Thomas Michl has urged a net-worth tax, and Hofstra law professor Leon Friedman has proposed a 1% tax on wealth owned by the top 1%. Even Donald Trump has proposed a one time 14.25% net-worth tax on Americans with more than $10 million in assets.

Wealth taxation is common in Europe. Most European wealth taxes have an exemption for low and moderate levels of wealth (especially the value of pensions and annuities). Economist Edward Wolff, who has studied these precedents carefully, suggests that America might begin with a wealth tax based on the very modest Swiss effort, with marginal rates between 0.05% and 0.3% after exempting roughly the first $100,000 of assets for married couples. He estimates that if this were done, only millionaires would pay an additional 1% or more of their income in taxes.

Europe also offers examples of much more aggressive approaches. Wealth taxation rates in 10 other European countries are much higher than Switzerland's—between 1% and 3%—and would yield considerable revenues if applied here. Wolff calculated that a 3% Swedish-style wealth tax in the United States would have produced $545 billion in revenue in 1998. Although an updated estimate is not available, nominal GDP increased about 19% between 1998 and 2002, and wealth taxes would likely produce revenues that roughly tracked that increase.

Some writers have held that wealth taxes are prohibited by the U.S. Constitution. There appear to be two answers to this. The first is legal: Ackerman, a noted constitutional expert, has argued at length in the *Columbia Law Review* that wealth taxes are not only constitutional, but represent the heart of both original and contemporary legal doctrine on taxation.

The second answer is political. We know that courts have a way of bending to the winds of political-economic reality over time. As the pain deepens, the courts are likely one day to recognize the validity of the legal arguments in favor of wealth taxation. Alternatively, political pressure may ultimately mandate further constitutional change, just as it did in 1913 with regard to income taxation.

There is no way of knowing for sure. But as with all important political change, the real answer will be found only if and when pressure builds up both intellectually and politically for a new course of action. The challenge, as always, is not simply to propose, but to act.

Section 4

Gender

THE UNITED STATES CONTEXT

In 2005, women held prominent posts in U.S. society. Condoleezza Rice was Secretary of State. Nancy Pelosi was the House Minority Leader, the highest Congressional position ever held by a woman, and there were fourteen women Senators and sixty-five women elected to the House of Representatives. These represent impressive gains from the past but they fall far short of equality. Women are only 15 percent of the 535 members of Congress. Moreover, gender inequality is a fact in wage differentials, possibilities for advancement in the workplace, equity in school sports, and the workload in families. There is a long list of occupations where women comprise 5 percent or less of the workers where the "glass ceiling" is the thickest (e.g., pilots, navigators, truck drivers, mechanics, carpenters, telephone installers, loggers, material-moving equipment operators, construction workers, and firefighters). Women are overrepresented (90 percent or more) in such occupations as secretary, cashier, dental hygienist, child care provider, hairdresser, and receptionist. Generally, the more prestigious the occupation, the better the pay and benefits, the lower the proportion of women.

Gender inequality is also manifested in stereotypical media portrayals of women and men; the differences in the socialization of girls and boys at home, school, and church; the greater difficulty that women face from voters when running for electoral office against men; the much greater household demands on wives; and religious traditions that make women subordinate to men.

9

Europe Crawls Ahead

MEGAN ROWLING

The level of representation of women in politics is slowly rising in Europe. One reason for this is the use of proportional representation in many European countries, where political parties are allocated seats in political districts according to the number of votes they win. Multiple seats may ease gender imbalances because parties are more likely to select female candidates if more than one seat per constituency is allowed. This article addresses some of the barriers facing women in politics, and how many European countries are slowly breaking down these barriers.

As Speaker of the Riksdagen, the Swedish parliament, Birgitta Dahl holds Sweden's second-highest political office. But when she was first elected back in 1969, as a 30-year-old single mother, she was regarded as "very odd."

"To be accepted and respected, you had to act like a bad copy of a man," Dahl recalls of her early years in politics. "But we tried to change that, and we never gave up our identity. Now women have competence in Parliament, and they have changed its performance and priorities."

Back then, women of her generation were eager for change. From the beginning, they based their demands on the right of the individual—whether male or female—to have equal access to education, work and social security. And as politicians, they fought hard to build a legal framework for good childcare and parental leave, for fathers as well as mothers. "We got this kind of legislation through," Dahl says, "even though it took 15 years of serious conflict, debate and struggle."

And their efforts paid off. Sweden now has the highest proportion of women parliamentarians in the world, at 42.7 percent—up from just 12 percent in 1969. Two of its three deputy speakers are also women. Other Nordic countries too have high levels of female representation: In rankings compiled by the Inter-Parliamentary Union (IPU), Denmark takes second place behind Sweden, with women accounting for 38 percent of parliament members, followed by Finland and Norway with around 36.5 percent. (Finland also has one of the world's 11 women heads of state.) These nations' Social Democratic and far-left governing coalitions have made impressive progress toward equality in all areas of society in the past 40 years. But the nature of their electoral systems is also very important.

Source: Megan Rowling. 2002. *In These Times* (July 22), pp. 15–17. www.inthesetimes.com. Reprinted by permission.

Julie Ballington, gender project officer at the Stockholm-based International Institute for Democracy and Electoral Assistance (IDEA), points out that the top 10 countries in the IPU ranking all use some form of proportional representation. This kind of voting system, in which parties are allocated seats in multi-member districts according to the percentage of votes they win, Ballington says, "offers a way to address gender imbalance in parliaments." With single-member districts, parties are often under pressure to choose a male candidate. But where they can contest and win more than one seat per constituency, they tend to be more willing to field female candidates. And by improving the gender balance on their slates, they widen their appeal among women voters.

Most European countries now use proportional representation or a combination of proportional representation and majoritarian voting, the system in use in the United States and the United Kingdom. In Europe, the widespread use of proportional representation has boosted the number of women politicians—particularly in the past three decades. And in the Nordic countries, where left-wing parties have enjoyed long periods in power and feminism has received strong support, the combination of these factors has led to significant progress toward gender parity in politics.

But even within Europe, some countries continue to lag behind. In Britain, which uses a single-member district plurality system, women members of parliament make up just 17.9 percent of the House of Commons. In the general elections of 2001, the ruling Labour Party stipulated that half those on its candidate shortlists be women. But research conducted by the Fawcett Society, a British organization that campaigns for gender equity, showed that some female hopefuls experienced overt discrimination and even sexual harassment when interviewed by local party members during the selection process.

"You are told things like 'your children are better off with you at home' . . . 'you are the best candidate but we are not ready for a woman.' They would select the donkey rather than the woman," said one candidate. Another complained: "They are absolutely adamant they will not consider a woman. . . . It was said to me . . . 'we do enjoy watching you speak—we always imagine what your knickers are like.' It is that basic." In light of such attitudes, it is not surprising that women candidates were selected for only four out of 38 vacant seats.

Thanks to new governmental legislation, however, the party is set to reintroduce the controversial method of all-women shortlists it used in the general election of 1997. The use of these shortlists saw the number of British women MPs double to 120 in that election, which swept Labour to power with a landslide victory. The technique was later ruled illegal because it was judged to discriminate against men. But in early 2002, the government returned to the idea, passing a bill that will allow political parties to take measures in favor of women when choosing parliamentary candidates—what's often referred to as "positive discrimination."

Judith Squires, a political researcher at Bristol University, believes that the new legislation got such an easy ride partly because it does not stipulate that parties must take action: "We had expected it to be a hard battle. But there has been a change of mood in the Conservative Party, and the fact that it is permissive, and there is a sunset clause [the legislation expires in 2015], all helped to push it through."

In France, where until the recent election women accounted for only 10.9 percent of National Assembly members, the government opted for a more extreme method: a law aimed at securing political parity between men and women. Now half of all contesting parties' candidates in National Assembly elections and most local ballots must be women. In National

Assembly elections, which do not use proportional representation, parties that deviate from the 50 percent target by more than two percent are fined a proportion of their public financing.

The law's first test in the municipal elections of March 2001 saw the percentage of elected women councilors in towns of more than 3,500 almost double, to 47.5 percent. But in June's National Assembly elections, the proportion of women deputies increased by less than 1.5 points, to just 12.3 percent—way below expectations. The main factor behind this disappointing result was the success of right-wing parties that ignored the new law, says Mariette Sineau, research director at the Center for the Study of French Political Life. "The big parties decided it was better to incur the financial penalty than to sacrifice their 'favored sons.' And this was particularly so with parties on the right."

Another problem with the law, Sineau explains, is that it does not apply to regional assemblies, "which is a shame, because most National Assembly deputies are recruited there." And the recent victory of the right suggests that France's ruling—and predominantly male—elite are in no hurry to change the system that has allowed them to hold on to power up until now, law or no law. As Chantal Cauquil, a French deputy at the European Parliament and member of the Workers' Struggle Party, argues, other aspects of French society must change before real parity can be achieved. "There's no doubt that economic and social conditions—which weigh on women earning the lowest salaries, in the most precarious situations, and with the biggest problems caused by a notable lack of child-care infrastructure—have a negative impact on women's political participation," she says. Moreover, governing parties of both the right and left are influenced by social prejudices and are not inclined to regard women as full citizens. It requires real political will to go against such prejudices and allow women to take on the same responsibilities as men."

Such deep-rooted but hidden obstacles, faced by women everywhere, are precisely why proponents of the use of gender quotas on lists for both party and national elections believe positive discrimination is essential. "Everybody hates quotas, and everyone wishes they weren't necessary," says Drude Dahlerup, professor of politics at the University of Stockholm. "But we have to start from the point that there are structural barriers. Then quotas can be seen as compensation." Currently, political parties in some 40 countries appear to agree, with quota systems in operation from Argentina and India to Uganda.

The use of quotas in Europe varies significantly from country to country and from party to party, but where a quota system is applied, it tends to lead to a rise in women's representation. In 1988, for example, Germany's Social Democrats adopted a system of flexible quotas, under which at least one-third of all candidates for internal party elections must be female—and between 1987 and 1990, the number of Social Democratic women in the German parliament, the Bundestag, doubled. In Sweden, parties didn't introduce quotas until the '90s, but the principle of "Varannan Damemas" ("Every Other Seat A Woman's Seat") has been widespread since the '80s. Dahl, the Swedish speaker, argues that "it is not only legislation that changes the world, but convincing people that change is necessary."

Yet, as Dahlerup notes, women in some Scandinavian countries have worked to improve gender equality since the end of World War I, and "other countries are not going to wait that long—they are showing impatience." "Critical mass," or the level of representation above which women make a real difference to the political agenda, is widely judged to be around 30 percent. And in countries such as France and the United Kingdom, where that is still a long way off, measures such as parity laws and all-women shortlists are a way to speed up progress.

Even in countries that are close to achieving political parity, however, women are quick to warn against complacency. Dahlerup emphasizes the case of Denmark, where quotas have been abandoned. "Young women say they don't want and don't need quotas. The discourse is that equality has already been achieved. But I think Denmark could go backward again, and that is dangerous."

Squires of Bristol University also talks about a backlash in Britain's Liberal Democratic Party against what younger women regard as "old-fashioned feminist policies." At the party conference last year, she says, many women in their twenties and early thirties lobbied against any form of positive discrimination, wearing pink T-shirts emblazoned with the words "I'm not a token woman." But Squires suggests that this attitude is somewhat misguided: "All parties [in the United Kingdom] have set criteria that discriminate against women. It is not a supply-side problem, it is a demand-side problem."

In an attempt to address this "demand-side problem," activists are targeting not only national political institutions, but also those of the European Union. The number of women members of the European Parliament increased from 25.7 percent in 1994 to 29.9 percent in the 1999 elections—not very impressive considering that some countries introduced proportional representation voting, and some parties alternated women and men on their lists to boost women's chances. More worrying perhaps is the gender imbalance in the Convention on the Future of Europe, a body charged with the important task of drafting a new treaty for the European Union. Its presidium includes only two women among its 12 members, and the convention itself only 19 out of 118 members.

"The establishment of the convention is a response to the need for transparency and democracy. How can we explain the fact that women are not included?" asks Denise Fuchs, president of the European Women's Lobby. "It is simply not coherent." The EWL has launched a campaign to rectify the problem and is lobbying to achieve parity democracy across all other European institutions as well.

Yvonne Galligan, director of the Belfast-based Center for Advancement of Women in Politics, points out that "there has been a groundswell of support for women in political life across Western Europe, but this has not yet translated into numbers in the United Kingdom, Ireland and the European Union." In May's elections in the Irish Republic, for example, women parliamentarians in Ireland's Dail gained just one seat, and are now at 12.7 percent, according to the IPU.

Galligan is now working with political parties to set targets for Ireland's local elections in a couple of years' time—a tough job, because most parties oppose any form of positive discrimination. Parity in Ireland isn't likely to happen for a long while yet, but Galligan believes the social backdrop is improving. She cites a controversial referendum in March, in which the Irish electorate narrowly voted against a proposal to tighten the country's strict abortion laws even further. "That raised the status of women," she explains. "The underlying question was, how do we perceive the role of women? Now that is carrying over into elections. People are waking up and saying that it's not right that there are so few women in politics."

But where a sea-change in attitudes has not already occurred, it is almost certainly emerging. Naturally, there are fears that the apparent resurgence of the right in Europe could reverse the trend. But most of those interviewed for this article say women have already progressed far enough to prevent a significant decline in representation.

As Linda McAvan, deputy leader of Britain's Labour MEPs, argues: "If we look at how things were 20 years ago, they have changed enormously. Young women are different now. They see what has been done by women politicians before them, and they want to do it too."

10

The Position of Women in Norway

PERNILLE LONNE MORKHAGEN

In two of the United Nations' indexes for gender equality, Norway was ranked as the most gender-equal nation in 2001. But, as this paper indicates, Norway still has some distance to go to achieve gender equality on all dimensions.

What is the position of women in Norwegian society? It depends on who we compare ourselves with. With Norwegian men? With women in Warsaw, Cape Town or Kabul? Our former prime minister, Gro Harlem Brundtland, now the head of the World Health Organization, has said that Norway is a leading country in the field of equal rights. Many other countries look to Norway for inspiration and ideas on how to promote sexual equality.

It's quite some time since equal rights was a major political issue and rallying cry among Norwegian women. For many years the changing governments and the political parties in the Storting, Norway's national assembly, have pursued such an active equal rights policy that the need for special activist organizations seems to have lessened.

In recent years we have seen two different reactions to the Government's active promotion of gender equality. One is that equal rights should focus on the rights of men from now on. Another reaction comes from the business sector and its organisations. The government is now stipulating that the boards of all private concerns are to include at least 40 percent women, in line with the requirements to the boards of public concerns. Business organisations consider this to be an unprecedented interference in the rights of private companies to run their own affairs.

EQUALITY FOR MEN

During the last decade, much of the work on gender equality has concentrated on men's rights in women's fora rather than on women's rights in men's fora. A number of prominent politicians and the former ombud for gender equality have said repeatedly that the battle for equal status must now focus on men and the male role.

This focus on men has already resulted in changes in maternity leave legislation. One of the really noticeable changes is that four weeks of the maternity leave is for the exclusive

Source: Pernille Lonne Morkhagen, "The Position of Women in Norway," Oslo: Ministry of Foreign Affairs, (May, 2002).

use of new fathers. If the father does not make use of his so-called father's quota to stay home with the baby for one month, the family loses its right to this portion of the leave period. How many countries in the world have a separate paternity leave for men?

After the special father's quota was introduced in 1993, the percentage of new fathers who took paternity leave increased from 45 to 70 percent during the first year. This arrangement is now firmly established. Most men now consider it a matter of course to use at least a part of their allotted leave.

In the last ten years, the Children Act has strengthened the rights of the father, or more correctly the child's right to have contact with both father and mother after a divorce. It is no longer an automatic process that the mother is awarded custody when parents divorce. In contested cases, the courts must concentrate primarily on the suitability of both parents rather than their sex. And when the parents move far apart after a divorce it is no longer the case that the parent who is not granted custody rights (read, the father) must pay travel expenses for the child/children moving from the one home to the other. This is a change that takes special consideration of the economic burden it was for men previously to maintain close contact with their children after a divorce.

MANY WOMEN IN POLITICS

In the present conservative/centrist government 8 of the 19 ministers are women. The minister of defence is a woman as is the minister of communications. But this is no record in a Norwegian context. The record is held by Gro Harlem Brundtland with her government of 10 men and 9 women.

In the mid 90s female representation in the Storting was 39 percent, the highest figure ever. 25 years ago, for example, only every fourth representative was a woman. After the previous general election, the number sank to 36 percent but in 2001 it rose to 37 percent. On a world basis the average is 13.9 percent.

After the municipal election in the autumn of 1999, there were 34 percent women in local government. In the county councils female participation is far better. In 12 out of 19 county councils there are now at least 40 percent women. Never previously have there been so many women in the local of county councils. Nevertheless, only 65 out of a total of 435 mayors are women. This is fewer than after the last local elections. 78 percent of deputy mayors and heads of political committees are men and in the municipalities there are only four women among the 19 chairpersons of Norway's county councils. In other words the percentage of women is not as high at all political levels.

Massive campaigns were waged in the 70s and 80s to get more women involved in politics, particularly in local councils. As a result there have been veritable election landslides, dubbed female coups, where voters have increased the representation of women by crossing out the names of male candidates and substituting the names of women candidates one or more times. This is especially true of local elections, where election rules allow this so-called cumulating. Many experienced male politicians lost their seats to less experienced women candidates this way.

The first female "coup" took place in 1971, provoked by a growing frustration in the female population. This was at a time when women were making their way into the work force in large numbers, while women's priorities were not achieving a corresponding impact in the political sphere.

Today it is a rarity for the political parties not to have a woman as the first or second name on the election lists. All of the major Norwegian political parties apart from the most conservative, the Party of Progress, have had or have women leaders. In present day Norway it is unthinkable for a political party, regardless of its ideology, not to have substantial female representation at a high level.

It is probably largely because of this "feminine political revolution" that foreigners consider Norwegian women to have attained a position of strength and equality.

THE GENDER EQUALITY OMBUD

The establishment of a special Gender Equality Ombud has made Norway known throughout the world as a country that values gender equality. Norway, which was the first country in the world to have a Gender Equality Ombud, consolidated its comprehensive legislation on equality in a separate Gender Equality Act whose 25th anniversary will be celebrated next year. It is the duty of the Gender Equality Ombud to enforce the act.

The act has been strengthened and revised several times. As early as 1981 a rule was introduced which stipulated equal representation for both sexes on public committees and boards. The rule was strengthened in 1988 with a "60–40 rule" for all committees with more than four members. In other words there were never to be less than 40 percent women on a public board or committee.

At the last count-up, in 2001, female representation on state boards, councils and committees was on average 41 percent. The year before it was 42 percent. Few now doubt that this law has contributed a lot towards creating a man/woman balance in these positions of power during recent years.

In 2002 it was in fact the Christian Democrat/Conservative government that introduced the requirement that private companies were also to follow 60–40 percent rule in their boards. This illustrates that point that it is the political parties themselves, almost regardless of ideologies, who have promoted gender equality over recent years. The heads of both individual companies and employer organisations protested vehemently against what they consider interference in their right to self-determination. But the government is crystal clear on the issue: It leads the way and stipulates that all public-owned enterprises are to have at least 40% women on their boards within one year. In 2005 the same rule will also apply to privately owned companies. But the law will only be enforced if the companies concerned have not voluntarily and independently increased the percentage of women on their board to at least 40 percent by this time.

One of the tasks of the Gender Equality Ombud throughout its almost 25 years of existence has been to monitor hiring in the public and private sectors. In Norway, it is illegal, for example, to advertise for a woman secretary. All appointment notices must be gender neutral, with the exception of advertisements for male or female actors or models. If the workplace seeking new employees is dominated by men, it is also common to encourage women to apply, with the reverse true for women-dominated workplaces.

Despite this, we have—as we will shortly learn—one of the most gender divided labor forces in the entire OECD area.

Another of the tasks of the Gender Equality Ombud is to ensure that pregnant women and those on statutory maternity leave are not squeezed out of their jobs. It is illegal to fire an employee who is pregnant or is on maternity leave. It is also illegal for an employer to prevent a man from taking statutory paternity leave if the family wishes him to tend to the child at home during its first year. In the previous Labour Party government there was for example a women minister who transferred a large part of her maternity leave to her husband.

THE HISTORY OF WOMEN'S LIBERATION IN NORWAY

There are long political traditions stretching back to the nascent fight for women's emancipation in the nineteenth century. As early as 1854, Norwegian women acquired inheritance rights. But it was not until the 1890s that married women gained the right to control their own wealth. Prior to the start of industrialization in the nineteenth century, the role of women was entirely subservient to men. Although Norwegian women received a modicum of education, the possibility for being independent was remote.

In 1882 women were given access to higher education, but it was not until 1903 that the first Norwegian woman received a doctorate at the University of Oslo. The first female professor came on the scene in 1912. By this time many women had already joined the work force as secretaries, teachers and industrial workers.

Industrialization gave women new opportunities in the cities, but the female factory workers had a hard life, with extremely long hours, a poor working environment and miserable wages. Equal pay was an unknown principle. Statistics from the turn of the century show that errand boys earned an average of 290 kroner a year, whereas a maid had to make do with 151 kroner.

Norwegian women won the right to vote in 1913, fifteen years after Norwegian men. They had been fighting a hard battle for political rights since 1885, when a women's suffrage organization was created, a year after the founding of the first women's rights association. These women's rights associations were far removed from the problems of the female factory workers, dominated as they were by liberal middle class women fighting for suffrage, the right to education, and the same legal rights in civil law for both sexes. However, towards the end of the last century and at the beginning of the 20th century, working class women also began to organize. The first to do so were the female matchstick workers. The various unions gradually helped in improving the unsatisfactory working conditions of the women.

We need only go back 30–35 years to find slogans such as "Women's right to work" being carried in the parades celebrating International Woman's Day on 8th March. A great deal has been achieved in the sphere of equal status since then. Young people will shake their heads in disbelief at their grandmothers' accounts of how they were expected to marry, bear children and stay at home. These same young people may also find it hard to believe that it was difficult to break out of this pattern and how conscience stricken they were at having to return to work only three to four months after a birth. Legislation on maternity leave is now quite different and it is normal for mothers of small children to have a job.

LITERARY MODELS

Forceful personalities among writers, teachers and socially committed women were quick to put the disadvantaged position of women on the agenda, and to do something about it.

One male writer was particularly active in the fight for women's rights: Henrik Ibsen's contemporary dramas feature strong female characters in leading roles who express their need for freedom. And the writer himself gave such a thundering speech to the Scandinavian Society in Rome in 1879 when he failed to get a majority to allow women members into the organization, that a woman fainted. Women writers have also provided poetic descriptions of women's role in society. The first of them was Camilla Collett, with her novel "The Governor's Daughter" ("Amtmandens Døttre") in 1855. The Norwegian author, Sigrid Undset, who won the Nobel Prize for literature in 1928, also described women and the reality they faced in both her contemporary novels and her works set in the middle ages.

A present day writer who has successfully described a Norwegian female psyche is Herbjørg Wassmo with her heroine Dina. The book was recently filmed with Marie Bonnevie playing the lead. Dina is a beautiful, strong and tempestuous woman from the north of Norway who is led by her instincts far more than by the men in her life. Perhaps this accords well with foreign conceptions of the Norwegian woman.

SPORTS IDOLS

In addition to the many competent and prominent women we can look up to in politics, it is in sports that Norwegian women have excelled in recent years. Ace marathon runner Grete Waitz has contributed a great deal to women's self-confidence and enjoyment of sport. To win the New York marathon 9 times in a row is an unparalleled achievement. She herself is modest and self effacing and has not been a vociferous advocate of women's rights. However, because of her athletic achievements she has had a tremendous impact on the participation of Norwegian women in sports, and on their self-image.

A host of talented skiers, handball players, swimmers and other athletes have followed in her footsteps. And lots of young girls are now learning to play soccer, exactly the same way that boys have done for generations. Norway's women's soccer team is also one of the best in the world.

These things should not be forgotten nor should their importance be underrated when describing the position of women in Norwegian society. The athletic prowess of Norwegian women is something we are proud of. It helps give women a healthy and robust self-image.

The American anthropologists/psychotherapists Akb Pillai and D. P. Pillai have in their research accurately described the Norwegian health ideal. In social relations Norwegian women are among the most natural we have ever seen. They dress modestly and use little make up. But this does not detract from their sex appeal. In the summer of this year the two anthropologists will issue the book "The Light of the Northern Star." In this the two authors cite hard work as the underlying reason why Norwegian women are so strong, self-confident and emancipated.

THE FLIP SIDE

Here we come to an important point. Norwegian women's prominent role in politics and sports represents one of the brighter sides of women's situation in Norway. If we look at the everyday life of Norwegian women and their situation 69 percent of Norwegian women today have paid employment outside the home as against 77 percent of Norwegian men.

Women thus constitute almost half the work force. A study reveals that among 16 European countries, Norway is in top position as regards working women.

But women do not work as much as men. Women work an average 30.3 hours a week while the average Norwegian man has a work week of 39.4 hours. In other words, many women work part-time, primarily to have enough energy left over to care for their home and family.

There are only a handful of women in leading positions in Norwegian business and industry, despite the fact that women make up nearly half the work force. Women executives are a rarity. In firms with more than 250 employees there are only 21 women directors as compared with 467 men. Furthermore, these women earn only half of what the men earn and wage growth is much slower than it is for men. In 240 of Norway's leading enterprises 26 percent have no women at executive level or on the board. 19 percent have women on the board. This is a smaller percentage than in many countries we naturally compare ourselves with. But it is positive that the female share of top leaders and board chairpersons in the business sector has increased somewhat in recent years. The increase is greatest in recruitment positions and among managers. But if developments continue at their present pace, it will take 115 years to get as many women as men onto the boards of private companies, says the Gender Equality Ombud. This is of course the reason why the government will use new laws to enforce affirmative action if the companies themselves do not voluntarily bring more women onto their boards.

WOMEN IN PUBLIC ADMINISTRATION

Central government figures are also disconcerting. Full-time women employees make up 45 percent of the civil service. Yet when it comes to the top echelon, women are not well represented. In 2002 only 10 percent of directors general were women and, for example, only 26 women among the 113 secretaries general. In the diplomatic corps only every tenth ambassador is a women while 97 percent of consuls are men. On the other hand, the gender balance in politically appointed ministerial posts has gradually improved: Of 35 state secretaries 12 are women.

The balance is uneven in local government too when we do not regard the councils as political arenas but as the country's biggest workplace. They are easily the country's biggest workplaces for women, with 75 percent women, the biggest concentrations of women being in schools and day care centres, nursing homes, the caring services and social welfare. Here too we find many women in low-paid jobs and part time jobs. When only full time employees are included in the figures women constitute less than 60 percent of the work force. But even when one only includes full-time employees, women in managerial positions make up only 25 percent of the total. Only 15 percent of department heads and administrative leaders in the municipal sector are women.

A telling example from the municipalities is the high percentage of employees who work with clients at social services offices and public health centers and in nursing and care-giving services. Eighty percent of the employees in these sectors are women, but only 34 percent of administrators are women. According to wage statistics compiled by the Ministry of Government Administration a few years ago, this means that only eight percent of the women who work in municipal nursing and care services will advance to managerial positions, while 48 percent of the men will attain a leading position.

There is only one area of local government in which there are just as many women administrators as men. Almost half of the country's health and social services officers are women. Women in leading positions are otherwise few and far between.

VISIBLE AND INVISIBLE BARRIERS

Why is this so? Many researchers who have done studies on women have tried to explain why women have achieved such a clear position in politics and ministry posts while remaining conspicuously absent from positions of power in working life.

Men, and in particular men who are themselves in leading jobs and who recruit new leaders, tend to explain this situation in terms of a shortage of qualified women willing to take on such work. They complain that there are not only too few women with the right qualifications, but that those suitable as candidates for the top jobs are reluctant to assume positions of power. A common explanation is that women have different priorities: home before careers. Men often say that they have no objection to women in top jobs, but that women themselves do not want to be there.

Such views are not wholly unfounded. Already burdened, many women and men do not want to take on even greater responsibilities in their daily lives. Another factor is that many women set such strict standards regarding the quality of their work, that they do not consider themselves qualified for promotion, even though they are objectively at par with the men who advance. In the words of Ingelin Killengren, Commissioner of the Oslo Police: "It is particularly the male middle managers who have to be more conscious of the fact that men are good at marketing themselves, while women are cautious and reserved. If managers are not aware of this, women will continue to be held back."

Others have called this barrier to top positions an invisible "glass ceiling." Well educated women in particular feel that they are not to the same degree urged to seek top jobs or contacted when new positions are to be filled.

"I've reached the glass ceiling and can go no further. With regard to board positions, these are based on personal relationships. Men have a network. They do not select on the basis of whether you are competent or not, but whether they trust you and know you" a women executive told the newspaper Aftenposten.

AFFIRMATIVE ACTION

Theoretically there are no sexual barriers. Norwegian women can advance on a par with men. The aforementioned equal rights legislation even demands that employers try to recruit more women further up the managerial ladder. The law clearly states that where one of the sexes is strongly underrepresented in an organization, this sex is to be preferred when new appointments are made, so long as the applicants have otherwise equal qualifications.

In jobs where formal education and seniority form the basis for weighing qualifications, comparing candidates is easy. Male teachers and male nurses, who are both a marked minority in their professions, are for example often preferred when appointments are made.

However, when recruiting to top jobs where women are underrepresented, formal qualifications are not the only concern. Here considerations such as an applicant's personal suitability, network of contacts and involvement in the community play a part as well. When well-qualified women are passed over, their exclusion is often explained in vague terms such as, "she wasn't suited for the job," "she lacks experience as a leader," and the like.

To bolster the self-confidence of women and to qualify women for managerial positions, courses have been arranged internally by many corporations and agencies and externally by trade unions and professional and trade organizations. However, it is difficult to document the effect of such courses. Some professional organizations also have so-called mentor arrangements for young women who aspire to a top job.

The Gender Equality Centre in Oslo has compiled a special women's data base. In it are stored the names of more than 2,500 women who qualify for leading positions or as board members. A number of young women are now copying the example of the men in another sphere. They are establishing formal and informal networks to provide each other with support and to exchange information. The effect of these measures is however not documented.

MORE EDUCATION

More and more young women are undergoing education at a higher level than before. 60 percent of all new students at universities and colleges are women. However much of the reason for Norway having what we call an extremely gender-divided labor market, is the fact that women have traditionally chosen to train themselves for the caring professions, whereas men have acquired economic or technical skills. In Norway there are few occupations employing an equal number of men and women.

Young women still tend to choose along traditional lines when selecting their line of study for the last three years of Norway's 13-year system. For several decades the authorities have tried to encourage young women, to pursue an education in typical male-dominated professions. In some areas these campaigns have been successful. A good balance has been achieved, for instance among medical and dentistry, law and journalism students. In other areas, the traditional gender distribution has become even more entrenched.

Symptomatic for this labour market differentiated along the lines of sex, is that the education chosen by women leads to low-paying jobs, whereas the jobs the men take yield higher wages and more prestige. A woman with a three year college education in nursing will get a far lower wage than a man with a three year course from a technical college. She will also be working within a system where the chances of promotion are fairly limited and wage increases are small and predictable. A man on the other hand will advance faster and demand wage increases in accordance with this.

WOMEN'S SUPPLEMENT

Recent pay settlements have to a certain degree attempted to rectify the imbalance between typical women's and men's occupations. On a couple of occasions, for example, a large number of women-dominated sectors have received an extra "women's supplement" on top of other pay increases. Teachers, for example, have had substantial wage increases in recent years. But other typical women's professions have not been so fortunate. Nurses, auxiliary nurses and day care centre teachers are dropping behind in wage development. But the overall trend is still positive. The Living Conditions survey reveals that there have been relatively fewer women in the low-wage group during the last twenty years. In 1980 there were slightly less than three times as many women as men in the low paid group, while before the turn of the century there were more than twice as many. But many more successful wage settlements are needed to iron out the differences. It must be correct to say that at the moment the most obvious fight for women's rights takes place during wage settlements. But despite the fact that wage differences are clearly obvious and are perceived as unfair by most women and men, a long hard battle remains to be fought before the work done by men and women is valued equally. Traditional attitudes in working life and educational patterns are not matters which equality-minded politicians have thus far managed to legislate away.

DOUBLE-WORKING FAMILIES

Despite our gender divided labour force there are a significant number of well-educated young women in Norway today who are making their way up the careers ladder in both the private and public sectors, and many who have encroached on the male-dominated professions. The problem is that many of these women feel torn between working as men do, and giving enough of themselves to the caring role they have outside their jobs.

There is little doubt that Norwegian women still retain the bulk of the responsibility for the home and children.

Time studies show that even in families where both parents work, the woman spends far more time on housework and being with children than the man. A time use study made in 2000 shows that 50% of mothers spend 10–19 hours a week on housework while 50% of the men spend less than 5 hours week on such work. 20 percent of the men spend at least 10 hours a week on housework while 78 percent of the women spend 10 to 30 hours a week on caring for the home. These time studies show that although women work full time outside the home, they spend far more time on household chores than their partners in full time jobs.

But this does not necessarily mean that the men are lounging on the sofa reading the newspaper. The study shows that they are at work. Men work far more overtime than the average woman.

Another point which emerges from the study is that there has been a quiet revolution on the home front. Women, particularly well-educated women, no longer define the role of "good mother" as someone who attends to the laundry and vacuums in the corners. Women spend far more time together with their children on active pursuits such as reading for them, playing with them, helping them with homework and taking them on trips and to their various leisure activities. Men too now give higher priority to being with their children than to doing traditional housework, to the extent that they are able to spend more time in the home.

PRAM-PUSHING MEN

A new generation of men who do do a lot on the home front is taking over. Many young men today have grown up with women's liberation and equality as important and natural ingredients of their formative years. When they become fathers, it will be just as natural for them to stay home from work when the children are sick, as for the child's mother to take time off from her job. Women and men have equal rights in this area too.

Now that the rules for maternity leaves have also been changed, we are now witnessing a host of pram-pushing men who take leave for a month or more before the baby is big enough to start in day care or is put in the hands of a child minder.

Although all statistics show that Norwegian women do most of the housework, a number of prominent men have begun to advertise the fact that they are not interested in a political career because it doesn't give them enough time to be with their children.

Quite recently a well-known politician did the opposite. He admitted that he had not attended any of his 9-year-old son's birthday parties. He gave priority to his work as a Storting (national assembly) representative. His statement sparked strong negative reactions.

The latest surveys on living conditions show that an increasing number of fathers of small children want to work less in order to be home more with their children. But here there is still a gap between theory and practice. For instance, it is very unusual for men to ask their boss if they can work shorter hours in order to take care of their children. They have an equal right to do this—on a par with women. But there are few men who devote more time to the family without being forced to relegate their career to second place. It is for this reason that so few people agreed with prime minister Kjell Magne Bondevik who said in 1998, when the cash benefits scheme was introduced, that it would give men the opportunity to be home with the children and thus promote gender equality.

CASH BENEFITS VERSUS DAY CARE CENTRES

The family of every one- and two-year-old who does not attend a day care centre receives a sum of 36,000 NOK (approx. euro 4,700)—per year. The sum is rather less if the child attends a centre with shorter hours, which thus is not so subsidized. The aim is to give the parents of young children the possibility, both economically and practically, to take care of their children themselves—rather than sending them to a day care centre.

Women's organisations, the more radical political parties and parts of the trade union movement protested vehemently when the then government of Christian Democrats and Conservatives introduced the scheme. They claimed that it would tear down much of what the fight for equality had achieved during the last 30 years and make it impossible to fulfill the goal of day care centres for all children by the turn of the century.

And what has happened? Analyses made so far show that three out of four children in the relevant age group receive a cash benefit. However, the parents are not working much less. One in five working mothers is now on shorter hours and a third of this number have become full time mothers. Only 4 percent of those receiving cash benefits are men. Of the 95,000 who work full day in the home, only 2,000 are men.

An unintentional effect of the new scheme is that families with one- and two-year-olds can use the cash benefit to pay au pairs or childminders to take care of the children while both parents continue to work. Whether very small children are better off with a childminder than in a properly regulated day nursery is a matter of opinion. One of the goals of the previous Labour Government was to shrink the market for unauthorized childminders who work for wages that go largely unreported. The authorities are also working to regulate private childcare providers by facilitating the opening of small publicly subsidized day nurseries in private homes.

Nevertheless, the goal of providing every child with a place in a day nursery has by no means been achieved. At the turn of the millennium only 77 percent of 3–7 year olds and 37 percent of 1–2 year olds had places in day nurseries.

PARENTS WITH TIME ACCOUNTS

Norway has yet another support scheme to increase flexibility and to give the parents of small children a chance to combine child care and a career.

At the same time as the father's quota was introduced, new parents received in 1993 another parental leave right, the so-called time account scheme. This means that parents of small children can choose various options in order to stretch the paid parental leave over a longer period by combining shorter working hours with child care at home. With the exception of three weeks before and six weeks after the birth that are reserved for the mother, and four weeks set aside for the father, the parents can split the parental leave between themselves. For example, they can choose a solution where both or one works less than normal in order to be home with the baby. This reduces the workload of the new family, while the parental leave rights ensure the same level of income.

So far, not very many young families have chosen this option. Many prefer to take their one-year leave in one go, with the person who is home with the child receiving 80 percent of their pay for one year, or full pay if the parental leave is 42 weeks.

In addition to this right for parents of very small children, Norway also has another type of right for employees who wish to spend more time with children who are a little older. All employees with children under 10 years of age have the right to reduce their position to 80 percent as long as it does not create major problems for the employer. There's little doubt that it is basically women who are availing themselves of this right.

NEW FAMILY PATTERNS

In recent decades the number of divorces has increased dramatically. Many families are breaking up, and quite a few of them are overstretched families with small children. Judging by the divorce rate in 2000, 46.8 percent of all marriages can end in divorce unless the pattern changes.

64 percent of children now live together with their married parents. The rest live with cohabiting parents, with a single mother or with a mother and a new step-family. Only a very small percent live together with their father or in a new step-family. Even the royal family illustrates the new family constellations. In 2001 Crown Prince Haakon married a single mother.

There are always many reasons for a divorce. But there is little doubt that the pressure of time and distribution of workloads can be contributory factors. Statistics show that it is often the woman who decides on divorce.

Single parents are those who are struggling most with financial problems today. And women almost always have the main responsibility for the children after the break-up of the marriage.

Nonetheless, there are also a large number of men who are responsible "part-time fathers," both in regard to paying child support and raising the children. Norway has a law whose purpose is to ensure that both parents maintain contact with their children after a break-up. There is an increasing tendency for fathers to take on the main responsibility for the children or that the parents decide to have the children split their time equally between mother and father. In Norway, there are quite a few children who live with each parent for a week at a time, or who shuttle back and forth between their homes on weekends and holidays.

WELFARE WITH AN AFTERTASTE

Despite the opportunities for reduced working hours and the tendency of women to work part time, many families feel they just don't have enough time for each other. Living standards and wage levels have in many cases made it necessary for both parents to work a lot, often more than they want to.

Overall, there is little doubt that parents have less time to spend with their children. Unpaid care-giving carries little prestige in today's society. Our children are to a larger degree being looked after by other paid employees and our old people are being taken care of by professionals. The countless at-home mothers who cared for their children and home and looked after their parents and elderly neighbors disappeared a long time ago. These tasks have become professionalized and paid, though at a far lower level than traditional men's work.

AN EQUAL SOCIETY?

In Norway we today in a rich and smoothly functioning society where few people fall outside the safety net of national insurance and pension schemes when they find they are unable to provide for themselves. Thanks to pension schemes, sickness benefits and national insurance benefits very few people live in dire poverty today. And we have rights in the workplace that many people in other countries no doubt envy, with respect to protection against dismissal, the opportunity to take care of our children and the opportunity to divide the workload between men and women.

We also live in a culture where women have a prominent position and where the general attitude is that nothing that is possible for a man is impossible for a woman. Other cultures may even find Norwegian women somewhat mannish due to their open and direct way of dealing with others.

At the same time our enlightened and equalized society has a flip-side, and that is that even though women have broken every barrier and entered every male bastion, the work women do is on the whole not valued as highly as the man's. Our highly regulated society has not been completely successful in creating a framework in which the care-giving tasks traditionally carried out by women alone are equally divided between women and men or provided by professions in a completely satisfactory manner.

It has been said that as long as men do not and are not expected to participate as much on the home front as women are now doing in public life, we will not have real equality in Norwegian society. We could add that as long as it is more difficult for a woman than for a man to get a top job, then Norway is not making full use of its human resources.

But if we compare ourselves with other countries, it's easy to see that we've come a long way.

Section 5

Sexual Orientation

THE UNITED STATES CONTEXT

Variance from the societal norm of heterosexuality is not a social problem, *the societal response to it is*. (Much of this section introduction is taken from Eitzen and Baca Zinn, 2006, Chapter 10, and Baca Zinn and Eitzen, 2005:271–272.) Consequently, people who differ from the socially approved sexual orientation (gays, lesbians, bisexuals, and the transgendered) are objects of derision and contempt by members of society and discriminated against by individuals and by the normal operation of society's institutions. Society imposes the norm of sexual identity (compulsory heterosexuality) through negative sanctions on those who are sexually different and by granting privileges to those in heterosexual relationships.

The Judeo-Christian tradition considers homosexual behavior a heinous sin. Thus, many (but by no means all) contemporary churches deny pastorates to gays and lesbians, refuse to conduct marriage ceremonies for them, and do not allow them as members unless they vow sexual abstinence.

The laws deny equal rights to gays and lesbians. Same-sex marriage is not recognized by the state, except in Massachusetts. Also, in 2005 Connecticut joined Vermont as the only states to recognize civil unions for gay couples providing them many rights and privileges afforded married couples. In response, many states have passed laws banning same-sex marriages. Congress has passed the Defense of Marriage Act, which denies federal recognition of same-sex marriage and allows states to ignore such unions licensed elsewhere.

Parenthood has become the latest battleground for lesbian and gay rights. The legality of homosexual parenthood varies from state to state, and the interpretation from judge to judge. Thus, there is considerable legal ambiguity regarding the rights of same-sex couples to adopt and to obtain custody of children following a heterosexual marriage.

Gay Americans won a historic victory in 2003, when the U.S. Supreme Court, reversing the Court's ruling in 1986, struck down a Texas law banning sodomy (oral or anal sex) as an unconstitutional violation of privacy. This invalidated anti-sodomy laws in 13 states.

The armed forces have always discriminated against gays and lesbians, with lesbians about three times more likely to be removed from the military for homosexuality than gays. The Clinton administration instituted the "don't ask, don't tell" rule in an attempt to reduce discrimination against homosexuals in the military. This meant that the military was not to ask its personnel about their sexuality, and to prosecute only if gay and lesbian service members were blatant about their sexual orientation. In short, as long as homosexual service members "stayed in the closet," they were allowed to remain in the military.

REFERENCES

Baca Zinn, Maxine, and D. Stanley Eitzen. 2005. *Diversity in Families,* 7th ed. Boston: Allyn & Bacon.
Eitzen, D. Stanley, and Maxine Baca Zinn. 2006. *Social Problems,* 10th ed. Boston: Allyn & Bacon.

11

Social Shift Opens Door to Gay Marriage Plan

CLIFFORD KRAUSS

Canada has become a more tolerant society, decriminalizing possession of small amounts of marijuana, permitting "safe-injection" clinics for heroin addicts, and allowing gay marriage. The author asserts that the main reason for this transformation is that Canada in the last generation has become a multicultural society.

TORONTO—Canada's decision to allow marriage between same-sex couples is only one of many signs that this once tradition-bound society is undergoing social changes at an astonishing rate.

Increasingly, Canada has been on a social policy course pursued by many Western European and Scandinavian countries, gradually moving more out of step with the United States over the last few decades.

Even as the government announced Tuesday that it would rewrite the definition of marriage, it was transforming its drug policies by decriminalizing possession of small amounts of marijuana and permitting "safe-injection" clinics in Vancouver for heroin addicts in an effort to fight disease.

The large population of native peoples remains impoverished, but there are growing signs that they are taking greater control of their destinies, and their leaders now govern two territories occupying more than a third of Canada's land mass.

Canada has never had a revolution or a civil war, and little social turbulence aside from sporadic rebellions in the 19th century and a splash of terrorism in Quebec in the 1960s and 1970s.

Regarding ease of social change, Canada is virtually in a category by itself.

The transformation of the country's demographics, for example, has been breathtaking since the 1970s, when the government of Pierre Trudeau opened wide the country's doors to Africans, Asians and West Indians as part of an attempt to fill Canada's huge, underpopulated hinterland. Eighteen percent of the population is now foreign-born compared with about 11 percent in the United States, and there is little or no public debate over whether a sea change in culture, demographics and even national identity is good or bad for the country.

In only the last generation, Toronto, Montreal and Vancouver, where a third of the population lives, have become multicultural polygots where the towers of Sikh temples and mosques have become mainstays of the skyline and where cuisine and fashion have become concoctions of spices and patterns that are in the global vanguard.

Toronto, once a homogeneous city of staid British tradition, is now a place where more than 40 percent of the people are foreign-born, where there are nearly 2,000 ethnic restaurants and where local radio and television stations broadcast in more than 30 languages.

"Everything from marriage laws to marijuana laws, we are going through a period of accelerated social change," said Neil Bissoundath, an immigrant from Trinidad who is a leading novelist here. "There is a general approach to life here that is both evolutionary and revolutionary."

He said that the balance goes all the way back to the ideals of the Tory founders of Canada, who remained loyal to the British crown and who instilled a laissez-faire conservatism "that says people have a right to live their lives as they like."

That philosophy was a practical necessity in a colony that was bilingual after the British conquered French Quebec, creating relative social peace by allowing greater religious freedoms than even Catholics in England had at the time.

The live-and-let-live approach was codified by the 1992 Charter of Rights and Freedoms, Canada's Bill of Rights. Being as young as it is, the charter occupies a vivid corner of the Canadian psyche. So when three senior provincial courts ruled recently that federal marriage law discriminated against same-sex couples under the charter, the Liberal Cabinet decided to go along and not appeal the decisions.

While the new law will have to be passed by the House of Commons, little organized resistance has risen.

Few here have complained that a national policy pertaining to something as intimate as marriage would be set by courts in Quebec, British Columbia and Ontario rather than by a federal body. In part that reflects the great relative political strength that regional governments have developed in what is known as the Canadian Confederation, where Canada's federal government is weaker than most central governments in the West.

But it also reflects poll results that show a majority of Canadians support expanding marriage to gay couples. Last year, the Quebec provincial assembly unanimously enacted a law giving sweeping parental rights to same-sex couples, with even the most conservative members voting in favor despite lobbying by the Roman Catholic Church.

"Canada has always been in the vanguard in relation to many societies in the world," Prime Minister Jean Chretien said Tuesday, speaking in French to reporters after he announced the Cabinet's decision. "We have met our responsibilities."

Nowhere has the social change been more dramatic than in Quebec, which as recently as the 1960s was a deeply conservative place where the church dominated education and social life. Since the baby-boomer generation launched the "Quiet Revolution" in favor of separatism, big government social programs and secularism, abortion and divorce rates there rose to among the highest in Canada while church attendance plummeted.

Now the pendulum is moving in the other direction, ever so slightly.

"There is a centrist mentality in Canada that translates into the political system not tolerating the Pat Buchanans nor the leftist equivalent," noted Michel C. Auger, a political columnist for *Le Journal de Montreal*. "There is a unified fabric here that is a lot stronger on social issues than it seems to be in the United States."

12

Gay Rights and European Citizenship

JOYDEEP SENGUPTA

The European Union leads the way in gay rights advances. Unlike the United States, where the government and state legislatures have been unwilling to grant gays and lesbians the "rights" of minority groups, the nations of Europe and Scandinavia have granted these group rights to prevent discrimination by the majority.

The European Union (EU) has been cautiously approaching the notion of the "European citizen"[1] as a person endowed with certain rights, privileges, and responsibilities traditionally held as the exclusive jurisdiction of nation states. Including gay rights within this evolving notion of EU citizenship requires a negotiation of rights in transnational space while utilizing the slowly widening apertures at the national level.

Citizenship is the legal expression of membership in the national family, carrying with it the obligation for its defense and welfare. Exclusions from the rights and duties of citizenship—such as banning homosexuals from the military or denying them the right to marry and create a family—are a symbolic ostracism from the national family. Attempts to redress the systematic exclusion of gays from full citizenship in Europe must reconcile a reprehensible history of injustice rooted in prohibitions on homosexuality in the Judeo-Christian religious traditions, and (with a few exceptions) in the criminalization, pathologization, or mere omission of homosexuality in legal code until the 20th century.

The progressive expansion of gay rights corresponds to the growing understanding of gays and lesbians as a "social group" having claims to rights similar to those of other minorities—ethnic, religious, and linguistic ones, among others—traditionally the target of discrimination. Many demands for greater rights and protections for gays and lesbians are similar to those sought by women or other minority groups, such as nondiscrimination in laws governing employment, housing, or access to public office and government services. On the other hand, most other minorities in Europe have not had to worry about laws governing marriage, property, inheritance, taxation, divorce, joint adoptions, custody rights, insurance and employer benefits, and immigration, as these rights have traditionally been derived automatically from heterosexual marriage.

Source: Joydeep Sengupta, "Gay Rights and European Citizenship," *The Gay & Lesbian Review* 9 (November/ December 2002), pp. 28–30.

The law plays a critical role in constructing group identity, affecting how the group is perceived by society at large. While minority legislation broadly addresses the group, the particular application of it to the individual forms the basis for contesting rights and benefits. Especially in the Anglo-American common law tradition, and to a large extent within continental civil law systems, the individual is afforded primary legal personhood; the individual, not the group, is the subject of the law. As Nathan Glazer has observed, the Fifth Amendment to the U.S. Constitution, which provided the legal foundation for the minority rights protections of the subsequent Fourteenth Amendment, emphasizes the "person" and the "citizen" in its guarantees for due process, privileges and immunities, and equal protection of the law.

In the U.S., right-wing opposition to civil rights advancements is sometimes veiled as a principled rejection of "special" rights for minority groups and women, since they explicitly recognize certain groups and provide protections that supposedly are not applicable to, say, white heterosexual males. In *Inclusion of the Other: Studies in Political Theory* (1998), Jurgen Habermas observes that the "legislation of identity," especially minority identities, in Western liberal democracies stands on precarious ground. Group rights are critiqued as weakening an individual rights culture, which has strengthened civil rights claims. Additionally, claims for state protection of a group's identity as distinct from the majority's religious and cultural value system are viewed as threats to national unity. Claims for rights by one group occasionally necessitates the controversial and divisive subjugation of the claims of another, such as religious conservatives and gay rights advocates. Habermas observes that "protection of collective identities comes into competition with the right to equal individual liberties (subjective *Freiheiten*)—Kant's one original human right—so that in a case of conflict a decision must be made about which takes precedence."

In an article in *Journal of Politics* (May 1996), Haider-Markel and Meier propose an explanation for the evolution of gay and lesbian collective rights in the American context. They claim that "two competing coalitions [are] often formed around conflicting ideological camps and/or partisanship, and are brought to a public vote."[2] The process resembles that of redistributive politics, except that groups seek to redistribute values rather than money through government action. The "government stamp of approval" is viewed as validation of their interests and affirmation of its rights as citizens. In *Multiculturalism and "The Politics of Recognition"* (1992), Amy Gutmann asserts that minority groups within pluralistic democracies seek "public recognition as equal citizens," thereby requiring two forms of legal respect from the majority: respect for unique identities, and respect for activities, practices, and world views. Thus, for group-identified sexual minority cultures, legislative protection serves not only to guarantee fundamental rights against prejudice or discrimination from the majority culture, but also to assert the right to enter into alternative social units and pursue autonomous cultural expression regardless of majority opinion against it.

In modern liberal democracies, group rights are broadly derived from the authority vested in elected leaders, who must then promote social justice while upholding the primacy of individual equality. This is complemented by a progressive, positivist legal culture in which the rights of minorities are upheld to prevent discrimination by the majority. Indeed, group rights have a long historical lineage in the West: Roman and Justinian law, for instance, provided special protections for politically weaker groups, such as women and slaves. In the utilitarian tradition of Jeremy Bentham and John Stuart Mill, protection of individual rights (entitlements) and liberties within the democratic state is favored over paternalistic prohibitions on behavior deemed harmful to the group. Mill's famous "harm principle" strongly resonates with the modern legal concept of "proportionality": Mill asserts that the potential tyranny of an all-powerful state must be restrained by forbidding state intervention in private choices that do not directly harm the general welfare of others.

The harm principle is what deprives the government of the right to interfere in the practice of private same-sex behavior between consenting adults, an act that does not inflict a proportional harm upon other citizens. In the gay marriage cases in Hawaii and Vermont, moral opposition or a paternalistic commitment to preserving "traditional values" is insufficient reasons for restricting rights. But the sweeping passage of anti-gay-marriage legislation in many states and at the federal level reveals that a moralistic ethic still wins the day with the argument that gay marriage would so harm the majority of citizens as to abolish the minority's claim to equal rights. Even John Stuart Mill, who advocated the full enfranchisement of one excluded group, women, simultaneously supported English efforts against colonized peoples, and he approved the imposition of "civilization" on traditional societies as a necessary evil.

In *History of Sexuality,* Foucault argues that in the 18th and 19th centuries, European society increasingly embraced a monolithic norm of heterosexual monogamy. This bourgeois norm translated into laws that restricted sexual behavior and forced the diverse sexual identities of Europe into the closet. As Foucault amply demonstrates, these identities were painstakingly enumerated in the law, which regulated extramarital sex, premarital sex, incest, sodomy in all its forms, miscegenation, prostitution, and so on. Thus did a category of "moral degenerates" join a number of other social categories—women, the landless, Jews, Gypsies, and so on—as legally excluded from the full benefits and privileges of citizenship. The persecution of what Foucault called "peripheral sexualities" thus shares a common heritage with the persecution of these other minorities.

Despite the continued occurrence of systemic homophobia and legally enforced inequality for gay and lesbian people in parts of Western Europe, the continent leads the world in gay rights advances. Legal equality began to emerge slowly with the growing acceptance of homosexuals in postwar Europe. All EU countries have decriminalized same-sex behavior, and most have repealed higher age-of-consent laws for homosexual acts. In the last two decades, dramatic advances have occurred in the areas of employment non-discrimination, access to reproductive technologies, partner recognition for taxation, immigration, and co-adoption, and protection from hate speech and hate-motivated violence. As in the U.S., support for equal rights varies regionally, being strongest in the north and the west, weakest in the south and east. Political support for gay rights in most EU countries rests on coalitions built by left-leaning parties, which have brought gay rights under their traditional banner of minority rights.

Scandinavian countries and the Netherlands continue to provide the most comprehensive legal protections to gays and lesbians. By 1989, Denmark had enforced employment non-discrimination, removed barriers to full military service, and led the world in the revolutionary Danish Registered Partnership Act or DRP. The DRP became the world's first national-level legislation recognizing the rights of homosexual couples almost on a par with heterosexuals (except in access to reproductive technologies from public health officials, church weddings, and joint adoptions). Currently all five Nordic countries offer some form of domestic partnership and adoption provision. In 2000, the Netherlands became the only government in the world to extended full marriage benefits, including adoption rights, to same-sex couples. Between 1999 and 2001, both France and Germany instituted partnership acts that permit the official registration of same-sex couples and many benefits of marriage. Within the EU, Belgium, Denmark, Finland, France, Germany, Holland, Sweden, and the UK all offer immigration rights for binational couples.

Still, the principle of equality for gay people does not have the status of an indisputable universal human right in the manner of, say, freedom from involuntary servitude. Two key international courts, the European Court of Justice (ECJ) and the European Court of Human Rights (ECHR), have enforced EU treaties and international human rights treaties with varying success when they've come into conflict with national laws. Created to interpret and uphold EU treaties, the ECJ has taken a conservative approach in adjudicating discrimination claims stemming from treaty provisions on gender equality. In ruling against granting equal employer benefits for homosexual couples otherwise available to heterosexuals, the ECJ has repeatedly recommended more explicit EU legislation on gay partnerships. While not an EU Court, the ECHR upholds the European Convention of Human Rights and Fundamental Freedoms (ECHRFF), to which the EU is formally committed through the Maastricht Treaty. For example, archaic sodomy laws in Northern Ireland were famously struck down in the *Dudgeon v. United Kingdom* case at the ECHR, and ruled a violation of the right to privacy. Catholic opposition to gay rights had preserved largely unenforced sodomy laws in the Republic of Ireland. In *Norris v. Ireland,* the ECHR ruled that Ireland should repeal its sodomy laws, and invalidated the Irish High Court's claim that the "Christian and democratic nature" of Ireland was sufficient justification for upholding the laws. The Irish Parliament complied in 1993, striking down all legal discrimination by instituting gender-neutral language.

But standard gay rights legislation for the whole EU remains sparse, causing wide regional disparities in the law. Unlike heterosexual marriage, for instance, same-sex marriage and domestic partnerships do not enjoy uniform reciprocal recognition among all EU states. As the European Court of Justice has repeatedly urged, more explicit EU legislation by way of directives on gay rights issues is necessary, since significant exclusions from the benefits of EU citizenship cannot be adequately addressed by national legislatures. The Treaty of Amsterdam of 1997 introduced for the first time a provision (Article 13) that authorizes the Community to "take appropriate action to combat discrimination [based on sexual orientation]." This article made possible a Council directive in 2000, the first explicit piece of EU legislation prohibiting discrimination on the basis of sexual orientation in private and public employment. While major gains have been made on nondiscrimination in employment, privacy rights, and sodomy laws, areas that are only now being addressed include same-sex marriage, reproductive choice, and immigration rights for gay partners.

With the fragmented, contested, and occasionally triumphant process of integrating a diverse continent, European leaders have long envisioned common values and principles upon which a shared democratic identity of contemporary Europe may be constructed. Embracing the human rights cause has been one such manifestation, and EU governments have consistently supported promotion of human rights worldwide, protection of existing mechanisms for human rights protection, strengthening of human rights organizations, and creation of new institutions for enforcement of international human rights law. In 2000, the European Council adopted the ambitious *Charter of Fundamental Rights of the European Union*, which provides a sweeping nondiscrimination provision: "[A]ny discrimination based on any ground such as sex, race, colour, ethnic or social origin, genetic features, language, religion or belief, political or other opinion, membership in a national minority, property, birth, disability, age or sexual orientation shall be prohibited."

Despite a lack of binding force, the Charter provides additional authority to EU institutions when interpreting community principles and adjudicating discrimination claims. Efforts to create a transnational European identity deeply rooted in respect for human rights requires stronger leadership of member states and continued commitment towards democratic values and minority protections. EU leadership has led to the repeal of anti-gay laws in several non-EU countries, as a condition of future membership. By strengthening support for human rights enforcement and providing moral leadership in promoting equal rights for sexual minorities, the EU can simultaneously consolidate its position as a modernizing, pluralizing, diversifying, progressive force, committed to just and humane social values. The answers that emerge on the citizenship debate must reach to the very soul of the European Union project, and what it seeks to become.

NOTES_____

1. See Title I, Article B, the Treaty on European Union, one of the key goals of which is "the introduction of citizenship of the Union," and "to develop close cooperation on justice and home affairs."
2. Key U.S. examples include Colorado Amendment 2 (1992); Oregon Ballot Measure 9 (1993); California Knight Initiative (2000), all of which sought to restrict gay rights and opposed broadening of existing definitions of family/marriage.

Section 6

Age

THE UNITED STATES CONTEXT

Similar to what is occurring worldwide, the population of the United States is aging. In 1900 about one in twenty-five residents was 65 or older. By 1950 it was about one in twelve. In 2000 one in eight was 65 and over and by 2030 it will likely be about one in five. In effect, by 2030 there will be more grandparents than grandchildren.

There are two major problems brought about by an aging society. (The following is from Eitzen and Baca Zinn, 2006, Chapter 5.) The first is that the Social Security system will become increasingly inadequate to meet the needs of the elderly. This program, when compared to similar programs in other industrialized societies, provides only minimal support. Instead of a universal system that allows the elderly to live comfortably, the Social Security program: (1) does not cover all workers; (2) pays benefits according to the length of time workers have paid into the system and the amount of wages on which they paid a Social Security tax; (3) provides such meager benefits for some that 30 percent of those relying exclusively on Social Security are *below* the poverty line; and (4) is biased against women. These problems will escalate in the future as more people become eligible for Social Security, people live longer, and relatively fewer workers, in comparison with the proportion who are old, pay into the Social Security system.

The second problem caused by the increasing numbers of the elderly in the United States is paying for health care. Of all age groups, the elderly are most affected by ill health, especially from age 75 onward. The United States does provide universal health care for those 65 and over through Medicare but this government program is insufficiently financed. From the perspective of the elderly, only about half of their health care bills are paid through the program, leaving them with substantial costs. The affluent elderly are not hurt because they can afford supplemental health insurance. The poor are not hurt because they are covered by Medicaid, a separate program that pays for the health care of indigent people. The problem is that with the high federal debt ($6.5 trillion in 2005) and huge budget deficits, the federal government and many of the states are slashing the funds available for Medicaid. The near-poor, however, do not qualify for Medicaid and they cannot afford additional health insurance.

More than four out of ten of today's elderly will use a nursing home in their lifetimes. This is a special concern for the elderly in the United States because nursing home care may cost as much as $3,000 to $5,000 a month. Nursing home patients must pay these costs until their assets reach a low point when Medicaid takes over. The problem, of course, is that this means that few resources remain for the surviving spouse. In other industrialized nations, the government pays for nursing home costs when needed.

REFERENCES

Eitzen, D. Stanley, and Maxine Baca Zinn (2006). *Social Problems,* 10th ed. Boston: Allyn & Bacon.

13

As Good As It Gets: What Country Takes the Best Care of Its Older Citizens?

MIKE EDWARDS

The American Association of Retired Persons (AARP) conducted a survey of sixteen nations on seventeen dimensions related to the quality of life of older people. The Netherlands ranked first and the United States was next to last. Even the highest ranked nations (i.e., the Netherlands, Australia, and Sweden), however, have room to improve.

Every week, Anna Sophia Fischer greets a clutch of tourists in the medieval central square of Utrecht and, with a spring in her step, guides them on a stroll among 14th-century Dutch monasteries and houses. She knows every arch, garden, and alley and, at 75, goes about her daily business by bicycle, as do the swarms of people around her. "You have to go by bike if you live in town," she says. (Could this be one reason that the Dutch live longer than we do—an average 78.6 years, compared with 77.3 in the U.S.?) A retired physician, Fischer is living her dream. "I wanted to do something different," she says. "I'm not rich, but I can do the things I want to do."

Wim van Essen, 69, is a former teacher, tall, vigorous, an ardent hiker, a fanatical chess player—and a one-man pep squad for the Dutch way of retirement. "You see how we live," he says, inviting a guest into his brick home in the leafy city of Amersfoort. There's a fireplace in the living room, a wildflower garden out back. Extra bedrooms upstairs await visiting grandchildren. On a coffee table are photos of Van Essen trekking in the Austrian alps with his wife, Lamberta Jacoba Maria, nicknamed Bep. (Every year, the two of them take a major trip, partly subsidized by the government.) The couple receive government and work pensions and various perks. All told, it's a wonderful life, based on what Van Essen calls "a beautiful pension," which, when everything is added up, comes to about $45,000 a year.

In a world that is rapidly aging, the Netherlands, perhaps more than any other country, has created a society in which people have the luxury of growing old well, according to a survey conducted by AARP THE MAGAZINE. We weighed 17 criteria (see chart, page [78]) in selected industrialized nations that approximate as closely as possible the lifestyle of most AARP members. We focused on key quality-of-life issues such as health care, work, education, taxes, and social programs.

But if you're already thinking of packing your bags, stop right there. The purpose of this report is not to encourage American retirees to immigrate to the Netherlands or to some of the other top scorers in our study. Most nations aren't keen to share their pensions and health care benefits with noncitizens just off a plane. Rather, our goal is to shed light on what retirees enjoy elsewhere in the world as a reference point for our own country's policies.

In the Netherlands, all citizens receive the full old-age pension at 65 if they've lived in the country for a minimum of 50 years between ages 15 and 64. Unlike our Social Security, however, the pension doesn't require a work history. The full amount per month is nearly $1,000 for singles and nearly $1,400 for couples, married or not. The old-age pension is in addition to an occupational, or employer-provided pension based on payments over the years by worker and employer. And every pensioner gets a "holiday allowance" of about $700, thoughtfully paid in May, just in time for spring.

Pension generosity is a major reason that, by international measurements, only 6.4 percent of the elderly fall in the bottom quarter of income distribution, as compared with the U.S. percentage of 20.7. Although the U.S. has a far larger per capita income than the Netherlands—$26,448 a year versus $17,080—it scores poorly in two other comparisons: First, all Dutch citizens have government insurance for medical conditions and nursing-home care; 45 million Americans have no health insurance at all. Second, prescription drugs are available to all Dutch citizens, with few if any copayments: Americans get drugs in many different ways and those without insurance pay top dollar. Even when Medicare drug coverage begins in 2006, most enrollees will still face substantial out-of-pocket costs.

How do the Dutch do it? How do their euros stretch further than our dollars? The key factor is lower costs. Although medicine isn't completely socialized—physicians and pharmacists, for example, aren't state employees—the government regulates almost all health expenses. That helps explain why, in the view of Professor Gerard F. Anderson of the Johns Hopkins Bloomberg School of Public Health, "in the U.S. we pay a lot more than anybody else for pretty much the same stuff." In analyzing health systems in the Netherlands and other industrialized nations, Anderson found that drugs, hospitals, and physicians' services were from 30 to 50 percent more expensive in the U.S., "and their health status is as good or better than ours."

Another factor is attitude. A strong feeling of "social solidarity," as Anderson sees it, makes Europeans inclined to be generous to older people, more willing to support them. "Their attitude is, we're in this together and sooner or later we're going to become older and we'll need some help," he says. "The U.S. attitude is, we're all rugged individualists and we're going to take care of ourselves, not others."

The Netherlands demonstrates its attitude toward older citizens (2 million are over 65) by showering them with numerous friendly perks, in addition to the big-ticket items such as pensions and health care. One example: seven days of free travel a year on the efficient rail system. "I go as far as possible," says Joris Korst, a 65-year-old civil servant in Nieuwegein. That's never very far in the Netherlands, which is only a third the size of Pennsylvania, but the destinations can be exhilarating—like the windswept beaches that Korst strolls in the West Frisian Islands. Museums, movies, concerts, campgrounds, and holiday bungalows are discounted, too. All this and a country that's worldly, prosperous, tolerant, steeped in art, and graced by canals, windmills, and tulip fields. What's not to like?

And the Winner Is . . . The **Netherlands**, which scored highest on key quality-of-life issues important to older people and society in general.

On a scale of 1 to 5, five is tops

	Netherlands	Australia	Sweden	Finland	Switzerland	Norway	Denmark	Japan	France	Canada	Ireland	Spain	United States	United Kingdom	Germany	Italy
Mandatory Retirement	1	5	1	1	1	1	1	1	1	1	1	1	5	1	1	1
Age-Discrimination Laws	5	5	4	5	1	1	1	1	3	5	5	5	5	1	1	3
Unemployment Rate	5	4	4	2	5	5	4	5	2	3	5	1	4	5	2	2
College Education	4	3	2	2	2	5	4	3	1	3	2	2	5	3	1	1
Per Capita Income	3	3	2	2	3	5	3	2	2	3	4	1	5	3	2	2
Total Tax Burden	3	5	1	2	5	2	1	5	2	4	5	4	5	3	4	2
Home Care	3	3	2	3	2	4	5	2	2	4	1	1	2	1	2	1
Retirement Age for Full Benefits	3	3	3	3	3	1	1	3	5	3	3	3	1	3	3	3
Public Pension Replacement Rate	4	1	4	3	3	2	3	2	4	1	1	5	2	1	1	4
Employers Pension Coverage	5	5	5	5	5	3	5	3	5	2	3	1	3	3	3	1
Economic Inequality	4	2	5	5	4	5	4	3	4	3	3	3	1	2	4	2
Economic Inequality for the Elderly	5	1	5	5	4	3	5	5	4	5	3	4	2	3	5	4
Public Spending on Social Programs	3	2	5	4	3	4	5	1	3	2	1	3	1	3	5	4
Total Health Costs	4	4	4	5	3	4	4	5	4	4	5	5	1	5	3	5
Universal Health Care	5	5	5	5	5	5	5	5	5	5	5	5	4	5	5	5
Universal Rx	5	5	5	5	5	5	5	5	5	4	5	5	3	5	5	5
Life Expectancy at Birth	2	4	4	2	4	3	1	5	3	3	1	3	1	2	2	3
TOTAL	64	62	61	59	58	58	57	56	55	55	53	52	50	49	49	48

UNDERSTANDING THE CHART

Mandatory Retirement Australia and the United States are the only countries on the list above that prohibit companies from making their employees retire at a certain age.

Age-Discrimination Laws The EU expects to have laws by 2006, but experts are skeptical that all countries will make the deadline.

Unemployment Rate In 2003, the Netherlands averaged lowest (3.89%); Spain, the highest (11.3%). The U.S. had 6%.

College Education The U.S. and Norway both get an A on this one: 28% of adults ages 25–64 have a college degree.

Per Capita Income Compared with the countries above, the U.S. has the highest average standard of living; Norway is next.

Total Tax Burden Sweden collects the most taxes (51.4% of GDP).

Home Care In Australia and Denmark, more than 20% of those 65 and older receive home help—from medical care to tidying up. (In the Netherlands, it's 12.8%; in the U.S., less than 10%.)

Retirement Age for Full Benefits Most grant benefits at 65. France is lowest—at 60—with citizens strongly protesting change; Denmark is 67.

Public Pension Replacement Rate Spain's retirement benefit as a percentage of an average worker's earnings is highest, at 88%. Spain also has a high tax burden and the lowest income.

Employers Pension Coverage About 50% of U.S. workers have pension coverage at work. In some countries—Finland and Australia—employer pensions are required by law.

Economic Inequality Using an international definition, this is the percent of those whose income is in the lower quarter.

Economic Inequality for the Elderly In the U.S., the elderly fare slightly better than the general population.

Public Spending on Social Programs Income-support programs, such as social security and welfare, vary widely. Scandinavian countries traditionally offer the most.

Total Health Costs Americans spend the most (14.6% of GDP); Finland and Ireland, the least (7.3%).

Universal Health Care The U.S. is odd man out: 45 million—41% have no health insurance, though most seniors have Medicare.

Universal Rx Canada has limitations and some gaps at the provincial level; 88% have coverage. The U.S. scores lowest, but changes in Medicare represent progress for the elderly.

Life Expectancy at Birth In the U.S., babies born in 2004 can expect to live to 77.3; in the Netherlands, to 78.6. Japan is highest at 81.9.

For more details on these criteria, go to www.aarpmagazine.org.

HEALTH CARE

The Dutch are accustomed to paying minuscule copayments for expensive treatment.

Dutch health insurance took care of teacher Van Essen when he needed a heart pace-maker. "He never saw a bill," his wife, Bep, recalls. Neither did civil servant Korst, who remembers that there were no charges when his wife, Trees, had cancer surgery followed by 32 chemotherapy treatments. "The whole country paid," he says, referring to the state-regulated insurance. In the U.S., those 32 treatments alone could have cost $30,000 or more, depending on the type and number of drugs used. Medicare might cover 80 percent, but the patient still could owe thousands.

Compare Trees's experience with that of Harold Powers, 79, and his wife, Ozelle, 82, retired educators in Tennessee. Powers paid about $200 of the bill for his bypass heart surgery because Medicare picked up 80 percent of the tab and his private Medigap insur-ance (which costs extra) paid most of the rest. But, in addition, he and Ozelle spend about $3,000 a year for medicines, and Medicare won't cover any of that until 2006. Van Essen, on the other hand, pays nothing for the medicine he takes to prevent migraines. In 2003, however, the Dutch health ministry proposed that everyone make a copayment of $1.75 for each prescription—but backed down when the people protested.

There is also a government limit on the amount a hospital may bill an insurance com-pany for a pacemaker—Van Essen's was $5,750, plus the expense of the procedure. In the U.S., a pacemaker can cost as much as a car—$15,000 to $20,000, just for the device. The whole procedure can zoom up to $50,000. In the Netherlands, government pressure on hospitals, doctors, and manufacturers helps to keep costs down.

These kinds of controls are not always painless. Just this past year, the Dutch govern-ment hit a nerve when it decided to boost the $6-per-hour cost of home care by 250 percent. Half a million citizens, most of them beyond the age of 65, have been receiving subsidized home visits by health professionals or workers who clean and tidy up (like most developed countries, the Netherlands wants to help people maintain their independence and avoid going into nursing homes as long as possible). However, at the increased rate of about $15 an hour, despite government subsidies, home care is rapidly climbing out of sight for many low-income retirees. This increase takes effect, moreover, at an awkward time when the country has a nursing-home waiting list of some 50,000.

Still, all things considered, the Dutch like their health care. In a Harvard School of Pub-lic Health survey (taken before the increase in home-care costs), 70 percent said they were satisfied with the system. The same study rated the satisfaction level in the U.S. at 40 per-cent. And this even when the U.S. spends far more on health care than any other nation in the world—an average of $5,440 per person, with a large share of that going toward retirees.

Canada, by the way, doesn't score much better. Just 46 percent say they are satisfied. Although Canadians receive low-cost prescription drugs, thanks to government controls, health services are underfunded and waiting periods for treatment are long.

Waiting. That seems to be the tradeoff. Someone who needs open-heart surgery in the Netherlands might have to wait 14 weeks before a time slot and hospital space become available. Hip surgery? You're maybe looking at eight weeks. Like much of Europe and also Canada, the Netherlands is short of hospital beds and medical staff. Dutch officials say no one has to wait for emergency attention, and some patients are being sent to Germany and Belgium for faster treatment. Still, the delays underscore a major difference between

Finland: Model Home

Drop a few coins into a slot machine in a local casino in Finland and you contribute to the care and comfort of retirees. Legal gambling in Finland is the exclusive province of the Slot Machine Association, a government-controlled nonprofit that pumps more than $50 million a year into the welfare of the country's 65-plus population (800,000 out of a total of 5.2 million).

Slot machine profits, for example, helped build the four-story Saga Senior Center, a complex of 138 units in Helsinki, with cheerful apartments that are emphatically uninstitutional and that allow older people to have their own space and their own life. "It's the classiest senior home in Finland," says Leif Sonkin, a housing expert. "It's really like a spa." Indeed. Sunshine pours through the glass roof of the atrium, nourishing a lush semitropical garden. The swimming pool is indoor-outdoor and heated in winter. In the basement are saunas, essentials of Finnish life, and a well-equipped gym. (Pay no attention to its thick steel doors: the government requires bomb shelters in all buildings, a holdover from Cold War days.)

"The Saga center isn't a place for rich people," says administrator Mariana Boneva.

A small apartment rents for about $600 a month. Most retirees can afford that, but "if they need it to live here, people can get a government housing subsidy," she adds.

Saga is owned by the non-profit Ruissalo Foundation. Although municipalities are charged by law with caring for older people, nonprofits have taken a major role; they operate more than half of Finland's "service housing" for the elderly. This shared responsibility is an extension of the egalitarian streak that started permeating policy in the 1950s, when Finland, along with Sweden, Norway, and Denmark, embraced an unabashedly liberal form of tax-supported welfare.

Finland's taxes are formidable. "I cannot say we love taxes," says Erkki Vaatanen, who lives with her husband, Orvokki, in the Wilhelmiina House, a new senior center. "But we know that schools, hospitals, and highways would go down if we didn't pay." Still, Vaatanen recently faced a drawback. After waiting a year for surgery for an arthritic wrist, she applied again, only to be told: "Little lady, you must wait two years more." So she went to a private physician for treatment and paid herself. —M.E.

Dutch and U.S. care. Says one not-so-happy Dutch resident: "I don't care what they say. If you need open-heart surgery here, you can die before you get it."

"In America we love responsiveness," says Anderson, the Johns Hopkins expert. "We're the best on responsiveness." But ready access to care, he adds, is one reason why Americans pay more than people in other countries. Anderson is among the many health specialists and economists who have been pointing out the built-in inefficiencies of U.S. care. Some critics argue that the huge number of health-insurance providers—HMOs, PPOs, Medicare, Medicaid, and all the rest—consumes far more in overhead than would one or two providers and that their many forms and complicated rules drive up hospital administrative costs. Others point to the huge sums spent advertising and marketing drugs and hospitals.

TAXES

The Dutch in particular pay quite a lot to take care of one another. The personal income tax rate in the Netherlands isn't Europe's highest, but it's well up there, with a top rate of

Sweden: Shrinking Benefits

In a suburb of Stockholm, care for Aina Karlsson, 85, arrives twice a day, seven days a week. In the morning a *vårdbiträde* (care assistant) helps her bathe and dress; in the evening she helps her get ready for bed. Once a month she cleans the apartment that Aina shares with her husband, Einar. And twice a week she takes Aina to a gymnasium for exercise.

Life expectancy in Sweden is 80.4, one of the highest in Europe. Good care could be one reason. Aina has been receiving *hemhjälp* (home help) assistance since she suffered a stroke four years ago. Cost to the Karlssons: $159 a month. "Not very much," says Einar, a retired union official. To the municipal government, which provides Aina's care, the real cost is about five times greater. And if the Karlssons couldn't afford even $159, the government would provide a subsidy. "That's why Swedish taxes are so high," Einar says cheerfully, noting that income taxes shrink his own pension of $4,400 a month by a third.

Sweden is democratic, capitalistic, high-tech, and industrialized, well known for Ikea and Volvo. It is also well known as a prime example of a welfare state. Social spending, which includes payments such as pensions and welfare, equals 28.5 percent of GDP. In the U.S. it's 16.4 percent.

The income tax rate tops out at a breath-taking 58.2 percent, and there's a 25 percent VAT tax on most purchases. "Of course, many people say taxes are too high," remarks Nils-Erik Hogstedt, a home-care manager. "But the complaint isn't against the elderly. The great majority favor the care." Adds Pernilla Berggren, the manager of a retirement home: "People in Sweden are used to the community doing everything. You grow up expecting society to help take care of Mom."

Tens of thousands use *hemhjälp*, which enables people to remain in their own homes. "Sometimes we visit just once a month to clean," says Chatrin Engbo, head of a Stockholm district care office. "But if needed, we may go several times a day and at night."

This sounds nice—but expensive. To contain costs, the government recently sanctioned sharps cuts in home care by the municipalities, a move that upset many. "Home care used to include visits just to sit and have coffee two or three times a week, or just to take someone for a walk," says Berggren. "We do the essentials, but we can't afford those social moments anymore."

Reductions are also in the pipeline for the pension system, but for now a worker on the job for 30 years is customarily rewarded with a pension that replaces about 60 percent of his pay. (In the U.S. the Social Security replacement rate ranges from about 30 to 60 percent.)

The government's worry about future solvency began in the 1990s. The percentage of 65-plussers, almost one in five of the 8.9 million Swedes, is one of Europe's highest. As with U.S. Social Security, pension payments made by active workers support retirees. With low birth rates and the increase of pensioners, experts estimate that by 2035 the system will be seriously out of balance, with about two workers supporting each older person. (By then, America will be in the same boat.)

Looking ahead, the parliament recently approved drastic, complicated revisions. Out the window went the defined-benefit pension—a set amount based on salary and years of service—replaced by a system based on contributions by worker and employer. The benefit will be indexed to wage growth, with a built-in expectancy that the rate will grow 1.6 percent annually. If wages don't grow that much, the benefit drops. The plan phases in fully in 2019, with the retirement of those born in 1954.

There's yet another new wrinkle: mandated private investments. Besides paying into the pension's main part (employee and employer contribute a total of 16 percent of the worker's wages), all workers are required to put an additional 2.5 percent into their choice of investments—an idea that has become popular among world pension experts. A voluntary form of this setup is favored by President George W. Bush.

Swedes were optimistic in 2000, when this change took effect, even though many were confused by the hundreds of funds, Swedish and foreign, competing for their kronor. The timing proved terrible. The return averaged 3.5 percent in 2001, and then *katastrof!* Or so said a civil servant who

saw a thousand dollars vanish from her stock account as markets toppled worldwide. More than 2 million Swedes lost 30 to 40 percent of their mandated investments. (By July 2004, the average fund had recovered nearly 19 percent.)

One likely outcome of the radically revised system: to earn higher pension benefits more Swedes will work beyond the typical retirement age of 60. Says Barbro Westerholm, president of the Swedish Association of Senior Citizens: "I've recommended to my children that they plan to work until they are 70." —M.E.

---

52 percent on any income over $60,000. (The top U.S. rate has been going down during the presidency of George W. Bush and now stands at 35 percent. A family of four with an income of about $60,000 would be in the 25 percent tax bracket.)

Almost half of Dutch taxes go to the universal pension fund, known as the AOW, which provides the basic pension that everyone receives at age 65. The AOW takes a salary bite of 17.9 percent. Most Dutch workers have an employer-provided pension based on payments by worker and employer—that's another salary bite of 6 or 7 percent.

Then comes a bigger bite: a 12.05 percent contribution to help pay for basic state health insurance, known as the AWBZ, which, like the basic pension, is universal. Besides paying for care for grave illnesses and a place in a nursing home (after a wait), it also covers part (but less now) of the cost of home care. Most workers also have government-regulated insurance with private or nonprofit companies for lesser medical expenses and medicines. Employers usually pay most of this cost: the worker's share is only about 1.7 percent of income.

On top of that formidable raft of outlays, there's also a stiff value-added tax (VAT tax) of 19 percent on most things you buy. And 12 percent on food. And a whopping tax of as much as 40 percent on new cars (plus roughly $6 for a gallon of gas). Yet costs like these haven't stopped Wilhelmina and Cornelius van der Hoop, both retired teachers, from driving all around Europe towing a trailer. The couple's combined pension is about $41,000 after all deductions. "We have no reason to complain," Wilhelmina says. "All those taxes help other people."

In fact, polls show that most Dutch citizens don't object to the large salary deduction that sustains the AOW. "The general attitude in the Netherlands—if you ask the man in the street—is that people who have worked their entire lives should be protected from poverty," says pension expert Maarten Lindeboom, an economist at the Free University of Amsterdam.

Dutch citizens with higher-than-average incomes usually invest in a private pension plan or annuities. That's what tour guide Anna Sophia Fischer did years ago. These investments put her annual income in the $60,000 range, where the taxman ordinarily takes a

O Canada!

The pain in her back was terrible, recalls Diane Tupper, who lives in a Vancouver suburb. When she finally got a consultation with a neurosurgeon—after waiting eight months—he said he could fix her spine. Then he delivered the bad news: "Our surgery waiting time is a year and a half to two years."

If Tupper, a 63-year-old lawyer, could hold out, her surgery would be free under Canada's universal-care system. But if she hopped over the border to St. Joseph Hospital in Bellingham, Washington, she could be in the operating room in days. The cost would be about $47,000. "I'm not a well-off person," Tupper says, "but I felt I didn't have any choice." Tupper took out two lines of credit, borrowed $14,500 from a friend, and went to Bellingham.

To many Americans, Canada may look like health care's promised land. Care for all 32.5 million citizens is paid for from taxes. Drugs are typically 30 to 50 percent cheaper than in the U.S.—which is why more than a million statesiders now get prescriptions filled in Canada.

But recently, Canada's system has fallen behind, hobbled by budget cuts, regulations, and shortages of physicians, nurses, and sophisticated equipment such as MRI machines. A recent survey put the backlog of unperformed procedures at 876,584. The waiting time for a hip replacement in Tupper's province, British Columbia, is nearly a year, even longer for a knee replacement.

Filling that gap are U.S. border cities such as Buffalo, New York, and Great Falls, Montana. Minot, North Dakota, attracts people needing CT scans and MRIs, for which they'd wait months in Saskatchewan. Randy Schwan of Trinity Health in Minot says Canadians are amazed to find that "a doctor says we've got to get a test, and the same day someone wheels them down the hall for that test." At the globally famous Mayo Clinic in Rochester, Minnesota, Canadians are the largest foreign-patient constituency.

Some provinces cover care outside of Canada under special circumstances. To trim the waiting list of cancer patients needing radiation treatment, Ontario picked up the bill for 1,650 people who went to the U.S. in 2000 and 2001.

So, get to a Canadian hospital's emergency room after a heart attack and you'll be treated promptly—with no worry about cost. But the system, once the nation's pride, has become, as one official says, "functionally obsolete." —M.E.

---

large bite. But thanks to reductions granted to people over 65, her tax is only about 30 percent of her income. As a former physician, Fischer is well acquainted with the fabled liberality of the health system. "If you want a sex-change operation, the government will pay for it," she says. "I do think that goes a bit too far." A recent innovation: marijuana available by prescription for pain.

A noticeable difference in Europe's treatment of older people is the absence of laws that forbid discrimination and age-based mandatory retirement. In the U.S., mandatory retirement has been illegal for most jobs since 1986. Says one Dutch pension expert: "Here it is automatic that at 65 the job is over." The European Union has mandated that its 25 member states introduce laws against age discrimination by 2006, but the word is that loopholes will permit mandatory retirement to continue. Laurie McCann, senior attorney with AARP Foundation Litigation, concludes that the EU is a long way from either "talking the talk" or "walking the walk" when it comes to eliminating age discrimination.

Today some 14 percent of Americans 65 and over—about 4.8 million people—are still on the job; that's one of the highest rates in the industrialized world. Most Europeans retire at 60 or so, taking advantage of pension generosity.

The need for a ban on mandatory retirement hasn't seemed all that urgent. Frits Velker, a foreman at a Dutch plumbing and sheet-metal company, was 59 when the company was sold. "I looked around and saw so many other people who had retired early," he says. So Velker did too. His company pension is about $27,000, and when he turns 65 he and wife Gerrie will receive about $14,000 a year from the AOW, the state pension fund. In general, a Dutch worker in the Netherlands can expect a total pension equaling about 70 percent of his salary if he worked for 40 years. Thanks to cost-of-living adjustments, former teacher Van Essen's pension is slightly higher—72 percent of his salary—even though his teaching career stopped after 38 years.

Such generous retirement benefits are under siege all across Europe (and Japan). Cutbacks and proposed cutbacks in care and pensions provoked angry strikes last year in France, Italy, Germany, and Austria. Even in Sweden, shining star of the Scandinavian welfare-state constellation, benefits have shrunk. With increasing concern, governments are facing challenging demographics: swelling ranks of longer-living older citizens and thinning ranks of workers able—and willing—to pay for benefits.

14

We Should Rejoice in an Ageing Society, So Long as We Plan Properly for It

HAMISH McRAE

Europe, like the United States, has a rapidly aging population. This arti-cle discusses some strategies for ensuring that adequate pensions will be available for people after they retire and suggests some methods for defer-ring retirements by adjusting mandatory retirement ages.

If we can get pensions right, demographic change may not be the disaster often painted. Provided we can afford it, living in an older society may be rather pleasant. There ought to be less pressure on resources, less congestion, less crime and a generally calmer society.

But only if we get pensions right. At the moment there are 3.2 people of working age for every person aged over 65. By 2015 that ratio will have fallen to 2.7 and by 2050, when the twentysomethings now entering the workforce will be drawing pensions, to 1.7. (If that sounds alarming, projections suggest that in Italy and Spain the ratio will be around 0.8 in 2050. There'll actually be more pensioners than workers.)

That is the problem with the present pay-as-you-go state pensions schemes, where each generation of working people pays the pensions of the preceding generation. When these were extended after the Second World War, there were about seven workers for every pensioner, so the burden on people of working age was quite modest. But the combination of earlier retirement and longer lifespans has changed the arithmetic. The average age of retirement and average lifespan for men crossed over in the US in the late 1950s. But it will only be in the next five or 10 years, when the baby-boomers born in the post-war era retire, that the arithmetic of these pay-as-you-go schemes becomes really unmanageable. So there is a short window when reforms have to be put in place. That is what the Government's pensions reform is about.

The UK is relatively lucky by European, though not US, standards. We are ageing more slowly than most Continental countries: the size of our workforce will be stable for some years, while that of most Continental countries will shrink. We have a high participa-tion rate—a larger proportion of the people of working age do actually work. And we have one of the most substantial private pension networks in the world. Private pensions, unlike

Source: Hamish McRae. 2002. *The Independent—London* (December 18), p. 16. Reprinted by permission.

state ones, are funded in the sense that there is a pot of money that can be drawn down to pay the pension. True that pot has in most cases been cut in size with the fall in share prices. But at least there are some funds.

So we have a more manageable problem than most countries—but not manageable enough. Whatever happens, young people now entering the workforce will have a bad deal from the state. They will have to pay far more in taxation than they will receive in pensions and other services. There is no way of changing that. But the greater the success of the Government in persuading people to save more and retire later, the less the burden on the people in jobs who have to pay for them.

So the tests to be applied to the Government's plans are simple. Will they encourage people to save more? And will they encourage people to stay in work longer?

Save more? Not sure. Whether people choose to save or not has long been something of a puzzle. Tax incentives to save probably have had some effect on the scale of saving, but there is also some evidence that people simply save differently. In other words people decide how much they want to spend and then look for the most tax—effective way of saving the rest. From a macroeconomic point of view, it really does not matter if people save in a company pension, a private pension, a PEP, Tessa or whatever. It is perfectly sensible, too, for people to dip into their retirement funds and invest the money instead in a flat or two for their university-aged children.

There is, however, one important reason for preferring people to invest in a structured way. If people have to set aside money each month and that money is deducted immediately from their wages, then the chances are that the pot really will be available for retirement and not cashed in early. We also know that the relative attraction of saving in a pension fund, rather than the various alternatives, has been decreased by the present Chancellor. His tax raid on pension funds in his first budget did not attract much attention at the time. But now it has begun to eat into the size of those pension pots—though most people will not feel anything until they come to draw their pensions.

So whatever view one takes of the changes to private-pension legislation proposed yesterday (and my instinct is that they are less important than they seem), the fact remains that this Government has, over its two terms, on balance discouraged people from saving more for retirement. But we will only know in 20 years when we see what happens to the long-term trend in savings.

So a possible fail on test one. What about test two, the working longer one?

Here I think there may be a pass. The adjustment of the state pension to reward later retirement will have two effects. There will be the direct one on people's desire to carry on working and defer retirement. But there will also be an indirect one on the job market. The signal to employers is that there will be many more older workers seeking to extend their working lives. That will encourage companies to think more, not just about the way they organise their pay scales but also about the way jobs are defined.

For example, most jobs are defined by hours worked. But that is only a secondary element in the work/pay relationship. What employers are really interested in is the amount of work done, not the time taken to do it. While time may be an appropriate element in the contract for most workers it is hardly relevant to the elderly. Maybe they take more time to do the job, but so what? They need to be paid for what they do, at their own pace, rather than how long it takes them.

The more that the Government can undermine the notion that there should be a single retirement age, the better. The idea that there should be a state retirement age was set by Bismarck, the German Chancellor, in the 1890s. He chose 70, by the way, at a time when the life expectancy of the German male was in the 40s.

But while these proposals to soften the single retirement are helpful, they won't be really convincing until the Government changes its own practices as an employer. Senior civil servants and diplomats retire on indexed pensions at the age of 60—often to go on to have a second career in the private sector. Many police and local authority workers retire early—police officers often on spurious health grounds. It is no good for the Government to preach to people that they have to work on to 70 or 75 and meanwhile allow their own employees to bunk off at 55.

Look, this is a start. At least we are talking about the problem. The more there is a vigorous debate, not just about pensions but about the whole nature of retirement, the better. The more we think as individuals what we are going to do in our "third age," the more likely we are to make decent preparation for it. On any measure of human values, it is far, far better for people to live to a healthy old age than to die unnecessarily young. So we should rejoice in our ageing society. But we have to plan for it.

PART THREE

Institutional Problems

Section 7

Families

THE UNITED STATES CONTEXT

The situation of families in the United States is similar in some respects to that found in other industrialized nations: a high divorce rate, both spouses in the workforce, and a relatively high number of single parents. Families in the United States differ considerably when compared to families in similar countries, however, in the relative lack of support they receive from the government and from their employers.

The United States has the highest incidence of unwed teenage births of any of the industrialized countries. Two obvious reasons for this are that it is much more difficult to obtain contraceptives and sex education is woefully inadequate in the United States. About 60 percent of all pregnancies in the United States are unplanned, occurring because contraceptives are misused or unreliable, or not used at all. Their cost is expensive. The free distribution of condoms in schools and health clinics is challenged by many in the United States because they believe that it leads to sexual promiscuity. Current law requires that schools will receive federal money if they use an abstinence-only message. In those countries with cheaper contraceptives and fully-informed sex education, teens who are as sexually active as those in the United States have much lower teen pregnancy rates (e.g., the rate in England and Wales is half that in the United States and one-tenth of it in the Netherlands).

The maternity and nursing benefits given to working mothers in the United States are the least generous in the industrialized world. Working mothers in Europe receive, on average, 80 percent of their wages while staying at home with their infants. The United States merely "permits" 12 weeks of *unpaid* maternity leave (a few employers provide paid maternity leave). Many industrialized countries provide paternity leave as well.

Child care is imperative for families where both parents are in the workforce or for working single parents. Child care in the United States is often expensive and difficult to find. By contrast, in France virtually all of 3-, 4-, and 5-year-olds attend preschools at minimal or no charge. Daycare facilities for younger children are heavily subsidized by the government.

15

Caring for Our Young: Child Care in Europe and the United States

DAN CLAWSON AND NAOMI GERSTEL

The United States compares poorly with European countries on how we care for our young children. In stark contrast with the United States, where child care is largely the financial responsibility of parents, France offers publicly funded child care for every child three to six years old. Child care in France is also considered part of the education system and is supported by all major political parties and groups. While the focus of this article is the contrast between the French and American child care systems, other European alternatives to child care are discussed.

When a delegation of American child care experts visited France, they were amazed by the full-day, free *écoles maternelles* that enroll almost 100 percent of French three-, four- and five-year-olds:

> *Libraries better stocked than those in many U.S. elementary schools. Three-year-olds serving one another radicchio salad, then using cloth napkins, knives, forks and real glasses of milk to wash down their bread and chicken. Young children asked whether dragons exist [as] a lesson in developing vocabulary and creative thinking.*

In the United States, by contrast, working parents struggle to arrange and pay for private care. Publicly-funded child care programs are restricted to the poor. Although most U.S. parents believe (or want to believe) that their children receive quality care, standardized ratings find most of the care mediocre and much of it seriously inadequate.

Looking at child care in comparative perspective offers us an opportunity—almost requires us—to think about our goals and hopes for children, parents, education, and levels of social inequality. Any child care program or funding system has social and political assumptions with far-reaching consequences. National systems vary in their emphasis on education; for three- to five-year-olds, some stress child care as preparation for school, while others take a more playful view of childhood. Systems vary in the extent to which they stress that children's early development depends on interaction with peers or some

Source: Dan Clawson and Naomi Gerstel, 2002. *Contexts* (Fall/Winter), pp. 28–35. Copyright © 2002 by American Sociological Association. Reprinted by permission.

version of intensive mothering. They also vary in the extent to which they support policies promoting center-based care as opposed to time for parents to stay at home with their very young children. Each of these emphases entails different national assumptions, if only implicit, about children and parents, education, teachers, peers and societies as a whole.

What do we want, why and what are the implications? Rethinking these questions is timely because with changing welfare, employment, and family patterns, more U.S. parents have come to believe they want and need a place for their children in child care centers. Even parents who are not in the labor force want their children to spend time in preschool. In the United States almost half of children less than one year old now spend a good portion of their day in some form of non-parental care. Experts increasingly emphasize the potential benefits of child care. A recent National Academy of Sciences report summarizes the views of experts: "Higher quality care is associated with outcomes that all parents want to see in their children." The word in Congress these days, especially in discussions of welfare reform, is that child care is good—it saves money later on by helping kids through school (which keeps them out of jail), and it helps keep mothers on the job and families together. A generation ago, by contrast, Nixon vetoed a child care bill as a "radical piece of social legislation" designed to deliver children to "communal approaches to child rearing over and against the family-centered approach." While today's vision is clearly different, most attempts to improve U.S. child care are incremental, efforts to get a little more money here or there, with little consideration for what kind of system is being created.

The U.S. and French systems offer sharp contrasts. Although many hold up the French system as a model for children three or older, it is only one alternative. Other European countries provide thought-provoking alternatives, but the U.S.-French contrast is a good place to begin.

FRANCE AND THE UNITED STATES:
PRIVATE VERSUS PUBLIC CARE

Until their children start school, most U.S. parents struggle to find child care, endure long waiting lists, and frequently change locations. They must weave a complex, often unreliable patchwork in which their children move among relatives, informal settings and formal center care, sometimes all in one day. Among three- to four-year-old children with employed mothers, more than one out of eight are in three or more child care arrangements, and almost half are in two or more arrangements. A very small number of the wealthy hire nannies, often immigrants; more parents place their youngest children with relatives, especially grandmothers, or work alternate shifts so fathers can share child care with mothers (these alternating shifters now include almost one-third of families with infants and toddlers). Many pay kin to provide child care—sometimes not because they prefer it, but because they cannot afford other care, and it is a way to provide jobs and income to struggling family members. For children three and older, however, the fastest-growing setting in the United States is child care centers—almost half of three-year-olds (46 percent) and almost two-thirds of four-year-olds (64 percent) now spend much of their time there.

In France, participation in the *école maternelle* system is voluntary, but a place is guaranteed to every child three to six years old. Almost 100 percent of parents enroll their three-year-olds. Even non-employed parents enroll their children, because they believe it is best for the children. Schools are open from 8:30 a.m. to 4:30 p.m. with an extended lunch break, but care is available at modest cost before and after school and during the lunch break.

Integrated with the school system, French child care is intended primarily as early education. All children, rich and poor, immigrant or not, are part of the same national system, with the same curriculum, staffed by teachers paid good wages by the same national ministry. No major political party or group opposes the system.

When extra assistance is offered, rather than targeting poor children (or families), additional resources are provided to geographic areas. Schools in some zones, mostly in urban areas, receive extra funding to reduce class size, give teachers extra training and a bonus, provide extra materials and employ special teachers. By targeting an entire area, poor children are not singled out (as they are in U.S. free lunch programs).

Staff in the French *écoles maternelles* have master's degrees and are paid teachers' wages; in 1998, U.S. preschool teachers earned an average of $8.32 an hour, and child care workers earned $6.61, not only considerably less than (underpaid) teachers but also less than parking lot attendants. As a consequence employee turnover averages 30 percent a year, with predictably harmful effects on children.

What are the costs of these two very different systems? In almost every community across the United States, a year of child care costs more than a year at a public university—in some cases twice as much. Subsidy systems favor the poor, but subsidies (unlike tax breaks) depend on the level of appropriations. Congress does not appropriate enough money and, therefore, most of the children who qualify for subsidies do not receive them. In 1999, under federal rules 15 million children were eligible to receive benefits, but only 1.8 million actually received them. Middle- and working-class families can receive neither kind of subsidy. An Urban Institute study suggests that some parents place their children in care they consider unsatisfactory because other arrangements are just too expensive. The quality of care thus differs drastically depending on the parents' income, geographic location, diligence in searching out alternatives and luck.

The French system is not cheap. According to French government figures, the cost for a child in Paris was about $5,500 per year in 1999. That is only slightly more than the average U.S. parents paid for the care of a four-year-old in a center ($5,242 in 2000). But in France child care is a social responsibility, and thus free to parents, while in the United States parents pay the cost. Put another way, France spends about 1 percent of its Gross Domestic Product (GDP) on government-funded early education and care programs. If the United States devoted the same share of its GDP to preschools, the government would spend about $100 billion a year. Current U.S. government spending is less than $20 billion a year ($15 billion federal, $4 billion state).

OTHER EUROPEAN ALTERNATIVES

When the American child care community thinks about European models, the French model is often what they have in mind. With its emphasis on education, the French system has an obvious appeal to U.S. politicians, educators, and child care advocates. Politicians' central concern in the United States appears to be raising children's test scores; in popular and academic literature, this standard is often cited as the major indicator of program success. But such an educational model is by no means the only alternative. Indeed, the

U.S. focus on the French system may itself be a telling indicator of U.S. experts' values as well as their assessments of political realities. Many advocates insist that a substantial expansion of the U.S. system will be possible only if the system is presented as improving children's education. These advocates are not longer willing to use the term "child care," insisting on "early education" instead. The French model fits these priorities; it begins quasi-school about three years earlier than in the United States. Although the French obviously assist employed parents and children's center activities are said to be fun, the system is primarily touted and understood as educational—intended to treat children as pupils, to prepare them to do better in school.

The 11 European nations included in a recent Organization for Economic Cooperation and Development study (while quite different from one another) all have significantly better child care and paid leave than the United States. Each also differs significantly from France. Offering alternatives, these models challenge us to think even more broadly about childhood, parenting and the kind of society we value.

NON-SCHOOL MODEL: DENMARK

From birth to age six most Danish children go to child care, but most find that care in non-school settings. Overseen by the Ministry of Social Affairs (rather than the Ministry of Education), the Danish system stresses "relatively unstructured curricula" that give children time to "hand out." Lead staff are pedagogues, not teachers. Although pedagogues have college degrees and are paid teachers' wages, their role is "equally important but different" from that of the school-based teacher. "Listening to children" is one of the government's five principles, and centers emphasize "looking at everything from the child's perspective."

The Danish model differs from the French system in two additional ways that clarify its non-school character. First, in the Danish system, pedagogues care for very young children (from birth to age three as well as older children ages three to six). The French preschool (*école maternelle*) model applies only to children three and older. Before that, children of working parents can attend *crèches*. *Crèche* staff, however, have only high school educations and are paid substantially less than the (master's degree-trained) *écoles maternelles* teachers. Second, while the *écoles maternelles* are available to all children, the Danish system (like the French *crèches*) is only available to children with working parents because it is intended to aid working parents, not to educate children.

The Danish system is decentralized, with each individual center required to have a management board with a parent majority. But the system receives most of its money from public funding, and parents contribute only about one-fifth of total costs.

Given its non-school emphasis, age integration, and the importance it assigns to local autonomy, the Danish system might be appealing to U.S. parents, especially some people of color. To be sure, many U.S. parents—across race and class—are ambivalent about child care for their youngest children. Especially given the growing emphasis on testing, they believe that preschool might give them an edge, but they also want their children to have fun and play—to have, in short, what most Americans still consider a childhood. Some research suggests that Latina mothers are especially likely to feel that center-based care, with its emphasis on academic learning, does not provide the warmth and moral guidance they seek. They are, therefore, less likely to select center-based care than either white or African-American parents, relying instead on kin or family child care providers whom they know and trust. U.S. experts' emphasis on the French model may speak not only to political realities but also to the particular class and even more clearly race preferences framing those realities.

MOTHERS OR PEERS

The United States, if only implicitly, operates on a mother-substitute model of child care. Because of a widespread assumption in the United States that all women naturally have maternal feelings and capacities, child care staff, who are almost all women (about 98 percent), are not required to have special training (and do not need to be well paid). Even for regulated providers, 41 out of 50 states require no pre-service training beyond orientation. Consequently, in the United States the child-staff ratio is one of the most prominent measures used to assess quality and is central to most state licensing systems. The assumption, based on the mother-substitute model, is that emotional support can be given and learning can take place only with such low ratios.

Considering the high quality and ample funding of many European systems, it comes as a surprise that most have much higher child-staff ratios than the United States. In the French *écoles maternelles,* for example, there is one teacher and one half-time aide for every 25 children. In Italy, in a center with one adult for every eight children (ages one to three years) the early childhood workers see no need for additional adults and think the existing ratios are appropriate. Leading researchers Sheila Kamerman and Alfred Kahn report that in Denmark, "what is particularly impressive is that children are pretty much on their own in playing with their peers. An adult is present all the time but does not lead or play with the children." In a similar vein, a cross-national study of academic literature found substantial focus on adult-child ratios in the United States, but very little literature on the topic in German-, French-, or Spanish-language publications. Why not? These systems have a different view of children and learning. Outside the United States systems often center around the peer group. In Denmark the role of staff is to work "alongside children, rather than [to be] experts or leaders who teach children." Similarly, the first director of the early childhood services in Reggio, Italy, argues that children learn through conflict and that placing children in groups facilitates learning through "attractive," "advantageous," and "constructive" conflict "because among children there are not strong relationships of authority and dependence." In a non-European example, Joseph Tobin, David Wu, and Dana Davidson argue that in Japan the aim is ratios that "keep teachers from being too mother-like in their interactions with students . . . Large class sizes and large ratios have become increasingly important strategies for promoting the Japanese values of groupism and selflessness." Such practices contrast with the individualistic focus in U.S. child care.

FAMILY LEAVES AND WORK TIME

When we ask how to care for children, especially those younger than three, one answer is for parents to stay home. Policy that promotes such leaves is what one would expect from a society such as the United States, which emphasizes a mothering model of child care. It is, however, European countries that provide extensive paid family leave, usually universal, with not only job protection but also substantial income replacement. In Sweden, for example, parents receive a full year and a half of paid parental leave (with 12 months at 80 percent of prior earnings) for each child. Because so many parents (mostly mothers) use family leave, fewer than 200 children under one year old in the entire country are in public care. Generous programs are common throughout Europe (although the length, flexibility and level of payment they provide vary).

The United States provides far less in the way of family leaves. Since its passage in 1993, the Family and Medical Leave Act (FMLA) has guaranteed a 12-week job-protected leave to workers of covered employers. Most employers (95 percent) and many workers (45 percent), however, are not covered. And all federally mandated leaves are unpaid.

The unpaid leaves provided by the FMLA, like the private system of child care, accentuate the inequality between those who can afford them and those who can't. Although the FMLA was touted as a "gender neutral" piece of legislation, men (especially white men) are unlikely to take leaves; it is overwhelmingly women (especially those who are married) who take them. As a result, such women pay a wage penalty when they interrupt their careers. To address such inequities, Sweden and Norway have introduced a "use it or lose it" policy. For each child, parents may divide up to a year of paid leave (say nine months for the mother, three for the father), except that the mother may not use more than eleven months total. One month is reserved for the father; if he does not use the leave, the family loses the month.

Finally, although not usually discussed as child care policy in the United States, policy makers in many European countries now emphasize that the number of hours parents work clearly shapes the ways young children are cared for and by whom. Workers in the United States, on average, put in 300 hours more per year than workers in France (and 400 more than those in Sweden).

CONCLUSION

The child care system in the United Sates is a fragmentary patchwork, both at the level of the individual child and at the level of the overall system. Recent research suggests that the quality of care for young children is poor or fair in well over half of child care settings. This low quality of care, in concert with a model of intensive mothering, means that many anxious mothers privately hunt for high-quality substitutes while trying to ensure they are not being really replaced. System administrators need to patch together a variety of funding streams, each with its own regulations and paperwork. Because the current system was fashioned primarily for the affluent at one end and those being pushed off welfare at the other, it poorly serves most of the working class and much of the middle class.

Most efforts at reform are equally piecemeal, seeking a little extra money here or there in ways that reinforce the existing fragmentation. Although increasing numbers of advocates are pushing for a better system of child care in the United States, they rarely step back to think about the characteristics of the system as a whole. If they did, what lessons could be learned from Europe?

The features that are common to our peer nations in Europe would presumably be a part of a new U.S. system. The programs would be publicly funded and universal, available

---

2002–2003 FEE SCHEDULE (PRICES EFFECTIVE UNTIL JULY 1, 2003)

Application Fee $50.00
(nonrefundable/annual fee)

Materials Fee $30.00 Full-time Enrollment
(nonrefundable) $20.00 Part-time Enrollment

Tuition Deposit* *amount equal to one month's tuition* (due in two installments)

a. Space guarantee Fee** $150.00
    (due upon acceptance to the school)
b. Balance due two months prior to starting date.

**See enrollment contract for refund conditions.

Full-Time	$859.00/month

Morning Preschool (9:00 a.m.–1:00 p.m.)
    three mornings $321.00/month
    four mornings $397.00/month
    five mornings $462.00/month

Afternoon Preschool (1:00 p.m.–5:00 p.m.)
    three afternoons $285.00/month
    four afternoons $350.00/month
    five afternoons $404.00/month

Kindergarten Program (11:25 a.m.–5:00 p.m.)
    three days $339.00/month
    four days $416.00/month
    five days $486.00/month

— Extended Care (hour before 9:00 a.m. and the
   hour after 5:00 p.m.) $5.25/hour
— Unscheduled Drop-in $6.25/hour

Participating Parents (P.P.) & Board Members receive tuition credit. P.P. credit is $25.00 per day of participation. Board credits vary with position.

2002–2003 Fee Schedule

Tuitions and fees for the U.S. preschool illustrated here, a nonprofit, parent-run cooperative that costs almost $1,000 per month.

Source: Kensington Nursery School.

to all, either at no cost or at a modest cost with subsidies for low-income participants. The staff would be paid about the same as public school teachers. The core programs would cover at least as many hours as the school day, and "wrap-around" care would be available before and after this time. Participation in the programs would be voluntary, but the programs would be of such a high quality that a majority of children would enroll. Because the quality of the programs would be high, parents would feel much less ambivalence about their children's participation, and the system would enjoy strong public support. In addition to child care centers, parents would be universally offered a significant period of paid parental leave. Of course, this system is expensive. But as the National Academy of Science Report makes clear, not caring for our children is in the long term, and probably even in the short term, even more expensive.

Centers in all nations emphasize education, peer group dynamics, and emotional support to some extent. But the balance varies. The varieties of European experience pose a set of issues to be considered if and when reform of the U.S. system is on the agenda:

- To what degree should organized care approximate school and at what age, and to what extent is the purpose of such systems primarily educational?
- To what extent should we focus on adult-child interactions that sustain or substitute for mother care as opposed to fostering child-child interactions and the development of peer groups?
- To what extent should policies promote parental time with children versus high-quality organized care, and what are the implications for gender equity of either choice?

These are fundamental questions because they address issues of social equality and force us to rethink deep-seated images of children and parents.

RECOMMENDED RESOURCES

Cooper, Candy J. *Ready to Learn: The French System of Early Education and Care Offers Lessons for the United States.* New York: French American Foundation, 1999.
Gornick, Janet, and Marcia Meyers. "Support for Working Families: What the United States Can Learn from Europe." *The American Prospect* (January 1–15, 2001): 3–7.
Helburn, Suzanne W., and Barbara R. Bergmann. *America's Childcare Problem: The Way Out.* New York: Palgrave/St. Martin's, 2002.
Kamerman, Shiela B., and Alfred J. Kahn. *Starting Right: How America Neglects Its Youngest Children and What We Can Do About It.* New York: Oxford University Press, 1995.
Moss, Peter. "Workforce Issues in Early Childhood Education and Care Staff." Paper prepared for consultative meeting on International Developments in Early Childhood Education and Care, The Institute for Child and Family Policy, Columbia University, May 11–12, 2000.
Organization for Economic Co-operation and Development. *Starting Strong—Early Education and Care: Report on an OECD Thematic Review.* Online. www.oecd.org.
Shonkoff, Jack P., and Deborah Phillips, eds. *From Neurons to Neighborhoods: The Science of Early Childhood Development.* Washington, DC: National Academy of Sciences, 2000.

ACKNOWLEDGMENTS

We would like to thank Amy Armenia, Michelle Budig, Mary Ann Clawson, Nancy DeProsse, Fran Deutsch, Eva Gerstel, Nancy Folbre, Joya Misra, Maureen Perry-Jenkins, Ruby Takanishi and Robert Zussman for comments and suggestions.

16

Support for Working Families: What the United States Can Learn from Europe

JANET C. GORNICK AND MARCIA K. MEYERS

Many industrialized countries provide far more support for working mothers and fathers than the United States. One reason for this is that the United States has left parents largely to their own devices when forced to balance work and child care, while most European nations provide working parents with public child care and generous parental leave policies. This article details the differences in support for working families in the United States and other countries, and outlines the changes that would be necessary to bring U.S. family policies up to speed.

Four decades of steady growth in female employment have gone a long way toward closing the job gap between women and men in the industrialized countries. One of the most striking changes in Europe and the United States has been the rise in employment among mothers with young children. Nearly 85 percent of U.S. mothers employed before childbearing now return to work before their child's first birthday. Although this is an encouraging trend from the perspective of gender equality in the marketplace, it is raising a new and difficult question about arrangements in the home: If everyone is working in the market, who is caring for the children?

Many parents in the industrialized countries find themselves navigating uncertain new terrain between a society that expects women to bear the primary responsibility for caring in the home and a society that expects, and increasingly requires, all adults to be at work in the market. Mothers and fathers are struggling to craft private solutions to this problem. But rather than resolving the question of who will care for children when everyone is on the job, these private solutions often exacerbate gender inequality, overburden the parents, and ultimately lead to poor-quality child care.

Although such problems are not unique to the United States, they may be more acute in this country because families have access to so little public support. The nation's policy makers and opinion leaders have been preoccupied in recent years with

Source: Reprinted with permission from Janet C. Gornick and Marcia K. Meyers, "Support for Working Families," *The American Prospect*, Volume 12, Number 1: January 1, 2001. The American Prospect, 11 Beacon Street, Suite 1120, Boston, MA 02108. All rights reserved.

the promotion of "family values." Compared with most of Europe, however, this country provides exceptionally meager help to children, their parents, and the workers—mostly women—who care for other people's children. And despite the current preoccupation with getting everyone—particularly poor mothers—into the work force, the United States does much less than European countries to remove employment barriers for women with young children.

THE PROBLEM OF PRIVATE SOLUTIONS

One private solution to child care adopted by many parents in the United States is the combining of parental caregiving and part-time employment. Because the parents who work reduced hours are overwhelmingly mothers—only 42 percent of American women work full-time year round—this solution exacerbates gender inequality in both the market and the caring spheres. Part-time work schedules, career interruptions, and intermittent employment relegate many women to the least remunerative and rewarding jobs; and these employment patterns contribute to wage penalties that persist long after the children are grown. In dual-parent families with children below school age, married mothers' labor-market income accounts for, at most, a third of families' total labor-market income across the industrialized countries; in the United States, it accounts for only one quarter.

Another private solution is the combining of substitute care for children and full-time parental employment. Although this works well for some families, many others find themselves overburdened by the demands of the market and the home. Women in particular often work the equivalent of a double shift, combining full-time paid work with unpaid caregiving. In a recent article in *Demography,* Suzanne Bianchi concludes that despite the increase in mothers' labor-market activities, their time spent with their children remained nearly constant between 1965 and 1998. Where do employed mothers get the time? The data suggest that they do less of everything else, including housework, volunteering, engaging in leisure activities, and sleeping.

More parental employment also means children spend much more time in substitute care. Recent increases in the use of child care in the United States have been particularly sharp for children below age one, 44 percent of whom are now in some form of nonparental child care. The extensive reliance on substitute child care imposes a heavy financial burden, consuming as much as 35 percent of household income for poor working families. It also raises concerns about the quality of care in children's youngest and most developmentally sensitive years. These concerns are particularly acute in the United States, where experts conclude that nearly two-thirds of the mostly private nonparental child care settings provide only fair-to-poor care.

The private-child-care solution to the work-family dilemma creates another, often overlooked problem: It impoverishes a large, low-wage child care work force dominated by women. Child care workers in the United States are among the most poorly paid members of the work force, averaging less than $7 per hour in earnings and usually working without employment benefits or realistic opportunities for career advancement.

While parents in the United States are left largely to their own devices, parents in most European welfare states can count on child care and parental-leave benefits to help them juggle work in the market and in the home. Although these policies have not fully resolved the problems of gender inequality and parental overburdening, they provide encouraging lessons about how government can help parents strike a balance between caring and earning.

Key to realizing greater gender equality in both the workplace and the home is recognizing that mothers and fathers alike deserve support in their market and caregiving roles. For a number of years, feminist scholars in Europe and the United States have debated the meaning of a woman-friendly welfare state. A universal-breadwinner perspective calls for welfare-state provisions that support and equalize women's employment attachments—for example, by providing extensive public child care. An opposing caregiver-parity perspective calls for provisions that grant women "the right to time for care" and remunerate women for care work performed in the home through generous maternity pay and other caregiver benefits.

Neither perspective fully resolves the tension between work and family life while promoting gender equality. Both fail to provide a satisfying vision of the welfare state—in part because they do not address the issue of fathers as caregivers. Women's widespread assumption of greater market responsibilities has not been equally matched by fathers' assumption of child care responsibilities in the home. Although men's involvement in care giving appears to be on the rise, Bianchi estimates that married fathers in the United States spent just 45 percent of the time their wives spent on caregiving in 1998—an increase of only 15 percentage points since 1965.

A bridge between the universal-breadwinner and caregiver-parity perspectives may lie in social policies that promote what British welfare-state scholar Rosemary Crompton calls the "dual earner/dual career" society. This is a society in which men and women engage symmetrically in both paid work in the labor market and caregiving work in the home. Central to the dual earner/dual career solution is the recognition that *both* mothers and fathers should have the right and opportunity to engage in market and caregiving work without incurring poverty in terms of money or time. For families with very young children (say, younger than age three), mothers and fathers would have the right to take substantial time off from market work to care for their children, without loss of income. For families with children from age three to school age, both parents would have the right to engage in flexible and reduced-hour employment, and they would have access to affordable, high-quality substitute child care.

This solution assumes that men would re-allocate substantial portions of time from the labor market to the home while their children are young. Hence, as American political theorist Nancy Fraser has suggested, "men [would] become more like women are now" in the allocation of their time.

The sweeping transformations of market and gender relations necessary to achieve a gender-egalitarian dual earner/dual career society are obviously not imminent. But the steep rise in maternal employment in recent years and the more modest rise in men's caregiving time suggest that some form of dual earner/dual career arrangement is already the reality for many families in the industrialized world. Given this reality, what can government do to help such families now and to promote greater gender equality in the future? The United States is arguably a leader in rhetorical support for the family and for equal employment opportunities—but it's a clear laggard in making the rhetoric meaningful. U.S. policy makers could take a lesson from the European welfare states, which finance extensive parental leaves during the earliest years of children's lives and provide high-quality early-childhood education and care services for older preschool children. Increasingly, these countries also incorporate incentives that encourage men to assume a larger share of caregiving work in the home.

FAMILY LEAVE

Although their family support programs vary substantially, nearly all of the industrialized welfare states provide generous maternity, paternity, or other parental leave during the first year of childhood, typically funded through some combination of national sickness, maternity, and other social-insurance funds. The most substantial leave benefits are provided in two Scandinavian countries that have consolidated maternity, paternity, and other parental-leave schemes. Norwegian parents are entitled to share 52 weeks of leave with an 80 percent wage replacement (or 42 weeks with full wage replacement) following the birth of a child, while Swedish parents can share a full year of leave with nearly full wage replacement, followed by three additional months at a lower rate. Most continental European countries provide somewhat shorter maternity leaves—usually three to five months—but they pay relatively high replacement rates: 80 percent to 100 percent.

Even beyond the child's first birthday, parents in some European countries have rights to partial leave and reduced-hour employment. In Denmark, for example, mothers have a right to 28 weeks of maternity leave after childbirth with high wage replacement, and fathers have a right to two weeks of paternity leave; once these leaves are exhausted, the parents can share 10 weeks of parental leave with high wage replacement, and then each parent is entitled to 13 weeks of child care leave at 80 percent of the parental-leave benefit level. Finnish parents can choose to stay on leave for up to three years while receiving a low, flat-rate benefit. And Swedish parents have the right to work as little as six hours per week, with job protection, until their children are eight years old.

Although generous leave policies have economic and social benefits for families with very young children, they can create new forms of gender inequality. The total percentage of paid parental-leave days taken by fathers amounts to less than 10 percent across the European welfare states and less than 3 percent in many. Because leaves are taken overwhelmingly by mothers, many women pay a price for their long absences from the labor market in the form of lost human capital and career advancement.

Several of the Scandinavian countries are addressing the gender gap in parental-leave taking by creating incentives for fathers to take the leave to which they are entitled. The most critical of these incentives is high wage-replacement rates. Because men tend to have higher wages than women, in the absence of full wage replacement it often makes economic sense for couples to decide that the mother should withdraw from the labor market. The 80 percent to 100 percent wage-replacement rates in most of the European countries reduce the economic disincentive for fathers to take full advantage of leave benefits.

A second important gender-equalizing policy is the granting of individual or nontransferable leave benefits to fathers as well as to mothers. In Norway and Sweden, four weeks of parental leave are reserved explicitly for fathers; in Denmark fathers have a right to two weeks of paternity leave. In all three countries, leave time reserved for the father but not taken is lost to the family. These "use or lose" provisions encourage parents to participate more equally in leave-supported caregiving. The Scandinavian welfare states have taken active steps to promote fathers' use of leave benefits. In the late 1990s, the Swedish government engaged in a public campaign to educate employers and unions about how fathers' parental leave can be good not just for families but for work organizations and society. Norwegian policy expert Anne Lise Ellingsaeter reports that in her country government officials are now pushing fatherhood onto the political agenda: "While employment for women was the main issue of policies in the 1980s," she suggests, the 1990s brought in "the caring father, and thus the domestication of men." The emphasis on fathers is expanding beyond the Scandinavian countries as well. Italy, for example, instituted use-or-lose days in 2000.

The European welfare states also provide instructive lessons about how to finance parental-leave benefits. Nearly all of the European leave programs are funded through either social-insurance schemes or general tax revenues. None relies on mandating employers to provide wage replacement for their own employees. Those countries in which social-insurance funds draw heavily on employer contributions do not "experience-rate"—that is, adjust contributions to reflect the number of leave takers at the firm level. These financing mechanisms reduce employer resistance by spreading the cost among employers and by supplementing employer contributions with general revenue funds. By reducing the cost to individual employers, these mechanisms also minimize the risk that employers will discriminate against potential leave takers who might otherwise be seen as unusually expensive employees.

How costly are these leave schemes? Spending on maternity, paternity, and parental leave is substantial and is rising in nearly all the European welfare states. Costs relative to population and gross domestic product (GDP) are surprisingly modest, however. As of the middle 1990s, annual family leave expenditures per employed woman (in 1990 U.S. dollars) were about $900 in Sweden and Finland, and about $600 to $700 in Norway and Denmark. France spent a more moderate $375 per employed woman. The higher-spending Scandinavian countries invested approximately 0.7 percent to 1.0 percent of GDP in family leave, while France spent 0.35 percent.

CHILD CARE

The European welfare states provide another critical form of support for dual earner/dual career families and for gender equality in the form of high-quality, public early-childhood education and care. They have developed two distinct models. The model in the Scandinavian countries is an integrated system of child care centers and organized family-day-care schemes serving children from birth to school age, managed by social-welfare or educational authorities. Nearly all employed parents have access to a place in the public child care system with little or no waiting time, and enrollment rates are high. In Sweden and Denmark, for example, one-third to one-half of children under age three are in some form of full-day, publicly supported care, along with 72 percent to 82 percent of children between the ages of three and five.

The model developed by the continental countries of France and Belgium is a two-phase system of child care. For younger children, full-day child care centers (*creches*) and some publicly supervised family-day-care schemes are provided under the authority of the social-welfare system. Beginning at age two and a half or three, children are served in full-day preprimary programs, the *écoles maternelles,* within the educational system.

Enrollment of young children in *creches* is high (30 percent in Belgium and 24 percent in France); it's nearly universal in the *écoles maternelles* for preschool-age children.

Although a large child care sector would seem to be unambiguously positive for gender equality in employment, it can exacerbate inequality if it impoverishes women who work as child care providers. In the European countries, although the child care sector is also mainly women, a large share of child care workers are public-sector employees. As such, they benefit from the good public-sector wages and benefits common in Europe. Relatively high wages for child care workers are tied to high standards for the education and training of child care professionals, who are typically required to have three to five years of vocational or university training. Higher educational standards have benefits that extend beyond the economic welfare of female child care workers. They also increase the quality of care that children receive.

Like leave benefits, early-childhood education and care services in European countries are financed largely by the government. Funding is provided by national, state or regional, and local authorities, with the national share typically dominant in services for preschool-age children. Care for very young children and, to a lesser extent, for preschool children is partially funded through parental co-payments that cover an average of 15 percent to 25 percent of costs. Because co-payments are scaled to family income, lower-income families typically pay nothing and more affluent families pay no more than 10 percent to 15 percent of their income.

Child care expenditures are large and growing in the European welfare states but—like leave expenditures—are modest in per capita terms. Total spending on direct child care in the mid-1990s was about $2,000 per child under age 15 in Sweden and Denmark; it served a large share of all children under the age of seven and many school-aged children in after-school care. In France expenditures totaled a little over $1,000 per child under age 15; they served nearly all three- to five-year-olds and about one-quarter of children under age three. These investments in early-childhood education and care constituted about 1.6 percent to 2.2 percent of GDP in Sweden and Denmark, and about 1 percent in France.

On all fronts, the United States lags behind Europe to a remarkable extent. The United States stands out as one of only a few countries in the entire world that fail to provide any national program of paid maternity leave. Until 1993 this country lacked even job protections for women at the time of childbirth. With the passage of the Family and Medical Leave Act (FMLA), workers in firms with at least 50 employees were granted rights to 12 weeks of unpaid, job-protected leave each year for child-birth or adoption or to care for a seriously ill family member. The exclusion of small firms leaves an estimated one-half of the U.S. work force without even this rudimentary benefit. Additionally, the absence of wage replacement presents an obvious problem: The congressionally established U.S. Commission on Leave reports that 64 percent of employees who need but do not take FMLA-based leave indicate that they cannot afford the loss of wages.

Some families in the United States receive short periods of paid leave through employer-based disability benefits. Five states provide public Temporary Disability Insurance (TDI) programs. Because the Pregnancy Discrimination Act applies to these programs, new mothers have a right to short periods of paid leave if they have either private or public disability benefits. As of the early 1990s, however, only an estimated one-quarter of U.S.

working women had coverage under these laws. The Institute for Women's Policy Research found that weekly benefits paid through the TDI programs average only $170 to $200 and that the duration of benefit claims ranged from five to 13 weeks.

The United States also stands out among industrialized countries for its paucity of public child care assistance. Unlike most of Europe, it has never embraced a national system for universal provision, funding, or regulation of early-childhood education and care. More than 40 percent of American children under age five spend 35 hours or more per week in non-parental care, and another 25 percent spend 15 to 35 hours.

Substitute care in this country is overwhelmingly private in both provision and financing. The U.S. government spends about $200 on direct child care assistance per child under age 15—about one-tenth of the spending in Sweden and one-fifth of that in France. Assistance is provided through two primary mechanisms: (1) means-tested subsidies, available on a limited basis for low-income families with employed parents, and (2) early-childhood education programs (mostly through the means-tested Head Start program) and state prekindergarten programs. Children in the United States now routinely start public school at a young age; about one-half of four-year-olds and 89 percent of five-year-olds are in (usually) part-day prekindergarten or kindergarten programs. But as few as 5 percent of children age three and younger, and of older preschool children outside prekindergarten and kindergarten, are in any form of publicly subsidized or provided care.

Some observers justify miserly child care expenditures in the United States by pointing to tax benefits for families who use child care. The federal government and several state governments exempt a portion of child care expenses from personal income taxes. While the federal Child and Dependent Care Credit is now used by a large number of families, low-income families with no tax liability receive no benefits, and the actual benefit for others is low. As of the mid-1990s, the federal tax credit expenditures totaled about $47 per child under the age of 15.

Unfortunately, the United States gets what it pays for. Minimally regulated private-child-care arrangements provide uneven and generally low-quality care. A research team from the National Institute of Child Health and Human Development recently estimated that only 11 percent of child care settings for children age three and younger meet standards for "excellent" care. In part, quality is poor because the care is provided by a minimally educated and inadequately trained work force. According to data collected by Marry Whitebook of the Center for the Child Care Workforce, some 22 percent to 34 percent of teachers in regulated child care centers and family child care settings do not have a high school diploma; Ellen Galinsky, president of the Families and Work Institute, reports that in unregulated family-and-relative child care settings, between 33 percent and 46 percent of caregivers have not completed high school.

Child care providers are a poorly educated work force in large part because families cannot afford to pay more highly trained professionals. Full-time child care for a four-year-old averages between $3,500 and $6,000 per year—more than college tuition at many state universities. Yet despite this expense, child care workers often earn poverty-level wages. Whitebook estimates that they earn an average of $6.12 per hour—slightly less than parking lot attendants and one-third the average salary of flight attendants.

Many of these poorly paid child care workers are women of color. And many are immigrants from developing countries who are in search of better economic prospects—and who often leave the care of their own children to even poorer women in their home country. [See Arlie Russell Hochschild, "The Nanny Chain," *TAP,* January 3, 2000.]

Although the European welfare states could teach the United States much about child care, they have not completely solved the dilemma of providing gender-egalitarian support for dual earner/dual career families. The supply of child care for children under age three is very limited in many countries, and for older preschool children in some. Also, both short- and longer-term leaves are still used overwhelmingly by mothers. A fully egalitarian package of family support policies is not completely realized even in the progressive Scandinavian countries, but there at least the framework for such policies is in place.

Learning across borders may have considerable cachet in contemporary policy debates, but drawing lessons from the European welfare states has fallen out of favor. Resistance to lessons from overseas has been fueled by vivid press reports of the collapse of the European welfare states. American reporters, particularly in the mainstream print and financial media, have been preoccupied in recent years with the death of the European welfare state. In 1992 the *Los Angeles Times* noted that "Britain . . . finished dismantling much of its welfare system in the 1980s under former Prime Minister Margaret Thatcher." The *San Francisco Chronicle* reported in 1993 that "nowhere is the dismantling of the social security net more drastic than in Sweden, . . . [though] similar retreats from the expansive days of social democracy are under way in virtually every European Community nation." And in 1995 *BusinessWeek* reported that "France . . . in recent weeks has been at the center of what may well be the last great Continental convulsion in this century: the dismantling of the European welfare state."

THE POPULAR WELFARE STATE

As Mark Twain is said to have observed about premature rumors of his demise, reports of the death of the European welfare state turn out to be greatly exaggerated. Spending trends in Europe suggest that while some countries have taken steps to curtail certain areas of program growth, overall social spending continued to rise throughout the 1980s and 1990s. Growth in expenditure was particularly steep in programs that support families and children. Between 1980 and the mid-1990s, per-child spending on family policy in the Western European countries increased by 52 percent. Within the arena of family policy, the growth in expenditures on maternity and parental leaves was quite high: Across Western Europe, average spending per employed woman doubled during this period.

Rising investments indicate that political support for family policies is strong in the European countries—a finding that is confirmed by public opinion research. Family policies are popular mostly because they are universally available. Family leave and child care have been institutionalized as middle-class benefits that support new parents, relieve parents of the financial burden of private child care, and provide high-quality early education for children—all without stigmatizing or isolating recipients. The public sees these programs as providing broader social benefits as well. Cross-national policy research has linked generous leave and child care benefits in Europe to much lower child poverty rates than in the United States, and to less disruption in employment among mothers with young children.

Steadily growing investments in family policies suggest that the European welfare states remain committed to supporting dual earner/dual career families. Translating these policies to the U.S. context remains challenging. One obvious concern is expense. One way to approach the question of cost is through a thought experiment: What if the United States were to commit the same share of its GDP to family policy as the Europeans do? This country currently spends about 0.2 percent of its GDP on child care and a negligible amount on leave. In contrast, France spends about 1.4 percent of its GDP on a generous policy package of family leave and early-childhood education and care. If the same spending share were applied to the U.S. GDP, we'd be looking at about $100 billion annually. As of the mid-1990s, U.S. expenditures on early-childhood education and care totaled only about $15 billion. Thus, in order to provide a package of leave and child care benefits similar to the one available to French families, we would need an additional $85 billion per year.

This figure very likely represents a high-end estimate. The actual bill would probably be lower than these figures suggest since children generally start school at a younger age in the United States than in France. It would also be lower if financing similar benefits consumed a smaller share of the GDP in the strong U.S. economy. Costs would be lower still if policies were partially means-tested or taxed for higher-income families. And recent research suggests that some of those expenditures would be recouped by productivity gains associated with lower employee turnover, fewer work absences, and a less stressed-out work force.

Nevertheless, it is clear that comprehensive family policies would require substantial new investments in the United States. Whether these investments are affordable is a relative question. It is easy to find examples of spending that might be used to offset new investments in family policy. According to the Center for Popular Economics, federal aid to U.S. corporations amounts to $75 billion to $200 billion a year. Former Assistant Secretary of Defense Lawrence Korb and the Center for Defense Information (founded by retired generals and admirals) have argued that the U.S. military budget could be cut by more than $150 billion a year without sacrificing high levels of military readiness. The United States could also find family policy revenues closer to home, by capping a variety of federal tax benefits that primarily reach our most affluent citizens. The mortgage interest deduction alone costs nearly $60 billion a year, local property tax deductions for homeowners cost $14 billion, and the exclusion of capital gains on inherited property costs $25 billion.

Providing real support for America's working families would require an exercise of collective political will. Fortunately, there are some hopeful signs. As more and more families find themselves squeezed for time between the demands of the workplace and the home, support for more expansive family policies may be growing, especially as parents find their budgets squeezed by the price of even mediocre child care. A recent survey conducted for the think tank Zero To Three found that four in five adults support "paid parental leave that allows working parents of very young babies to stay home from work to care for their children." Policy officials are taking at least tentative steps in the direction of policy expansion. Forty-two states now have some form of prekindergarten services. In June 2000, the U.S. Department of Labor issued regulations that allow states to extend unemployment insurance to mothers out of work owing to childbirth. By cross-national standards, these developments are meager. But they may signal a welcome shift in the United States from rhetoric to action in the valuing of children, families, and equal opportunities for women.

Value for Family Tax Dollars:
How Does the U.S. Stack Up?

RACHEL HENNECK

This report outlines how Americans' income tax dollars will be spent in 2005, what American families get in terms of government benefits and what families in other advanced industrialized countries get. [Henneck] compare[s] the quality and cost burden to families of health care, child care, and family allowances between these countries. [Henneck] find[s] that the portion of the tax cuts going to American middle-class families is not nearly enough to offset the costs of health care, child care and college education, and middle-class families can often lose out on quality of services. On the other hand, citizens of European countries such as France, Sweden, Norway and Germany have access to different tax-funded programs that make the same services much less expensive to families and put higher quality within families' reach, while they also provide basic cash benefits that go much further than the typical American middle-class tax cut. They may end up paying more in taxes, but they get much more in return for what they do pay than American families get.

THE FEDERAL BUDGET: WHERE DOES $100 IN INCOME TAX GO?

• Military and defense spending eat up more income tax money than any other government program, consuming about $30.[1]
• $18.60 is spent paying interest on the national debt.
• $20.27 goes to health care programs.
• $6.58 to income security (broken down as: SSI, $2.13; Earned Income Tax Credit refunds, $1.94; Temporary Assistance for Needy Families, $1.03; child tax credit refunds, $0.52; foster care and adoption assistance, $0.37, rest of small programs including child care subsidy, $0.58.
  • $3.67 goes to education
  • $3.44 goes to veterans' benefits
  • $2.69 goes to nutrition programs
  • $2.14 goes to housing
  • $1.72 goes to environmental protection
  • $0.94 goes to job training

Source: Rachel Henneck, "Value for Family Tax Dollars: How Does the U.S. Stack Up? A briefing paper prepared for the Council on Contemporary Families," April 15, 2005. www.contemporaryfamilies.org.

• $10.51 goes to various other programs (including non-military international affairs, general science, space and technology, energy, agriculture, commerce and housing credit, transportation, community and regional development, labor and social services other than train-ing/employment services, justice, general government, and undistributed offsetting receipts.[2]

Over the next ten years, the debt is expected to increase from just over 33 percent of GDP to 54 percent.[3]

In January 2001, interest payments on the debt were projected to be $715 billion over the 2002–2011 period. Now the Center on Budget and Policy Priorities estimates $2.5 trillion over the same period and then $3.4 trillion in interest payments from 2005–2014. By 2014, interest payments are expected to burn up no less than 13 percent of the total federal budget.[4]

WHAT AMERICAN FAMILIES GET:

Most American family benefits from the government come through the tax code, rather than in the form of direct payments or services as European countries typically provide.

The dependent exemption reduces a household's taxable income by $3100 per quali-fying dependent.[5] For a married couple filing jointly earning $30,000 per year with two children, the exemption could reduce taxable income by about $620. At $50,000 per year, the same family could save $930.[6]

The child tax credit is available up to a maximum of $1000 per child. It is refundable.[7]

The child and dependent care tax credit allows families to credit their expenses for child care up to a maximum of $3000 for one child or $6000 for two or more children.[8] The average cost for one child's yearly fees in a child care center is $7020,[9] so it could be said that this credit is worth considerably more to families with fewer than three children.

The Earned Income Tax Credit program helps lift the incomes of many poor work-ing families above the poverty line. This program costs about twice as much as Tempo-rary Assistance to Needy Families. The Earned Income Tax Credit is available to families within the following income and filing status limits:

• Single head of household with one child: adjusted gross income of $30,338 or less;
• Married filing jointly with one child: adjusted gross income of $31,338 or less;
• Single head of household with two or more children: adjusted gross income of $34,458 or less;
• Married filing jointly with two or more children: adjusted gross income of $35,458 or less;
• Single head of household with no child: AGI of $11,490 or less;
• Married filing jointly with no child: AGI of $12,490 or less.

The credit is refundable and maxes out at $4000.[10]

Tax credits are available for higher education expenses, but programs that provide direct financial aid for college are being slashed. The Pell Grant program is expected to be cut by $550 million in 2006.[11]

• The Hope Credit is available at a maximum of $1500 per student enrolled at least half-time in an undergraduate program during the first two years.
• The Lifetime Learning Credit is available at a maximum of $2000 per return, for all years of postsecondary education or education for improving or acquiring job skills. There is no limit on the number of years this credit can be received.[12]

Homeowner families can benefit from the mortgage interest deduction. However, this is "a government subsidy that goes primarily to the most affluent."[13] The more expensive the home, the more one pays on mortgage interest, and the more one can deduct. In the mid 1990s, about half of all tax subsidy for homeownership went to the 5.1 percent of households with yearly incomes of $100,000 or more.[14] Tax subsidies for homeownership cost the government more than the entire budget of the Department of Housing and Urban Development.[15]

Along with the EITC, the direct family subsidies and services available to poor families include Temporary Assistance to Needy Families and Head Start.

• Temporary Assistance to Needy Families (TANF) is the program most people are referring to when they talk about "welfare." It provides modest cash assistance to the most impoverished U.S. citizen families for a lifetime maximum of five years, in stretches of two years at a time. Federal policy requires that recipients participate in work or work-related activities at least 30 hours per week, and most states have not modified that requirement, except to allow exceptions for people with very small children or temporarily incapacitated adults.[16] States are not obligated to provide child care assistance to make adherence to the work requirements easier for families. Many states still do, but federal funding for child care has not increased since 2002, and the number of children receiving child care assistance has fallen each year.[17] Families who qualify for TANF also qualify for Medicaid and food stamps.

• Head Start is a high-quality free preschool and family support program for impoverished families with young children, created in the mid-1960s as part of the War on Poverty effort. Studies have shown over the years that Head Start has had a positive effect on families as well as children's long-term educational and employment prospects.[18] Currently, funding for Head Start is so low that only 20 percent of eligible children are being served.[19]

**WHAT AMERICAN FAMILIES DON'T GET THAT FAMILIES IN
OTHER ADVANCED INDUSTRIALIZED COUNTRIES GET:**

Health Care

In every other advanced capitalist country, citizens enjoy the right to health care. Families do not have to forego routine care for financial reasons, and can't be forced to choose between paying for health care and other basic needs, a common and stressful scenario for many American families.

National health care can provide better freedom of choice for patients than many private insurance plans in the U.S. In France, for example, citizens have the right to choose among health care providers, regardless of income. They can choose between private practices, not-for-profit facilities, universities and general hospitals. There is no problem with waiting lists. For more than 96 percent of the population, health care is either free or 100 percent reimbursed. The system is funded by taxes on workers' salaries, pensions and capital, and indirect taxes on alcohol and tobacco.[20]

Canadians manage to enjoy longer life expectancy and a lower infant mortality rate than the U.S. while spending a smaller proportion of their GDP (10 percent) than we do on health care to provide full medical coverage to all citizens.[21]

Child Care

In France and the Scandinavian countries, which are characterized by high rates of maternal employment, high-quality preschool and child care are universally provided for preschool-aged children. Families typically pay a small percentage of their income for the services. Subsidies are also available for families to hire child-minders to work in their homes, although they mostly choose to use the child care and preschool centers because they are of such high quality and accommodate families' work hours well. In France, they are considered essential for preparing children for first grade.[22]

College Education

In Sweden, students are not charged for tuition.[23] In Germany, where states were only very recently given the option to charge tuition, families bore only about $190 of the cost of university fees during the 1997–1998 academic year,[24] and the cost to families hasn't risen much since then.

Like Germany, the UK only recently began to charge tuition fees. Currently, a yearly fee of $1641 is charged to students from households making $30,534 or more. Scotland decided to roll back the tuition fees and replaced it with a sort of mandatory loan program called the "Graduate Endowment Scheme," which requires students to pledge to "contribute" $3053 (broken down into monthly payments) to the "Graduate Endowment Fund of Scotland" after they graduate and attain annual income of about $15,000.[25]

Family Allowances

Family allowances in most northwestern European countries are set at modest levels, comparable to the tax benefits many U.S. families with children could take advantage of in 2004. But unlike tax deductions and credits, these allowances are paid reliably to families each month, helping families plan their budgets and meet their immediate needs, and they do not require the families to correctly calculate their benefits in order to claim them. Also, they are less subject to the vagaries of political debate, while the U.S. Child Credit is scheduled [to] decline in coming years.

In Austria, the family allowance is the highest-value provision to families. It is a universal cash benefit based on the presence, age and number of children in a household. In 2001, the benefit was equal to about $110 per month for a child between the ages of three and ten years. It's higher for children younger than three and for children between the ages of 10 and 19, and higher still for children between age 19 and 26. In addition to this benefit provided to all families, supplemental benefits are available to moderate-income families with infants or who have three or more children.[26]

In France, the basic universal tax-free family allowance is paid to all families once their second child is born. In 2003, the monthly allowance paid for two children was about $143, and for three children, about $336. Allowances increase as children get older. The allowances are usually adjusted annually to reflect price changes and to remain at a level equal to about half the French minimum wage. Family allowances are a very important component of income for low-income families: they are worth 13 percent of median income.[27]

Parental Leave

Americans who work for medium- to large-sized firms have access to up to 12 weeks' unpaid parental leave via the 1993 Family and Medical Leave Act (FMLA). Due to the exclusion of small companies, about half of workers are not even eligible, and even more cannot afford to take unpaid leave—78 percent of workers who needed to take family leave but did not made their choice because they couldn't afford the missed paycheck.[28] American women who decide that it's best to take time off around the birth of their child—or who can't opt to work for a period of time due to childbirth complications—usually face a choice between unpaid leave or quitting their jobs. This substantial loss of wages due to motherhood largely explains the persistent wage gap between mothers and men. In her study of family policies in the U.S., economist Heather Boushey found that the current wages of mothers who worked before the birth of their first child and whose employers provided paid maternity leave to them were 9 percent higher than the wages of mothers who had not taken leave.[29] Paid leave policy for all mothers in the U.S. could go a long way toward leveling the economic playing field between men and women.

In the absence of federal paid leave policy, California, New Jersey, New York, Montana, Missouri and Minnesota have created their own various partially-paid leave schemes, using temporary disability insurance funds from payroll deductions and other sources of funding. The most generous is California's newly established leave program, which provides workers who pay into the state's disability insurance program (13 million of California's 16 million workers) with six weeks of job-protected leave at about 50 percent pay (up to a limit of $728 per week) to care for a new baby or an ill child, parent, spouse or domestic partner. Employers are allowed to require workers to use up to two weeks of their vacation time before receiving paid leave benefits. If employers will not give the leave, workers can quit and still collect benefits, which are funded completely by payroll deductions for disability insurance.[30] This program costs each taxpayer only about $50 per year—and it is worth much more to the workers who can take parental leave without forgoing all of their pay.

The relative generosity of these programs still pales in comparison to what European working parents are entitled to by their parental leave policies, which often replace a large percentage of parents' salaries. In Norway, for example, there are separate provisions for maternity, paternity, parental and family leave. Maternity leave is a mandatory nine-week period (three weeks before the due date and six weeks after birth) paid at 80 percent of the mother's wage. To qualify for this benefit, the mother must have been employed six out of the last ten months prior to giving birth. Mothers who do not meet this stipulation are entitled to a different benefit, a "modest, lump-sum, tax-free cash benefit."[31]

Paternity leave consists of a four-week period for fathers paid at 80 percent. Any of this leave not taken by fathers cannot be transferred to the mother's available leave balance. In cases where the mother has not been in the labor force, fathers can still take a two-week, unpaid but job-protected paternity leave.[32]

Parental leave (or adoption leave) is a period of 52 weeks at 80 percent pay or 42 weeks at 100 percent pay. It is to be shared between mothers and fathers at their own discretion, and is subject to the same maternal employment requirement as maternity leave.[33]

Family leave is provided as ten fully paid days per year to care for one sick child under age 12, 15 paid days for two or more children, or, for single parents, 20 paid days.[34]

COST, QUALITY OF SERVICES, AND THE ROLE OF TAXATION: HOW FAMILIES IN OTHER RICH COUNTRIES GET MORE BANG FOR THEIR BUCK

Most Americans who have some idea of the sort of social and health programs provided to citizens of rich European countries are under the impression that the taxpayers have to fork over an inordinate share of their income to government bureaucracy in exchange for these benefits. They assume that the American private system must be more financially efficient because it doesn't involve so much "wasteful" government administration and it allows people to choose for themselves where, how, and whether to spend their money for social and health services on the free market.

But this analysis reveals that in terms of the important family services and benefits discussed in this paper, European families get more in exchange for their tax dollars than Americans. They may pay more in taxes, but it means that all families' needs for health care, child care, education and income supplementation are met. Meanwhile, low- and middle-income American families struggle to afford the same services on the private market, and the tax cuts they get don't really help to offset these rising costs.

It doesn't matter whether one is looking from the vantage point of the government, insurance providers, health care providers, employers or consumers: Health care in America is expensive and the costs are becoming more and more difficult for employers and consumers to meet. Between 2000 and 2003, family health spending increased three times faster than income for married couples with kids, so that health care expenses absorbed half the growth of their income.[35] In 2002, the average household spent 4.8 percent of its income on health care—that's $2350 for a household making $50,000 annually or $1440 for a household making $30,000.[36]

Medical costs are pushing many American households into bankruptcy. From their sample of almost 2000 bankruptcy filings from 1999, Warren, Sullivan and Jacoby found that 25 percent of debtors identified a medically-related reason for seeking bankruptcy. Sometimes the medical reason was actual medical bills with no insurance coverage, but more often it was the loss of earnings due to absenteeism that the worker incurred due to illness or disability, or because the worker had to take care of someone else who was ill or disabled. Among debtors age 65 and up, nearly 50 percent seek bankruptcy for medical reasons. One fifth of all debtors reported that their family had no health insurance.[37]

The cost of health care to even middle-income families is painfully high. It may come as a surprise, then, that the U.S. government and employers spend much more per capita than European governments spend, even while the U.S. provides a much smaller proportion of the population with health coverage. This is what Garfinkel, Rainwater and Smeeding found in their study of OECD nations' social and health expenditures. Combining government spending and employer spending on health insurance, the U.S. spends over twice the OECD annual median amount of per capita health care expenditure—$4631 in the U.S. versus $1983 at the OECD median level.[38]

Sadly, this increased spending doesn't translate into better care and health for the population. We have a lower level of health service usage than the OECD median level, and our life expectancy (77.1 years) ranks 21st out of 30 OECD countries' life expectancies.[39]

France, which has a higher life expectancy and lower per capita health care spending than the U.S., manages to provide greater choice and better outcomes at no cost to patients. They can choose between different health care service models and 80 percent of workers enjoy supplemental insurance coverage provided by their employers.[40]

The French as well as the Swedish come out ahead of American families with their universal child care programs, in terms of the proportion of income families pay for the service and the quality of care. In America, poor families who have to purchase child care pay 22 percent of their incomes for child care while more affluent households pay only 6 percent (it is important to note that most poor American families do not pay for child care because [they] make informal arrangements with family, friends and neighbors). Swedish families pay only one to two percent of their income on child care, and French families at all income levels usually pay seven to eight percent.[41]

The difference in quality between American child care and subsidized child care in France and Sweden cannot be underestimated. While high-quality child care does exist in America, it is generally restricted to those who can either pay dearly for it or those who can qualify for a place [in] one of the few subsidized full-day full-year Head Start centers.

Preschool teachers in France and Sweden are required to have the equivalent of bachelor's degrees, and they are paid living wages. In the U.S., educational standards for preschool staff are much lower, and they are practically nonexistent for child care workers. Even in licensed, regulated child care centers and homes, 22 to 34 percent of staff lack a high school diploma. The proportion is greater in unregulated child care settings. Better-educated early childhood care/education staff are harder to attract and retain in the U.S., where child care workers earn barely half the average wage of working American women, and preschool staff earn only two-thirds the average U.S. wage. In addition to the discrepancy in staff quality, it is disturbing to note that health and safety regulations are enforced by routine inspections in only 17 states.[42]

In addition to health and child care services, European governments also fund programs that provide direct cash benefits to most families. These family allowances provide about the same monetary value as U.S. family tax benefits, but they are a more reliable support to families than either America's disparate, fluctuating set of family-related tax benefits or its low-income cash assistance program, TANF. Tax savings once a year are rather abstract and intangible compared to monthly benefit checks.

CONCLUSION

No one likes paying taxes. It's nice to keep more of your income to spend on what you wish. But the rising costs of health care, child care, college tuition and foregone wages for parents who stay home with their kids force most families to pay all the money they save on taxes, plus a whole lot more, on these family essentials. In the long run, Americans might have more disposable income, and certainly more disposable time for family life, if we shifted tax and spending priorities.

ACKNOWLEDGMENTS_____

I give my sincere gratitude to the following skillful, knowledgeable people who gave their time and expertise to this project: fellow CCF intern AnneMarie Murdock, CCF Director of Research and Public Education Stephanie Coontz, Timothy Smeeding at the Maxwell School at Syracuse University, Steven Wisensale at the University of Connecticut, Nancy Folbre at the University of Massachusetts at Amherst, Janet Gornick at the Baruch College at CONY, Paula England at Stanford University, David Kamin at the Office of Budget and Management, Anita Dancs at the National Priorities Project, and Ruth Carlitz at the Center on Budget and Policy Priorities.

NOTES_____

1. National Priorities Project. "NPP Income Tax Chart." 8 April 2005. http://www.nationalpriorities .org/taxes/incomeTaxChart05.html
2. National Priorities Project. "Where Do Your Tax Dollars Go? Notes and Sources." 8 April 2005. http://www.nationalpriorities.orgrTaxDay2005/sources.pdf
3. Kogan, Richard, David Kamin and Joel Friedman. "Deficit Picture Grimmer than New CBO Projections Suggest." Washington, D.C.: Center on Budget and Policy Priorities, 2004. http://www.cbpp.org/l-28–04bud.htm
4. Ibid.
5. Internal Revenue Service. "Publication 17: Your Federal Income Tax." 5 April 2005. http://www.irs.gov/publications/pl7/chO3.html
6. Kamin, David. Office of Management and Budget, telephone call. 12 April 2005.
7. Ibid.
8. Internal Revenue Service.
9. Shellenbarger, Sue. "As Cost of Child Care Rises Sharply, Here's How Families Are Coping." *Wall Street Journal.* 21 October 2004. D.1.
10. Internal Revenue Service.
11. "Fiscal Shenanigans." *New York Times,* late edition. 3 June 2004: A.26.
12. Internal Revenue Service.
13. Dreier, Peter and John Atlas. "Give the Middle Class a Break: Replace The Mortgage Deduction, Which Benefits the Well-Off, With a Tax Credit to Increase Homeownership." *Los Angeles Times.* 20 January 1995.
14. Ibid.
15. "Building the American Dream: Asset-Building as a Foundation." New York: Demos, 2004. http://www.demos-usa.org/pubs/Building_PBrief.pdf; Steuerle, C. Eugene. *Contemporary Tax Policy: Chapter One.* Washington, D.C.: The Urban Institute, 2004. http://www.urban.org/pubs/CTP/chapterone.html
16. "State Policies Regarding TANF Work Activities and Requirements." 9 April 2005. http://www.spdp.org/tanf/work/worksumm.htm
17. Ewen, Danielle. "The Senate's $6 Billion Child Care Provision: A Critical, But Modest, Investment." Washington, D.C.: Center for Law and Social Policy, 2005. http://www.clasp.org/publications/6_billion.pdf
18. Kennedy, Edward M. "Keeping Faith With Our Children: Why Early Childhood Education Is the Best Investment We Can Make." *The American Prospect Online.* 1 November 2004.
19. NHSA: The Dismantling of Head Start is Already Underway." 27 October 2004. http://www.saveheadstart.org/102704release.html
20. "The French Healthcare System." Embassy of France, 2003. http://www.info-france-usa.org/atoz/health.asp
21. Wisensale, Steven. A letter to the author. 12 April 2005.
22. Gornick, Janet and Marcia Meyers. *Families That Work: Policies for Reconciling Parenthood and Employment.* New York: Russell Sage Foundation, 2003.
23. The International Comparative Higher Education Finance and Accessibility Project (ICHEFAP). "A Brief Description of Swedish Higher Education." 10 April 2005. http://www.gse.buffalo.edu/org/IntHigherEdFinance/region_europe_Sweden.htm
24. Johnstone, D. Bruce and Preeti Shroff-Mehton. *Higher Education Finance and Accessibility: An International Comparative Examination of Tuition and Financial Assistance Policies.* Buffalo: Center for Comparative and Global Studies in Education, State University of New York, 1999.

25. ICHEFAP. "A Brief Description of the Scottish Higher Education System." 10 April 2005. http://www.gse.buffalo.edu/org/intHigherEdFinance/region_europe_scotland.htmi

26. Clearinghouse on International Developments in Child, Youth and Family Policies. "Clearinghouse Countries: Austria." 10 April 2005. http://www.childpolicyintl.org/countries/austria.html

27. "Clearinghouse Countries: France." 10 April 2005. http://www.childpolicyintl.org/countries/france.html; Rainwater, Lee and Timothy M. Smeeding. *Poor Kids in a Rich Country: America's Children in Comparative Perspective.* New York: Russell Sage Foundation, 2003.

28. National Partnership for Women and Families. "Paid Family Leave." 11 April 2005. http://www.nationalpartnership.org/default.aspx?tabid=116

29. Boushey, Heather. "Family-Friendly Policies: Boosting Mothers' Wages." Washington, D.C.: Center for Economic and Policy Research, 2005. http://www.cepr.net/publications/labor_markets_2005_04_06.pdf

30. Edds, Kimberly. "California Adopts Family Leave: Law Mandates Paid Time Off." *The Washington Post* 24 Sept. 2002: A.03.

31. Clearinghouse on International Developments in Child, Youth and Family Policies. "Clearinghouse Countries: Norway." 10 April 2005. http://www.childpolicyintl.org/countries/norway.html

32. Ibid.

33. Ibid.

34. Ibid.

35. Mishel, Lawrence, Michael Ettlinger and Elise Gould. "Less Cash in Their Pockets: Trends in Incomes, Wages, Taxes and Health Spending of Middle-Income Families, 2000–03." Washington, D.C.: Economic Policy Institute, 2004.

36. United States Department of Health and Human Services. "Effects of Health Care Spending on the Economy." 31 March 2005. http://aspe.hhs.gov/health/costgrowth/index.htm

37. Jacoby, Melissa B., Teresa A. Sullivan, and Elizabeth Warren. "Rethinking the Debates over Health Care Financing: Evidence from the Bankruptcy Courts." *New York University Law Review,* Volume 76, Issue 2 (May 2001).

38. Garfinkel, Irwin, Lee Rainwater, and Timothy M. Smeeding. "Welfare State Expenditures and the Redistribution of Well-Being: Children, Elders, and Others in Comparative Perspective." Prepared for the conference of the Association of Public Policy Analysis and Management, Atlanta, GA, 29 October 2004.

39. Ibid.; Gould, Elise. "Health Care: U.S. Spends More, Gets Less." 26 October 2004. Washington, D.C.: Economic Policy Institute, 2004. http://www.epinet.org/content.cfm/webfeatures_snapshots_10202004

40. "The French Healthcare System."

41. Gornick and Meyers.

42. Ibid.

_____Section 8_____

Schools

THE UNITED STATES CONTEXT

Public education in the United States has many problems. Foremost, schools are vastly unequal in resources because their finances depend largely on the local economy. This means, for example, that urban schools are poorly financed, yet they have the highest concentration of poor children, minority children, and children of recent immigrants. Educational policy, for the most part, is not a federal issue but rather divided into 50 state programs and 15,000 local district programs. Thus, there are wide differences in curricula, standards, and emphases depending on the locality. It is estimated that school districts need at least $100 billion to repair or replace deteriorating facilities. Many high school graduates are barely literate. Compared to their peers in other industrialized countries, U.S. students by the 12th grade do not fare well in mathematics and science. Latinos, the largest racial/ethnic minority in the United States, have a 30 percent dropout rate from high school, compared to 12 percent for African Americans and 9 percent for whites. Colleges and universities, the most important gatekeepers, are so expensive that they are less and less available to the children of middle-class parents and certainly children of the working class, and, obviously, the working poor and the poor. This leads, of course, to a two-tiered society.

As a result, educational performance in the United States varies by locality and the social and economic background of students. Most notably, the United States falls short on a number of indicators used to compare the industrialized nations on education (e.g., high school graduation rates, the gap between the highest and lowest performing students, per pupil expenditures as a percentage of income per person, early childhood education, and the number of days spent in school each year).

18

Early Childhood Education and Care:
International Perspectives

SHEILA B. KAMERMAN

In testimony before the U.S. Senate Committee on Health, Education, Labor, and Pensions, Professor Kamerman compared early childhood (preschool) education in the United States with those programs in other industrialized countries. In doing so, she described three major models of early childhood care and education.

I am Sheila B. Kamerman, a professor at Columbia University School of Social Work, director of the University-wide Institute for Child and Family Policy, and co-director of the Cross-National Studies Research Program. I have been carrying out research on child and family policies in advanced industrialized countries for more than 25 years and have studied early childhood education and care policies and programs throughout the industrialized world.

Early childhood education and care (ECEC) is high on the child and family policy agenda of all advanced industrialized countries today and many developing countries as well. Equitable access to good quality ECEC programs supports both the education and social needs of young children and their families. In more and more countries young children are spending two or three or even four years in these programs before entering primary school. In some countries access to these programs is a legal right—at age one in most of the Nordic countries, at age two in France, and age three in most of the other continental European countries such as Belgium, Germany, and Italy. In all countries there is stress on expanding supply unless there are already enough places to cover all children whose parents wish them to participate; and there is an ongoing stress on improving quality.

The term "Early Childhood Education and Care" (ECEC) includes all arrangements providing care and education for children under compulsory school age regardless of setting (schools, centers, or carers' homes), funding (public or private), hours (part-day, full school day, full work day), or curriculum. There are three major "models" of early childhood care and education programs in the industrialized countries:

1. a program that is designed to respond to the needs of working parents as well as children, covers the normal workday and year, serves children from the end of a paid parental

Source: Sheila B. Kamerman, "Early Childhood Education and Care: International Perspectives," Testimony before the United States Senate Committee on Health, Education, Labor, and Pensions, March 27, 2001.

leave lasting 1–3 years depending on the country, and is administered under social welfare auspices (or sometimes, education) (for example, Denmark or Sweden);
2. a program that includes preschool for children aged 2 or 3 to compulsory school entry (typically age 6), administered under education auspices, and provides supplementary services for children whose parents' work day and year do not coincide with the school day and year; and a second program for children under age 3 usually under a separate administrative agency but sometimes under education auspices as well, that also begins when a country's paid maternity and/or parental leave ends (for example France or Italy);
3. a fragmented system that maintains two parallel systems (or non-systems) of care and education, but that is beginning to move toward integrating the two streams (for example Britain or the U.S.).

The dominant model in Europe is that of the preschool program for children aged 3 to compulsory school entry, and a separate program for the under 3s. A full understanding of European early childhood education and care programs, however, requires an understanding of the role played by paid parental leaves in providing infant care. I have described all three models including infant and toddler care programs and parental leave policies elsewhere (Kamerman, 2000 and 2001), but now I will focus on the preschool programs.

In Europe, these early childhood education and care programs are increasingly available to all children this age because they are considered good for children regardless of their parents' employment status. They enhance children's development and prepare them for formal primary school as well as providing care for those children whose parents are in paid employment. Most important, they reflect the growing consensus within the OECD (Organization for Economic Cooperation and Development) group of countries that care and education are inseparable in programs for preschool-aged children. In many countries, these programs are free, at least for the core program covering the normal school day, while others charge modest income-related fees; and all are voluntary. Nonetheless, when places area available, all children attend.

This morning, I will comment briefly on some aspects of these ECEC programs:

- the extensiveness of the programs serving children aged 2 ½ or 3 to compulsory school entry, at ages 5–6 or 7 depending on the country;
- the general trend towards universal access for all children whose parents wish them to participate;
- the movement towards locating these programs under "education" rather than social welfare auspices;
- the interest in improving the quality of the programs;
- the conviction that these services are essential for all children, not just those with employed parents or those who are poor or otherwise disadvantaged; and
- the recognition that they are not cheap, but nonetheless worth investing in.

ELIGIBILITY, COVERAGE, AND TAKE-UP

To repeat: ECEC programs in Europe are largely universal, voluntary, and available to all children aged 3–6 regardless of family income or problem. Some countries do give priority to employed or student parents. Where places are available, just about all children are enrolled in center or school-based programs, for example: about 98 percent in Belgium and France, 95 percent in Italy, 80–85 percent in Denmark, Sweden, and Spain. (See Table 18.1.) (Coverage is lower for children under age 3, ranging from about 30 percent in France to almost 60 percent of l and 2 year olds in Denmark, and the services are delivered in centers or in supervised family day care homes.)

FINANCING AND COSTS

In countries with the preschool model, the core program covering the normal school day is free and the supplementary ("wrap around") services are heavily subsidized and charge income-related fees. In countries providing a full work day program, fees are also income-related but heavily subsidized for all. In almost all countries governments pay the largest share of the costs, with parents covering only about 11–30 percent (in contrast to the 55–70 percent of costs that parents bear in the U.S.) According to a recent study, public investment in ECEC per child in 1996 ranged from $4511 in Sweden and $2951 in France to $600 in the U.S. (Meyers and Gornick, 2001). Countries use a range of financing mechanisms including direct funding (the primary financing strategy), subsidies, tax benefits, and employer contributions. Affordability remains a barrier to equitable access, especially when parents bear the major share of financing these programs. The programs are not cheap anywhere and especially not in those countries desiring a quality system.

STAFFING AND COMPENSATION

Staffing is an important component of the quality of ECEC programs. Although there is no consistent pattern of staff training and qualifications, there is consensus that staff require specialized training and that compensation should be equitable across ECEC programs and primary school. There is some concern regarding scarcity of males among staff, and some effort—in some countries—to actively recruit male staff. And there is some recognition, also in some countries, of the importance of staffing that reflects the ethnic and racial diversity of the children served.

QUALITY

There is no agreed on definition of—or standards concerning—quality of ECEC programs cross-nationally. The current OECD study of ECEC in 12 countries should provide more information about quality when the final report is issued. U.S. researchers have carried out the most extensive efforts designed to identify the variables than account for the most significant differences regarding program quality—and the consequences for children's socio-emotional-cognitive development. These variables have been identified as group size, staff-child ratios, and caregiver qualifications, in addition to health and safety standards. These criteria have been further refined and supplemented so that current indicators of quality would include caregivers' education and training, salaries, and turnover rates—among the dimensions of quality that can be regulated, and staff:child interactions and relationships among those variables that require direct observation.

Both public and publicly funded private programs in Europe are subject to the same government regulations regarding quality, but countries vary in the type and extent of regulations and whether they are imposed by the national government, the state government, or local, and the degree of enforcement. Of some interest, the standards specified for most of the countries are not far removed from the recommended standards of U.S. scholars.

Peter Moss, the coordinator of the former European Commission Network on Child Care, attempted to carry out a study of child care quality in the European Union in the early 1990s and concluded that quality is a relative concept, reflecting the values and beliefs of the society in which the programs are embedded. Nonetheless, all the countries discussed here recognize the value of quality as it relates to subsequent outcomes. The importance of integrating care and education regardless of the administrative auspice of the program, is emphasized as is the need for a stated, explicit educational mission.

The research literature on outcomes and impacts of ECEC is enormous and well beyond what can be addressed here. The most extensive, systematic, and rigorous research has been carried out in the U.S. But clearly there is important and relevant research that has been carried out in many other countries, too. Among the most influential European studies is the research of Bengt-Erik Anderson (1985; 1990), the Swedish psychologist who followed several groups of children from infancy to high school and beyond, and compared them on the basis of various tests and teacher observations/evaluations. Comparing "early starters" in day care centers (those entering at 9–12 months of age) with those in family day care and home care, those entering at a significantly later age, in family day care, and/or experiencing shifts in care, showed more negative results. The research found distinct advantages by age 8 for early day care starters and those enrolled in center-based care. Positive differences were found in language and all school academic subjects. Teachers found the early starters more outspoken, less anxious in school situations, more independent, and more persevering. (It must be remembered that these children were in consistently high quality programs.)

French research has documented the value of the *ecole maternelle* (the French universal preschool program) in achieving readiness for primary school and reducing primary school problems and school "failure." French research has found that their preschool has particularly strong positive impacts on the most disadvantaged children, and as a result are expanding access to the *maternelle* for children from age 2, with priority given to those living in disadvantaged communities. In Italy, too, researchers found that children ended up better prepared for primary school if they had a preschool experience (and better prepared for preschool if they had a still earlier group experience).

To summarize: the major current policy trends include:

- integration of care and education under education auspices
- a stress on universal access, not limiting access to poor, disadvantaged, or at risk children;
- a goal of full coverage of all children whose parents want them to participate
- substantial public investment
- increasing emphasis on staff qualifications and training
- ongoing concern with quality
- expanding the supply of toddler care (care for 1 and 2 year olds)
- extending the duration of paid and job-protected parental leaves.

CONCLUSIONS

I have summarized the highlights: What are the implications, the emerging issues?

The movement toward universal preschools has clearly emerged as the dominant model of ECEC in Europe. Several countries have already achieved full coverage, regardless of

TABLE 18.1: Child Care by Auspice, Age of Child, Locus of Care, Quality, and Access/Coverage

COUNTRY	AUSPICE	AGE	LOCUS OF CARE	QUALITY	ACCESS/COVERAGE (%)[a]
Austria	Welfare Public or private, non profit	3–6	Preschool	No national standards; Vary by state: Staff child ratios 3:20.	80%
		0–3	Centers		3%
Belgium	Education	2½–6	Preschool	1.7:14 FDC Home, max 7 staff.	97%
	Welfare Public or nonprofit	under 3	Centers	1:19; 1.5:20–25. 2½:7 (incl. .5 nurse) in centers: 3–4 ch. max in FDC Homes.	30%
Canada	Education	5–6	Preschool	Set by Province.	50%
	Welfare Public; non-profit and for profit	under 5	Centers and FDC Homes		45%
Denmark	Education	6–7	Preschool	set locally.	100%[b]
	Welfare Largely public	6 mos.–6 years.	Centers and FDC Homes (esp. for under 3s)	generally, 1:5.5, 3–6 1:2.7, under 3.	3–6: 83%[c] 0–3: 58%[a]
Finland	Welfare; largely public	1–7	Centers and FDC Homes (also for under 3s)	1:7, 3–7 year olds 1:4, under 3s FDC Homes, max 4 preschoolers	3–6: 73%[d] 1–3: 48%
France	Education	2–6	Preschool	National health, safety, and staffing standards. 1:10 2 year olds 1:27 others staff=teachers	3–6: 99%
	Largely public health and welfare	3 mos.–3 years.	Preschool, centers and FDC Homes	1:8 toddlers; 1:5 infants 1:3 FDC	2–3: 35% 0–3: 29%
Germany	Education, public and private non-profit	3–6	Preschool	1:10–14	85%[c]
	Welfare; public and private non-profit	under 3	Center and FDC (largely)	1:5–7.5	5% (West German States) 50% (East German States)

Country	Auspices	Age	Type	Standards	Coverage
Italy	Education	3–6	Preschool	3:25	95%
	Welfare, public and private non-profit	under 3	Center	no national standards 1:3 under 3s is customary in most regions.	6%
Spain	Education, public and private non-profit	0–6	Preschool	National standards 1:25 3–6 year olds	3–6: 84%
			Center	1:18 2–3 year olds 1:10 toddlers 1:7 infants 1/3 staff "trained"	0–3: 5%
Sweden	Education, largely public	0–6[f]	Center	No national standards; local government sets standards. 2:3½ children 3–6	3–6: 80%
			Centers and FDC Homes	1:3–5 children under 3 FDC: 1:4–8	1–3: 48%[a]
U.K.	Education	3–4	Preschool	2:26	3–4: 60%
	Welfare public, private, non-profit, and for profit	0–4[g]	Centers and FDC Homes	National standards 1:4 for 2–3s 1:3 for under 2s	
U.S.	Education	5–6	Preschool	No national standards State standards vary widely	95% of 5 year olds @ 50% of 3–4 year olds in either preschool or center care
	Education and Welfare Largely for profit and private non-profit	0–4	Preschool and Centers; FDC for under 3s.	32 states require 1:4 ratios for infants. Half the states have 1:5 (or lower) ratios for toddlers.	0–3: 26%

Source: Kamerman, S. B. (Ed.) (Forthcoming). *Early Childhood Education and Care: International Perspectives.* NY: Institute for Child and Family Policy, Columbia University.

[a] The age of entry and access/coverage need to be seen in the context of the duration of the maternity/parental leave.
[b] Some also attend child care center for part of day.
[c] All children one year old and older with working parents, now guaranteed a place in subsidized care.
[d] All children under 7 with working parents, now guaranteed a place in subsidized care.
[e] Coverage in kindergarten for all children 3–6 is the goal.
[f] Sweden has now lowered school entry to age 6.
[g] Compulsory school entry is age 5.

parents' employment status or income or problem; and this is clearly the goal in those countries that have not yet achieved it. These programs are viewed as good for children and access is assured, sometimes as a matter of legal right and sometimes out of societal conviction. These programs are increasingly viewed as a "public good." Regardless of the early focus on formal education, program goals have been broadened now to include socialization and enhancing development in addition to cognitive stimulation and preparing children for primary school. There is strong conviction regarding the value of these programs for all children and there is increasing recognition of the appropriateness of public financing for programs that should be available to all children, free of charge. The key issue for the future, in most countries with this model, is increasing the availability of supplementary services to meet the needs of employed parents.

Quality remains an issue everywhere and there appears to be growing consensus on the important dimensions even though the recommended standards have not yet been achieved in most countries. Educational philosophy varies among countries but countries increasingly see these programs as "education" in the broadest sense, incorporating physical, emotional, and social development along with literacy and numeracy.

Public financing is the dominant mode in all countries. Parent fees play a minor role in meeting the costs. Costs are high for good quality programs but there appears to be growing recognition of their value and its importance. Government subsidies are generous and given to providers, in most countries.

Finally, the continued rise in labor force participation rates of women with young children coupled with the growing recognition of the value of good quality early childhood education and care programs for children regardless of parents' employment status, suggests that the pressure for expanding supply, improving quality, and assuring access will continue in all countries, despite variations in delivery.

REFERENCES_____

Andersson, B. Several reports out of a longitudinal study of the impact of out-of-home child care on children at different ages, 1985–1990. Stockholm, Sweden: Stockholm Institute of Education.

Baudelot, O. (1988). *Child care in France,* Paper prepared for the National Academy of Science/ National Research Council Working Group on Child Care Internationally. Woods Hole, MA.

Sheila B. Kamerman, ed. *Early Childhood Education and Care: International Perspectives.* New York: ICFP, 2001.

Sheila B. Kamerman, "Parental Leave Policies: An Essential Ingredient in Early Childhood Education and Care Policies," *Social Policy Report,* SRCD, Vol. XIV, No. 2, 2000.

Marcia Meyers and Janet Gornick, "Early Childhood Education and Care: Cross-National Variations in Service Organizations and Financing," In Sheila B. Kamerman, ed. *Early Childhood Education and Care: International Perspectives.*

Ministere de L'Education Nationale, De La Recherche et de la Technologie, (France) Decembre, 1999. "Observation a l'entrée au CP des eleves du "panel 1997."

Moss, P. (1996). *Quality targets in services for young children.* Brussels, Belgium: European Commission, DGV, Childcare Network.

Musatti, T. (1992). *La giornata del mio bambino.* Bologna, Italy: Il Mulino.

Pistillo, F. (1989). Preprimary care and education in Italy. In P. P. Olmsted & D. P. Weikart, *How nations serve young children: profiles of child care and education in 14 countries.* Ypsilanti, MI: HighScope Press.

19

Denmark: Lessons for American Principals and Teachers?

RICHARD MORRILL

Schools in Denmark have many qualities that U.S. schools could benefit from by adopting. Social supports reduce the differences in income and wealth, which levels the playing field for students. Students in elementary school remain together with the same teacher for several years. The typical classroom consists of a heterogeneous mix of social classes and interests. There is no ability grouping. Tests and quizzes are virtually unknown through grade 6. The use of threats and punishments to discipline and motivate children is relatively absent. There is a high degree of group work and the use of cooperative projects.

The U.S. and Denmark, long NATO allies, share many things, but attitudes and beliefs with regard to the proper role of government, the alleged efficacy of unregulated free markets, and what constitutes a civilized society vary considerably in the two countries. Whereas policy making in the U.S. has long been characterized by the conflict of competing individual rights and special interests, Danish policy making seems to exemplify a concern for the common good and decision making by consensus.

In Denmark, making sure that no one is left behind is more than expedient political rhetoric. Deciding policy on the basis of its impact on the least advantaged members of the society is taken as a given, even by politicians in the Conservative Party. Vast differences in income and wealth—so typical of the U.S. in recent decades—are regarded by the Danes as a primary cause of social pathologies. Consequently, Danish social policy since the early 20th century has sought to foster social harmony by avoiding great gaps in income and wealth between social and occupational groups. This is not to say that there is no diversity in Denmark or that the individual freedoms and creativity of the Danes are being stifled. On the contrary, it would seem that a higher percentage of Danes are empowered to develop themselves as individuals because of the support they receive from society.

The differences in attitudes and beliefs between the U.S. and Denmark are especially noticeable in the area of education. Because education has been a political hot potato in the

Source: Richard Morrill, "Denmark: Lessons for American Principals and Teachers?" *Phi Delta Kappan* 84 (February 2003), pp. 460–463.

U.S. for some time, it might be instructive to take a closer look at Danish attitudes toward such issues as testing, classroom management, and the role of the schools in socialization.

I base my arguments here on a decade of firsthand observations of Danish child-rearing practices and schooling. From October 1990 to February 2000, I lived and worked in Denmark. During the latter years of that period, my son attended a community-run preschool day-care center, kindergarten, and grades 1 through 4 of a public school.

THE 'CLASS TEACHER' SYSTEM IN DENMARK

The major difference between the American public schools and the Danish public schools at the primary and lower-secondary levels—that is, grades 1 through 9—is that Danish children and their parents know that from first grade at age 7, the same 20 or so classmates, more or less evenly divided between boys and girls, will remain together for the next several years. Danish children will also have the same "class teacher" year after year.

The typical Danish class will consist of a mix of children from various family backgrounds (working class, merchant class, professional class) and exhibiting a variety of interests (artistic, athletic, cultural, etc.). No attempt is made to group the children by ability within the individual "classes." Rather, it is more likely that the class will be formed on the basis of residential patterns. Children who live and play together in the same neighborhood will be grouped in a class.

Once composed, the class will stay together with the same "class teacher" as it progresses through the primary and lower-secondary grades. Typically, though not always, the "class teacher" is the teacher with whom the class has its Danish language and literature lessons. During the primary grades, the class will usually have a second and third teacher who divide up the responsibility for teaching math, science, social studies, music, and art. By the lower-secondary grades, a class may have as many as five or six teachers.

One of the main responsibilities of the "class teacher" is to coordinate the activities of the class with the other teachers and to mediate whenever members of the class have academic or behavioral problems in lessons taught by the other teachers. The result of having the same "class teacher" stay with the class year after year is that the teacher and the class members get to know one another well and develop a good working relationship.

Similarly, it is possible for the "class teacher" to develop a close working relationship with the parents over the years. The "class teacher," the students, and the parents can develop a relationship of trust and a feeling that "we are all in this together." The same relationships and feelings develop among the parents of the children in the class, and the parents typically meet a few times a year in a parents' council (*forældreråd*) in order to socialize and exchange views and concerns about the progress of the class.[1]

This "class teacher" arrangement offers many advantages with regard to classroom management and parent participation, and it is a measure that could easily be adopted by American administrators and teachers who are willing to think outside the box.[2] One of the most beneficial effects is psychological. When a class and a teacher know that they will be working together over a period of several years, they are generally motivated to find ways to get along with one another. Neither pupil nor teacher can afford to adopt the attitude that next year each will be rid of the other.

Instead, what happens is that each child has a ready-made group to rely on and interact with during his or her developing years. Traditionally in Denmark, birthday parties, class parties, trips, and so on are arranged at the level of the school class. A child may well have good friends outside the class, but many of a child's social activities will be focused on the class. It is considered extremely bad form not to invite a classmate to a social event. Consequently, no child has to worry about being excluded or being a social outcast. There is a peer group that will include him or her as a matter of course. This sense of belonging should not be underestimated as a positive aspect of the "class teacher" system.

Another benefit, alluded to above, is that the "class teacher" has extensive knowledge of each child and can closely monitor his or her strengths and weaknesses. Children cannot fall behind, unnoticed, because the "class teachers" are always aware of how their charges are doing—academically, emotionally, and physically.

There is also a benefit for the teacher. Instead of becoming complacent or burnt out from teaching the same subject at the same grade level year after year, the teacher can look forward to dealing with new material in the year to come and remains fresh as a result. The Danish teacher who accompanies the same class from the first to the sixth grade before starting over with a new class of first-graders knows the joy of seeing pupils progress over the intervening years, whereas the American teacher who spends year after year moving different classes from one grade to the next may come to doubt that he or she has made much difference in the pupils' lives.

TESTING AND THE EXTERNAL EXAMINER

Tests and quizzes—and, indeed, the use of grades and grade report cards—are practically unknown in the primary grades (grades 1 through 6) and are much less frequently used in the lower secondary grades in Danish schools than in American schools. This should not be construed as evidence that the Danish teachers and parents are less aware of the abilities and achievements of their pupils than are their American counterparts. On the contrary, they follow closely the work of their children inside and outside the classroom.

The lack of emphasis on testing in Danish schools reflects the teachers' commitment to teaching basic concepts and skills to all their pupils instead of using the academic material as a means of sorting (and labeling) pupils into groups of winners and losers. If anything, Danish teachers want to avoid for as long as possible the labeling of a pupil as a failure, which is what tests often do. The lack of emphasis on testing also reflects the Danish teachers' skepticism about the utility of tests and quizzes as motivating factors. Making a competition out of learning may be compatible with the American culture, but it poses something of a threat to the value that the Danish culture places on cooperation and social unity. It also detracts from the pleasure of learning for the sake of learning.

In the context of testing, it should be mentioned that the Danish school system, like the American one, is a decentralized system.[3] The Danish Ministry of Education has developed standards for the various subject areas and has issued curriculum guidelines, but these are advisory in nature rather than mandatory. In this respect, the Danish education system is much more like the education system in most American states than it is like the centralized system in France.

decentralized

Local schools and teachers have great latitude in deciding how they will teach the subject concepts and skills that the ministry has identified as important. To a very considerable extent, the use of the same textbooks results in a uniformity of learning from school to school, but Danish teachers do develop and use their own materials to a degree unknown in most American schools.

When the students reach the end of the mandatory lower-secondary education in the ninth grade, from which they will pass on to an academic high school or to vocational education, they have been relatively free of the artificial pressures of testing throughout most of their school careers. However, at this stage they are required to pass a series of written and oral examinations on required and elective subjects.

A student's responses are read (or heard, as the case may be) and evaluated by two persons: the teacher who taught him or her the subject matter being tested and an external examiner who is an experienced teacher in the same subject area at another school. Together, the two examiners reach a consensus on the appropriate score for the student's performance on the test. Danish grades range from 13 (excellent); through 11, 10, and 9 (gradations of very good); to 8 (good or average); to 7 and 6 (fair, but still passing); and on to 5 and 3 (not passing). From this, it is clear that there is more room to spread out student scores than in a system restricted to A, B, C, D, and F.

The point to be made, though, is that in Denmark testing is regarded as much less essential to the process of educating the young than is the case in the U.S. Testing is not necessary for purposes of accountability because of the excellent involvement of parents with the "class teacher." Parents know, without needing test scores, what the school is doing for their children. Nor, seemingly, is testing needed for the purpose of motivating pupils to learn the material. Certainly, the idea of teaching extensively to the test, as frequently happens in the U.S., is foreign to Danish teachers and parents.

SCHOOL AND CLASSROOM DISCIPLINE

The first major cultural difference that an American in Denmark notices is the prevailing attitude toward disciplining and motivating children. In Denmark, the use of intimidation and force—threats and punishments—in order to motivate children is generally regarded with disdain and is conspicuous by its relative absence. While it is common to hear parents in the U.S. say mean things to their children or scream at them in such places as Wal-Mart, I have never experienced anything similar in 10 years of shopping in the Danish *Brugsen* (cooperative grocery store). Nor were children, not even intransigent children who threw fits and balked at putting on their snowsuits, for example, shaken and jerked around and spanked the way they often are in the U.S.

In the same way, such practices as sending pupils to stand in the hall, sending them to the principal's office, or suspending them from school are not common in Denmark. Nor are pupils scolded as harshly in Denmark as they often are in American schools. The sight of a fourth-grader coming out of the assistant principal's office with tears streaming down his face is a phenomenon virtually unknown in Denmark.

From the Danish point of view, the problem with the American emphasis on punishment as a means of correcting student misbehavior is three-fold: 1) it assumes that children are better motivated by fear than by praise and encouragement; 2) it creates an unpleasant reign-ofterror atmosphere in the classroom and the school that affects the psyche of all the children; and 3) it teaches the child that problems and conflicts are to be resolved by the use of power rather than the use of reason and persuasion. The idea of using authoritarian measures to pre-pare citizens for life and work in a democratic society is a nonstarter in today's Denmark.

STAGES OF DEVELOPMENT

The work of Piaget and Erikson on the progression of the individual through stages of cog-nitive and psychosocial development is emphasized in Danish teacher training and is taken seriously in practice. For this reason, Danish children enroll in first grade at age 7, after having attended a kindergarten class with no academic activities the previous year.

The Danes deem it unrealistic and doomed to failure to start children on cognitive exercises at an age younger than 7. The mark of a good Danish teacher is his or her ability to design and put into use educational activities that are appropriate to a child's particular stage of development.

GROUP WORK

Danish classrooms are characterized by a high degree of group work and the use of many cooperative projects in which pupils work together and help one another and ensure that everyone in the group has learned from the experience. Danish classrooms do *not,* for the most part, cater to competitive individuals whose success or failure depends on outshin-ing their classmates. In the Danish schools, to see classmates helping one another is to see something beneficial to the individuals involved and to the society. Cheating, in the sense of one pupil helping another, is not a problem in this context.

Perhaps it is a bit unfair to compare the policies and practices of an essentially homo-geneous society such as Denmark—characterized by a single racial group, a single lan-guage, and a single religion—with the multiethnic, multicultural society that is the U.S. But child rearing and schooling are universal concerns in modern societies. If the Danes have found effective ways of dealing with the problems of testing and classroom manage-ment, then perhaps the Americans could benefit from a study of that nation's school poli-cies and procedures.[4]

The Danish "class teacher" system has so many positive aspects that it would seem to merit adoption. Whether American communities would permit the adoption of the Dan-ish approach to student discipline and motivation is, on the other hand, highly question-able. Only very secure school administrators and teachers would dare change from the punishment-oriented approach that typifies American schools today. Likewise, as more and more states (and now the federal government) impose various kinds of mandatory testing, the possibility of reemphasizing learning and deemphasizing testing seems more and more remote. That Danish students generally outscore American students in international math and science competitions would seem to suggest that increased emphasis on testing is not what American schools need. Ironically, we may be so locked into a peculiarly American cultural pattern today that we cannot learn from European educational innovations in the way that we did in the 19th century, when, for example, we were able to adopt and use the ideas of Pestalozzi, Herbart, and Froebel.

NOTES_____

1. Parent participation in Danish school activities is described in Birte Ravn, "Formal and Informal Parental Involvement in School Decision-Making in Denmark," *Childhood Education,* vol. 74, 1998, pp. 375–78.
2. The Danish "class teacher" system has been described for American readers in Birgitte Birkvad, "Teacher Professional Development in Denmark," *Phi Delta Kappan,* April 1997, pp. 611–14.
3. The Danish tradition of a decentralized education system has been described in Jens Bjerg and Staf Callewært, "Danish Education, Pedagogical Theory in Denmark and in Europe, and Modernity," *Comparative Education,* March 1995, pp. 31–48.
4. Readers seeking an English-language briefing on the Danish approach to special education should turn to Niels Egelund, "Special Education in Denmark," *European Journal of Special Needs Education,* vol. 15, 2001, pp. 88–98.

20

Globalization and Education:
What Students Will Need to Know
and Be Able to Do in the Global Village

R. D. NORDGREN

The author argues that globalization requires new skills, experiences, and knowledge. He cites Sweden as an example of a country that prepares its young people to meet the challenges of globalization by teaching them to work together and collaborate, and by giving them the opportunity and space to learn at their own pace. For U.S. schools to meet the new challenges of globalization, a restructuring of education must take place that empowers students, focuses the curriculum on teaching students to get along and accept diversity, and deemphasizes testing.

While attending a school board meeting in Sweden, I sat in on a seminar given by a local principal to a roomful of parents and teachers. She told us that whatever we remember about our schooling days is no longer important, explaining that we were schooled in the Industrial Age, which was much different from today's world. In addition, she said that we had no idea of what is important in education today if our only frame of reference was our own schooling. Schools in her community, including her own school, she contended, are geared to enable children to succeed in the Global Village.

Once this was said, the audience remained silent—amazingly silent. As a former middle and high school administrator, I could not imagine telling a community resource team of parents and teachers that their own schooling experience was of no use in designing their children's education. American parents, especially the ones who frequent schools for these types of meetings, often believe that they are educational experts because they endured 13 years of schooling. Many teachers, unfortunately, despite years of curricular and instructional reform efforts, still revert to the way they were taught five, 10, or even 30 years ago. But the Swedish principal was correct. Our children do need to be educated for globalization: an economic, political, and cultural force that dominates the developed and developing worlds.[1]

Source: R. D. Nordgren. 2002. *Phi Delta Kappan* (December), pp. 318–321. Reprinted by permission.

BUREAUCRATIC SCHOOLS AND SCHOOL SYSTEMS

Large American school districts are essentially Taylorist bureaucracies that depend on autocratic leadership and "sheep-like" adherence to rules and regulations set by politicians and administrators at the state and local levels. Schools have essentially the same structure, with their own policies dictated by the administration. In addition, teachers dictate policies within their classrooms that require students to also adopt obedient sheep-like behaviors in order to be "successful."[2]

The vast majority of business organizations today are not bureaucratic but rely instead on work teams, shared decision making, and a great deal of risk taking in an effort to compete in the global market.[3] The Swedes understand this, and their national curricula for both noncompulsory and compulsory education show that understanding.[4] While the student standards for most U.S. states specifically list what a student must *know* on page after page, the Swedes ask their students to *be* what research suggests is important for living in a democracy: collaborative and responsible.[5] These Swedish curricula resemble cultural value statements rather than what we Americans would consider curricula.

LEARNING EARLY WHAT IS TRULY IMPORTANT

On a recent trip to Sweden, my hosts were an assistant principal and his wife, who is a middle school teacher. I asked her about the academic progress of their 7-year-old son, who was in his first year of compulsory education (noncompulsory education goes from age 16 through age 19, though 98% of those in that age group do attend school).[6] Her answer was, "Fine, I guess." She paused for a few seconds then went on, "If there were any problems, his teacher would let us know."

I was very confused and actually a bit stunned. Here she was a teacher with a husband who was an administrator, and she didn't know how her son was doing in school? She read my shocked and perplexed expression and said, "In Sweden, we spend the first few years concerned about how well children get along, how well they work together." After some time, she said, "You know, I guess it doesn't matter whether or not a child can read and write if he's going to end up in prison." How right she was. Statements like this from other Swedish educators, along with my own observations of the tremendous degree of autonomy and trust given to the Swedish students, led me to compare their national curricula with various state standards in the U.S.

I felt compelled to first compare Swedish children's test scores to those of American students. If so little emphasis is given to academics, I reasoned, surely Swedish students must not be learning much. The results of the Third International Mathematics and Science Study showed that the Swedes gave U.S. students a real beating when it came to math and science.[7] Maybe learning to get along at an early age and deemphasizing the importance of such expectations as "every child will learn to read by the third grade" (as nearly every politician from Washington to the local school board has advocated) has some merit.

GLOBALIZED ORGANIZATIONS

Studying the phenomenon of globalization, I found that, while the competition between organizations has become much more intense, the culture within these organizations will need to be increasingly more collaborative.[8] Work teams will dominate organizations, and

children need to learn to survive and succeed within them.[9] Globalization also r
blurring of political boundaries as goods are produced and sold around the wo₁
tremendous speed and efficiency. Multinational corporations have plants and o....
nearly every corner of the world, and their workers have to understand and appreciate a
wide variety of cultures.[10]

The literature on what will be needed to succeed in the new global economy lists the
following as the most important: 1) the ability to work cooperatively and collaboratively
within teams and across cultures; 2) the ability to solve problems, including resolving conflicts within teams; 3) the acquisition of technological literacy, as well as the possession of
a marketable technological skill and some understanding of how technology can be used
to enhance one's personal life as well as one's organization; and 4) the willingness to take
risks by being an entrepreneur who is willing to initiate change and think creatively.[11]

In bureaucratic American school environments, it is difficult, if not impossible, to
teach any of these skills, with the possible exception of the technological skills. This is
in large part because modeling, as most educators know, is among the most important
aspects of teaching and learning.[12] If the school systems, schools, and classrooms depend
on top-down management and emphasize success on knowledge-based standardized tests
and control of student behavior, how can students be expected to know how to thrive in
global organizations? It is only logical that, after 13 years of living in a bureaucracy, the
students will pick up bureaucratic behaviors (such as mindless obedience)—behaviors useless in the global work force.

WHAT EDUCATION CAN DO TO HELP

What can we educators do to ensure that our students can be successful in the age of globalization, so that they can help maintain America's standard of living and support those of
us who are baby-boomers in our retirement? Here I offer some suggestions derived from
the vast literature on globalization and the global workforce.

1. *Restructure education.* Okay, we've been doing this for decades—or at least trying.
Where has it gotten us? We still teach roughly the same knowledge, using the same pedagogical methods that were used with us (and our parents and grandparents) in the Industrial
Age. But we need to do something else. We need to flatten the organizational structures of
schools and school districts to allow for real decisions to be made at the schools, not by
district-level bureaucrats. These decisions need to be made mostly by teachers, who are in
touch with their students.[13]

2. *Empower students.* This statement may strike fear in the hearts of teachers and
administrators, as well as some parents. But how can our children learn to survive in a
work world that depends on people who are autonomous and can be trusted if we do not
foster such trust? We educators often complain that students lack responsibility. How
can they take on responsibility if we continue to control their every decision? Swedish students, I might add, are required to develop their own learning plans, which are,
essentially, their own curricula. This is a national requirement, but it is done willingly
by students who have internalized the benefits. They feel it is their right to have control
of their own education.[14]

We also must foster creativity and other entrepreneurial skills, both of which will be
crucial in the globalized world. No longer can one expect to work for an extended number

of years for a single company; we cannot even count on a particular company's existing from one year to the next. Students will need to learn to take risks, to "think outside the box," not simply to perform obediently the often mundane, repetitive tasks asked of them in our schools today.

3. *Change the curricula.* I contend that much of what we ask students to learn is useless. But I am hardly suggesting that we eliminate academics. We must, instead, focus on teaching students to get along with one another, as they do in Sweden. What are the biggest concerns in schools and in our society in general? Conflicts between people. While the recent spate of school shootings has focused attention on the most extreme behaviors, ordinary fights in elementary, middle, and some high schools are commonplace. Principals of Swedish schools were hard pressed to remember the last time there was a fight in their schools.

4. *Deemphasize testing.* Finally, we should contain our enthusiasm for quantifying all that students do. In our zeal for standardized testing, we are subjecting our children to stressful situations that are unnatural in the real world. Moreover, the very content of the tests is suspect. How useful is the information found on these tests for students who will need to succeed in the Global Village? This is a question that all school districts, state departments of education, and even the U.S. Department of Education need to ask themselves.

A TRANQUIL LEARNING ENVIRONMENT

What I found in Sweden was that students in high schools got along wonderfully with no apparent conflicts, despite an increasing amount of racial and cultural diversity (one in eight Swedish children is an immigrant or has parents who are immigrants).[15] The Swedes' emphasis on teaching values at an early age seems to pay off when the students get older. Can you imagine the increased amount of learning that might take place in our schools if few personal, racial, or ethnic conflicts existed? (Swedes are, however, quick to note that they, too, are struggling to deal with the great influx of immigrants in the major cities of Stockholm, Götheborg, and Malmö. They do believe they are succeeding in enculturating them into the Swedish culture by means of special immigrant programs based on developing citizens with dual cultures.)

If we start teaching character and values early on and allow the academics to be picked up later, then perhaps we, too, could have high schools like those in Sweden, where students go completely unsupervised between classes—and sometimes during classes. After 15 minutes observing a Swedish language classroom, I was asked by the teacher to go with him to have coffee and rolls. I wondered aloud about the students and what they would do for the next 75 minutes of class. He said that they knew what they needed to do. And he trusted them to do it. Besides, he is only a facilitator of learning, he told me, and so he is not always needed and may sometimes actually be a hindrance to the learning of his students. Learning cannot be forced, he reminded me. The students must want to learn. Knowing that they can be trusted to learn allows students to assume a great deal of personal responsibility.

CAN WE CHANGE?

Other American educators who have gone to Sweden and I have asked one another, Can this style of schooling be replicated in the U.S.? After years of working in middle schools and high schools, I know that we could not do so overnight. The majority of our students simply lack the sense of responsibility to flourish in such an environment. But that lack it is not their fault. Our school structures and our pedagogical methods have not allowed us to trust students enough to help them acquire that responsibility. As I was reminded by a high school principal in Sweden, "Democracy is trust; trust is responsibility." Not only does our economy depend on a drastic change in the way we conduct schooling, so too does our democracy.

NOTES

1. David Held et al., *Global Transformation, Politics, Economics, and Culture* (Stanford, Calif.: Stanford University Press, 1999).
2. William Glasser, *Choice Theory in the Classroom* (New York: HarperPerennial, 1998).
3. Karolyn J. Snyder, Michelle Acker-Hooevar, and Kristen M. Snyder, *Living on the Edge of Chaos: Leading Schools into the Global Age* (Milwaukee: ASQ Quality Press, 2000).
4. Peder Sandahl, *A School for the Future: The Ideas Underlying the Reform of the Upper Secondary Education in Sweden* (Stockholm: Skolverket, 1997); and Regeringskansliet, *Curriculum for the Compulsory School System* (Stockholm Ministry of Education, 1999).
5. Delaine Eastin, "Getting to the Heart of the Matter: Education in the 21st Century," in David D. Marsh, ed., *Preparing Our Schools for the 21st Century (1999 ASCD Yearbook)* (Alexandria, Va.: Association for Supervision and Curriculum Development, 1999), pp. 12–24.
6. Annika Rydman, *Education for All: The Swedish Education System* (Stockholm: Skolverket, 2000).
7. National Center for Education Statistics, *Highlights of the Third International Mathematics and Science Study (TIMSS): Overview and Key Findings Across Grade Levels* (Washington, D.C: U.S. Department of Education, 1999).
8. William Greider, *One World, Ready or Not* (New York: Simon & Schuster, 1997); John Micklethwait and Adrian Wooldridge, *A Future Perfect: The Challenge and Hidden Promise of Globalization* (New York: Random House, 2000); and Thomas L. Friedman, *The Lexus and the Olive Tree: Understanding Globalization* (New York: Farrar, Straus and Giroux, 1999).
9. Charles C. Snow, Scott A. Snell, and Sue Canney Davison, "Use Transnational Teams to Globalize Your Company," *Organizational Dynamics,* Spring 1996, pp. 50–67.
10. Micklethwait and Wooldridge, op. cit.
11. Joseph B. Mosca, "The Restructuring of Jobs for the Year 2000," *Public Personnel Management,* Spring 1997, pp. 645–47; "A Learning Plan for 2005," *Training & Development,* November 1999, pp. 28–29; and Barbara D. Davis and Thomas R Miller, "Job Preparation for the 21st Century: A Group Project Learning Model to Teach Basic Workplace Skills," *Journal of Education for Business,* November/December 1996, pp. 69–73.
12. William Glasser, *The Quality School: Managing Students Without Coercion* (New York: HarperPerennial, 1998).
13. Michael W. Apple, "Between Neoliberalism and Neoconservatism: Education and Conservatism in a Global Context," in Nicholas C. Burbules and Carlos Alberto Torres, eds., *Globalization and Education: Critical Perspectives* (New York: Routledge, 2000), pp. 57–78.
14. Glasser, *Choice Theory in the Classroom.*
15. Rydman, op. cit.

Section 9

Work

THE UNITED STATES CONTEXT

As noted elsewhere in this text, pay for work in the United States is highly skewed, with Chief Executive Officers at large corporations making as much as 500 times the pay of the average blue-collar worker. This gap is actually understated because it does not include stock options, paid insurance, travel subsidies, country club memberships, huge retirement settlements, and other perquisites that are commonly provided to corporate executives but not to their workers. The gap between the pay and benefits of corporate executives and their workers is much higher in the United States than in any other industrialized nation.

Public policy in the United States actually accentuates the gap between the rich and the poor. For example, blue-collar workers cannot write off their lunches at work but executives get a tax break for their business meals. The tax code also gives breaks for "business travel" and even for owning second homes, advantages only to those in the upper tier. Moreover, while wages are taxed fully, profits made from the sale of stocks, bonds, land, houses, and other property are taxed at a lower rate. Also, Congress recently made it easier to pass wealth on to heirs by increasing the amount exempt from estate taxes. At the same time, Congress has chosen *not* to provide universal health insurance, a living wage, subsidized child care, universal preschool for four- and five-year-olds, and free public education through college as found in other industrialized nations.

A major difference between the United States and other industrialized nations is that is has a relatively weak and declining labor union movement. The proportion of workers in unions fell from 27 percent in 1978 to 13 percent in 2004. This erosion in the numbers of union workers, coupled with the rise of international competition and accelerated capital mobility, has weakened their bargaining power.

Summarizing the situation of U.S. workers, Larry Williams and Mary Otto say:

> *Americans are working longer hours than their counterparts in any other industrialized nation; a growing share of the workforce has no pension and health benefits; and the income gap between the rich and rest of society continues to widen. From these crosscurrents emerges a snapshot of a divided society in which the middle class is running harder and harder to support a bountiful lifestyle while the wealthiest can afford unimaginable luxuries and the poor find work but little security in a world that appears to be leaving them behind. (Williams and Otto, 1999:1E)*

REFERENCES

Williams, Larry, and Mary Otto. 1999. "Mild Unrest Marks Modern Labor Day." *Denver Post* (September 6):1E,5E.

21

Europe's Work-Time Alternatives

ANDERS HAYDEN

This essay describes the conditions of work and workers in Europe, which include relatively few hours of work week, paid vacations of four to six weeks, paid parental leave, flexible work schedules, and career breaks and "job rotation." The irony is that the European model results in greater productivity per hour of labor than in the United States.

It's late October. You've been working hard all year and feel like you're ready for some time off. How about taking *the rest of the year?* If you've been working as much as the average American employee, you've already clocked as many hours as a full-time worker does over an *entire* year in many European countries.

Of course, Europeans don't just stop work nine to ten weeks before the New Year. Instead, European nations have introduced a wide range of shorter work-time policies. Their goals, which vary in importance in each country, include: improving the quality of life for working people, promoting work-family balance and gender equity, creating opportunities for skills-upgrading and lifelong learning, and reducing unemployment by better distributing the available jobs.

While Western Europe is not a worker's paradise, its various shorter work-time policies are valuable examples of ways in which public policies can foster "time affluence" alongside material affluence.

THE GROWING INTERNATIONAL WORK-TIME GAP

One of the first products of the Industrial Revolution was a dramatic increase in work hours for most people, with 13- and 14-hour days, 70- or 80-hour weeks, or more, common in many countries in the nineteenth century. In response, working people embarked on a difficult struggle for work-time reduction, which, over time, has delivered achievements such as the eight-hour day, the two-day weekend, and paid vacations.

The United States was once an international work-time reduction leader. Henry Ford's auto plants introduced a 40-hour week in 1926, while German auto-workers had to wait

TABLE 21.1 Average annual hours actually worked per person in employment

COUNTRY	1979	1990	2000	%CHANGE 1979–1990	%CHANGE 1990–2000	%CHANGE 1979–2000
Canada	1832	1788	1801	−2.4	+0.7	−1.7
France	1806	1657	1562*	−8.2	−5.7	−13.5
Germany (West)	1696	1548	1462	−8.7	−5.6	−13.8
Italy	1722	1674	1634*	−2.8	−2.4	−5.1
Japan	2126	2031	1840*	−4.5	−9.4	−13.5
Korea (South)	2734**	2514	2474	−8.0	−1.6	−9.5
Netherlands***	1591	1433	1343*	−9.9	−6.2	−15.6
Norway	1514	1432	1376	−5.4	−3.9	−9.1
Sweden	1516	1546	1624	+2.0	+5.0	+7.1
UK	1815	1767	1708	−2.6	−3.3	−5.9
U.S.A.	1845	1819	1877	−1.4	+3.2	+1.7

Source: OECD, 2001

*   1999 figures

**   1983 figure

*** Figures for the Netherlands are for dependent employment.

Figures for all other countries are for total employment.

until 1967 for a similar standard. In the 1930s, the U.S. and France were among the first countries to legislate a 40-hour week, and Congress seriously considered a 30-hour bill. By contrast, Saturday was a regular working day in the Netherlands until the 1960s, and Sweden did not reach a 40-hour standard until 1973.

After World War II, the American shorter work-time movement ground to a halt, while many European nations caught up with and surpassed American standards. From 1979 to 2000, France, Germany, the Netherlands, and Norway benefited from work-time reductions of nearly 10 percent or more (Table 21.l). Work hours have also fallen dramatically in South Korea and Japan, which now has a lower annual estimate than the United States.[1]

BRINGING THE WORKWEEK BELOW 40 HOURS

While many Americans long for the days when they worked only 40 hours per week, several European countries have recently reduced the standard workweek below 40 hours.

The boldest recent initiative is France's 35-hour week, which was announced in 1997 and became the legislated standard in 2000. The "shorter workweek" has taken many flexible forms, including extra days off (an average of 16 per year), shorter daily hours, and alternating four- and five-day weeks. In 2001, France's national planning agency found "indisputable" evidence that work-time reduction was creating vast numbers of new jobs, helping to bring unemployment down from 12.5 percent in 1997 to an eighteen-year low of 8.6 percent.[2]

A recent major study found that the majority of French workers (60 percent), said that shorter hours had improved their quality of *life,* versus only 15 percent with a negative experience. The effect on quality of *work,* however, has been more mixed. Roughly half said the 35-hour week had not changed their working conditions, with others equally divided over whether conditions had improved or deteriorated.[3]

Where complaints exist, increased workloads, as a result of insufficient new hiring, and the effects of increased work-time flexibility[4]—such as more evening and weekend work in return for shorter hours overall—are often the culprits. France's 35-hour week is still a work in progress.[5] But despite some concerns and controversies, it has delivered important employment and quality of life improvements overall.

Rather than a dramatic legislated leap forward, the Netherlands (36 or 38 hours), Denmark (37), Norway (37.5), and Belgium (39 in 1999, 38 in 2003) have relied on national agreements between employers and labor unions to gradually cut the workweek. By 1996, almost one-quarter of German employees enjoyed a 35-hour week through their collective agreement.

A shorter workweek is not only on the agenda in Europe's wealthier northern nations. In the 1990s, Portugal cut its workweek from 48 to 40 hours. Portuguese unions, like those in Greece, are now campaigning for 35 hours. Shorter hours are also gaining ground in Spain, where 1.4 million workers had a 35-hour week by the end of 2001.

Not all European countries have been making similar progress. For example, in the United Kingdom—Europe's "long-hours capital"—one in six employees works more than 48 hours a week Still, on average, even British workers put in far fewer hours annually than do Americans.

FOUR TO SIX WEEKS VACATIONS FOR ALL

Many Americans, who have no legally mandated right to paid vacations, suffer from "vacation deficit disorder." A typical U.S. worker earns only 13.8 vacation days per year, while 22.5 million private sector workers have no paid vacation at all.[6] President Bush, who took a full month off in 2001, is one notable exception.

Across the Atlantic, the European Union (EU) Working Time Directives requires a minimum of four weeks paid leave each year for all employees, and several EU countries have five weeks (25 working days) of vacation by law. Dutch, German, and Italian workers have gained roughly 30 vacation days, on average, through collective bargaining (Figure 21.1).[7]

In 1998, a national strike shut down Denmark over the demand for a sixth week of vacation, later phased-in through five additional paid leave days. Some might think that Danish workers were asking for too much, but the strike is best seen as a struggle by working people to share in a booming economy, and *as an enlightened choice of time over money* as the way to take that share. In 2002, Sweden announced plans to catch up with its neighbor by phasing-in five more paid leave days, which employees can choose to take as vacation time, individual days off, or shorter daily work hours.

PAID PARENTAL LEAVE

Spending time with newborn children is one of the most important reasons to scale back hours of paid work. The Family Medical and Leave Act gives American parents the right to a mere twelve weeks of *unpaid* leave after birth or adoption. In Western Europe, parental leave is generally much longer and *paid.*

Sweden's system is one of the most developed; parents can take 15 months of job-protected leave per child, at up to 80 percent of their previous pay. The leave can be taken flexibly, at any time, until the child reaches eight years of age. A "father's month"—30 days reserved for the father—encourages men to play a role in child care. In Norway, parents can take 42 weeks of leave at 100 percent of their previous wage, or 52 weeks at 80 percent. German parents have a very lengthy leave entitlement—up to three years, full-time or part time—but the rate of pay is relatively low: about $300 per month for two years or $450 per month for one year.[8]

THE RIGHT TO CHOOSE SHORTER HOURS
WITH EQUAL CONDITIONS

Some European countries, most notably the Netherlands, have recently shifted emphasis from collective work-time measures, such as a shorter standard work-week, to individualized options. In 2000, a new Working Hours Adjustment Act gave Dutch workers the right to reduce their hours of work, while part-timers can request longer hours. Germany introduced similar legislation later the same year.

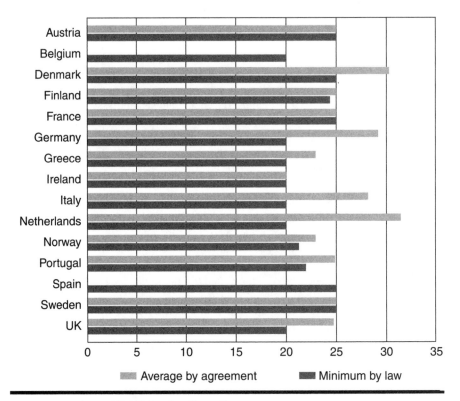

FIGURE 21.1 Annual Paid Vacation Days, Europe

If a Dutch or German worker wants a four-day week for four days' pay, for exam[ple] the employer can only refuse if he or she can show it is not possible without serious hard-ship for the firm. This promises to be a very significant reform, giving people more power to balance work with the rest of their lives.

The right to adjust one's work hours is part of the Netherlands' promotion of a "1.5 jobs model" for families—in which *both* men and women are empowered, and encouraged, to work 75 percent of their regular hours when they have young children. Some Dutch col-lective agreements also include "multiple choice" options—giving employees the choice between additional income, days off, or periods of leave. Among other uses, this could allow working parents to "buy time" while caring for children.

A 1996 Dutch law that outlaws discrimination between full-timers and part-timers in terms of hourly pay, benefits, and promotion opportunities makes the shorter-hours option more attractive. This principle of equal treatment for shorter-hour workers is now becom-ing law across Europe, in response to the 1997 EU Part-Time Work Directive.

Some other countries give workers with special needs the right to reduce their hours. Belgians over the age of 50 have the right to work an 80 percent or half-time schedule. The option of combining part-time work and a part-time pension for workers nearing retirement is also becoming more common in countries such as Germany.

Swedish parents can choose to work three-quarters of their normal hours until their children are eight years old. Norwegian parents with young children also have the right to choose shorter hours, and to combine part-time work with part-time, paid parental leave in flexible ways.

CAREER BREAKS AND "JOB ROTATION"

Several European countries allow employees to take breaks from their careers for training, family reasons, or other personal projects. In 1994, Denmark introduced an innovative system of paid educational, child-care and sabbatical leaves that allows "job rotation" between the employed and unemployed, and creates opportunities for skills upgrading.

Finland, the Netherlands, Norway, and Sweden have introduced similar measures, and Germany plans to do so. Each country's model differs slightly, but the basic idea is that an employee can take up to one year off and receive unemployment benefits or a paid allowance. The cost is balanced by the money saved when an unemployed person is hired as a replacement.

Belgium's "career break" program has evolved into a new "time credit" system. As of 2002, employees can take a one-year leave (full-time or half-time) from their job during their career and work a four-day week for up to five years, while receiving a paid allowance. In effect, this is like an extension of the public pension system, one that allows people to enjoy time off before retirement and to balance their careers with family responsibilities.

FUNDAMENTALLY DIFFERENT CULTURES?

Some argue that inherent differences in national cultures, such as deeply-rooted differ-ences in work ethic, are the reason why Europeans spend less time at work than Americans do. But this explanation is not entirely convincing. As mentioned, the U.S. was once an international work-time reduction leader. As late as the 1970s, Americans worked less and had a stronger desire for shorter hours than did Germans, for example.[9] If differences in work-time culture exist today; they are a recent development and not fundamental components of national character.

The work-hour advantage of some European countries *is*, however, related to "social democratic" institutions and policies, such as progressive taxation, public funding of health care and college education, and relatively low income inequality. Minimum wages in Europe are living wages, much higher than in the U.S., which help working people to have a decent life without excessively long hours.

A strong link also exists between work-time reduction and the percentage of workers covered by collective agreements,[10] which suggests that the relative weakness of American unions at present is a key factor in the growing international work-time gap.

However, widespread concern over the corrosive effects of long hours does give the U.S. Labor Movement—the folks who brought you the weekend and the eight-hour day—one important issue around which to rebuild.

LONG HOURS: THE PRICE OF SUCCESS?

Some people argue that long hours are necessary to succeed in the global economy. *The evidence suggests otherwise.* There is, however, a question of how one defines "success."

One point of comparison is unemployment. Some critics of work-time reduction note that the U.S. unemployment rate (5.6 percent in fall 2002) is lower than that in Europe's largest economies, Germany (9.8 percent) and France (9.0 percent). But these critics fail to recognize that unemployment in the Netherlands (2.9 percent) is only half that in the U.S., and is also lower in shorter-hours nations such as Denmark (4.3 percent), Norway (3.8 percent), and Sweden (5.1 percent—not to mention the fact that if America's two million prisoners were added to the unemployment roles, its rate would be much higher, bringing us close to French and German levels.[11]

There's certainly no evidence here to suggest that only the American long-hours model can deliver low unemployment. In fact, work-time reduction has been an important job-creation tool in some countries, such as the Netherlands, although, on its own, it is no guarantee of low unemployment.

Now, what about productivity? Several shorter-hours innovators in Europe—Belgium, France, the Netherlands, and Norway—are actually more productive *per hour* of labor than is the United States.[12] Higher hourly productivity in these countries is almost certainly due, in part, to shorter work-time's beneficial effects on employee morale, less fatigue and burnout, lower absenteeism, higher quality of work, and better health.

Take Norway, for example. In 2001, its hourly productivity was 10 percent higher than the United States, but its annual Gross Domestic Product (GDP) per person was about 17 percent lower. The main difference was that Norwegians were working 29 percent fewer hours than Americans. (It's also worth noting that Norway's poverty rate is one-quarter, and its incarceration rate *one-tenth*, as high as the United States'.)

In the final analysis, the issue largely boils down to how nations choose to benefit from the capacity to produce more in each hour of labor. Is there more to the good life than maximizing output and consumption? Are work-family balance and a less stressful pace of life equally valuable? If so, then it's time to ask how the United States can regain its status as a world leader in creating not only material affluence, but time affluence, as well.

NOTES

1. International work hours comparisons are imprecise due to differences in how hours are calculated in various countries. The Organization for Economic Co-operation and Development statistics provide a general idea of international comparisons, and a good sense of the trends within each country. Figures from the International Labor Organization show longer hour estimates for each country, but a similar difference between hours worked by Americans and their counterparts in Europe.

2. Due to the global economic slowdown, French unemployment crept back up to about nine percent in 2002.

3. European Industrial Relations Observatory, October 2002. "Government issues assessment of 35-hour week legislation." European Industrial Relations Online http://www.eiro.eurofound .ie/2002/10/Feature/FR0210106F.html

4. The exchange of greater work-time flexibility for employers, which involves more variation in weekly hours in response to business needs and in return for shorter overall hours for employees, has been a controversial point in several European countries.

5. In October 2002, a newly-elected conservative government passed amendments to make the 35-hour week more "flexible" and allow more overtime. Critics of the changes fear that those firms that still have not moved to a 35-hour week will have no incentive to do so, leaving the workforce divided between 35-hour and 39-hour workers.

6. Average vacation days for an employee with five years of service in a medium or large firm, according to the Bureau of Labor Statistics. See also Helene Jorgense, "Give Me a Break: The extent of Paid Holidays and Vacations." *Center for Economic Policy and Research* (September 3, 2003). Economic Policy and Research Online http://www.cepr.net/give_me_a_break.htm

7. Figure 4. Data from the European Industrial Relations Observatory, 2002. European Industrial Relations Online http://www.eiro.curofound.ie/2002/02/Update/TN0202103U.html

8. Some critics say the German parental leave is actually too long, and in a climate of traditional "male breadwinner" values, encourages women to drop out of the workforce.

9. Bell, Linda, and Richard Freeman. "Why do Americans and Germans Work Different Hours?" *National Bureau of Economic Research Working Paper* No. w4808 (July 1994). Online http:// papers.nber.org/papers/W4808

10. Organization for Economic Cooperation and Development. "OECD Employment Outlook." *OECD* (June 1998): 166–7.

11. "Output, demand, and jobs," *The Economist* (October 31, 2002). http://www.economist.com•

12. Van Ark, Bart and Robert H. McGuckin. "International comparisons of labor productivity and per capita income." *Monthly Labor Review* (July 1999): 36–41. Online http://www.bls.gov/ opub/mlr/1999/07/art3full.pdf. Van Ark's more recent calculations are reported in "Leisure often responsible for GDP gaps." *Toronto Globe and Mail* (July 8, 2002): B8.

22

Finland Experiments with a Six-Hour Workday: A Family Friendly Policy?

ELLEN MUTARI AND DEBORAH M. FIGART

Many employers claim that to remain competitive, they must operate 24 hours a day, 7 days a week. In the United States, employees work longer hours than in any other industrialized country. A Finnish experiment with 6-hour work days (and a 30-hour work week) has shown that employees benefit by having more time for family, and employers benefit by increases in efficiency and quality of services and decreases in absenteeism.

"I feel that I have more time for my family," said a child care teacher in Finland, in response to a shift to a 6-hour working day. Being less hurried, she added, had an enormous impact on everything in life. Her reactions were echoed by dental nurses, physiotherapists, child care assistants, and other public servants across Finland.

Between 1996 and 1998, the Finnish state experimented with a 30-hour work week. Workers who participated said they enjoyed more time for other activities: 80% said they had more time for rest and relaxation; 75%, for spending with family and children; 72%, for fitness and exercise; and 68%, for housework. Overall, employees who worked fewer hours reported less conflict between work and family responsibilities.

Even though the Finnish experiments were not driven by the aim of furthering gender equity, they contain important lessons—both positive and negative—for achieving that goal. Enabling people to balance work and family responsibilities is a prerequisite for gender equity. While the United States and many other countries have promoted part-time jobs for mothers, this strategy tends to create female job ghettoes, such as part-time and low-paid jobs in clerical, cleaning, and food-service occupations. In contrast, shortening the work week for everyone creates good jobs for working people, men and women. Reducing the standard work week can alleviate the stress of overwork, allowing everyone to combine paid employment with fuller and more satisfying lives.

FLEXIBLE HOURS AND THE FINNISH MODEL

In recent years, many employers in the advanced industrial countries have been claiming that, in order to remain competitive, they must operate on a "24/7" basis (24 hours a day, 7

Source: Ellen Mutari and Deborah M. Figart. 2001. *Dollars & Sense* (September/October), pp. 32–44. Reprinted by permission of Dollars & Sense, a progressive economics magazine. www.dollarsandsense.org.

days a week). More and more, they are insisting on flexibility in how they schedul
it is no longer enough, they say, for employees to work just Monday through Frid
5. Throughout the European Union (EU), employers have increased weekend hours, part-
time employment, and temporary work. In 1993, the EU even issued a directive setting the
work week at a maximum of 48 hours—but allowing the maximum to be averaged over
time. For example, employees can work 60 hours one week and 36 hours the next. Since the
averaging can occur over a 6-month to one-year period, employees can work long hours for
many weeks before working a stretch of shorter hours. In the United States, employers have
dramatically increased the use of overtime; as a result, many U.S. workers are regularly
clocking over 40 hours of work per week.

These flexible hours options are typically implemented in a gendered way. For example, in the United States and Europe generally (though not in Finland), employers in male-
dominated industries usually require employees to work overtime, while employers with
primarily female work forces tend to run part-time and weekend shifts. These differing
approaches reinforce the unequal sexual division of labor in the household. Since women
are spending fewer hours at paid work, there is less pressure on men to share the unpaid
household labor. These arrangements also perpetuate wage inequality between men and
women, since part-time jobs tend to pay less than full-time work.

Like other European countries, Finland is facing pressure to reduce and reorganize
paid work time. The impetus for change has come both from employers, who want to
use buildings and equipment more fully, and from unions, which are advocating job creation through shorter work hours. So far, the two sides have negotiated flexible scheduling
arrangements through collective bargaining at the national level. As part of the shift toward
flexibility, employers have gained more freedom to negotiate work time issues at the local
and firm levels.

But in contrast with many other countries, Finland has coupled flexible scheduling
with an ongoing commitment to *full-time* work for women as well as men. The proportion
of women in Finland who work full-time is far greater than in other wealthy industrial societies. In Finland, 87% of employed married women work at full-time jobs, compared with
only about 66% in Denmark and France, 55% in Sweden and Germany, and less than half
in the United Kingdom. Only 20% of employed married women in the Netherlands work
full time. Throughout Europe, only a small percentage of employed men (generally less
than 10%) work part time, and they are usually young men pursuing education and older
men nearing retirement.

What accounts for the difference? The Finnish government provides social supports
that encourage women to pursue full-time rather than part-time employment. Most women
return to work immediately after paid maternity leave, using state-financed child care.
Schools and child care centers are organized on the assumption that both parents work full
time: children are not sent home from school until the typical daytime work shift ends. (In
the United States, of course, the school day usually ends at 3:00 PM, but the work day often
extends to 5:00 PM, 6:00 PM, or later. The not-so-subtle message is that parenting and full-
time work should not be combined.)

As a consequence of these state policies, men and women in Finland, both single and
married, work about the same number of hours and participate in the labor force at about
the same rate. In addition, men and women work about the same number of hours whether
or not they have children. According to a recent study of married couples, Finnish men

with children work three hours more per week than their single (and presumably childless) male counterparts. It is not unusual for men with family responsibilities to put in extra time at work; this happens in most industrialized countries. What is unusual is that, in Finland, women with children tend to work at their jobs one hour more per week than women without children. In other countries, women with children usually reduce their hours on the job. In addition, 83% of Finnish working women are unionized, as compared with 75% of men, again suggesting the importance for many women of paid work and their identity as workers. Nevertheless, Finnish women continue to perform the bulk of the household labor, although men have increased their involvement in recent years.

These factors—state support for balancing work and family, a society in which mothers working full time is considered normal, and union representation of working women—influenced the kinds of flexible hours policies the Finnish government adopted. The work-time experiments instituted a seemingly gender-neutral scheme that reduced the length of the full-time work week for *all* employees. Instead of relegating women to part-time employment, they had the potential to change work norms altogether, so that it would be acceptable for all employees to work less. Yet balancing work and family was a fringe benefit of the shorter hours program, rather than a core goal.

THE 6 + 6 EXPERIMENTS

The most notable Finnish undertakings—the so-called "6 + 6" experiments—combined *longer operating hours* for employers with *shorter and less stressful working hours* for individual workers. Usually the traditional single eight-hour shift was replaced with two six-hour shifts.

The 6 + 6 plan originated with a recession in the early 1990s, when many municipalities downsized their workforces. As a result, unemployment increased in the public sector, and the remaining employees were overworked. Unions, political parties, and the government sought a solution. Starting in the mid-1990s, the Finnish government, with some financial support from the European Social Fund (an EU program whose mission includes job creation), provided partial subsidies to municipal governments if they hired back some of their laid-off workers in conjunction with the 6 + 6 trial. The national government agreed to cover up to half of the cost of rehiring unemployed workers. The subsidies were, unfortunately, only temporary measures to stimulate employment during a period of high unemployment.

Between June 1996 and December 1998, 20 municipalities participated in the 6 + 6 plan. The new scheduling patterns were concentrated in social services and health services, especially areas such as libraries, administrative services, legal services, home health-care and dental-care agencies, and child-care centers.

As with many schemes to reduce work hours, employers and unions differed over whether compensation would be reduced along with hours or whether increased productivity would allow weekly wages to remain constant. Some municipalities held weekly wages steady, while others decreased them by as much as 10–15%. On average, employees worked 20–25% fewer hours, but their weekly wages fell by only 7%. In effect, the average worker's hourly wages increased. The additional cost to employers was partially offset by the government subsidies for rehiring workers and by increases in productivity.

Employers reported that the experiments proved beneficial, even if they had to pay some of the increased labor costs. According to University of Jyväskylä researchers Timo Anttila, Jouko Nätti, and Mia Väisänen, most employers changed from one eight-hour shift to either two or three six-hour shifts. They found that customers were happy with extended hours of service, the efficiency and quality of services improved, and absenteeism decreased.

Women were far more likely to participate in the experiments than men. Despite women's high rate of employment in the money economy, jobs in Finland, as elsewhere, are sex-segregated. Women constituted 75% of eligible employees in the social service agencies where the experiments took place. But 94% of all employees who opted for the 6 + 6 experiment were women. Although the 6 + 6 model was not explicitly intended to facilitate a better balance between work and family life, women employees viewed this as one of the primary benefits and rushed to take advantage of the new scheme.

Although the work week for participants in the experiments averaged 30 hours, employees did not have to work a six-hour shift; in fact, only 40% actually did so. Another 35% took extra days off instead, and 21% took extra weeks off. Yet those who took the 6-hour shifts reported the most satisfaction. According to Anttila, Nätti, and Väisänen, although participants found extra days or weeks off to be "a tempting opportunity," those who took extended periods of time off found that their everyday routines remained unchanged. When the free time was distributed more evenly on a daily basis, employees found it easier to balance work and family responsibilities—especially if they had children.

According to one physiotherapist who tried the experiment, the new arrangement resulted in "big changes." Under the new system, she said, "I don't have to, like [a] maniac, rush to collect my child from care. . . . Now I have more time for myself and [can] take care of [my] home more." Researchers Anttila and Nätti found that the increased leisure was "chiefly spent in rest and recreation, time with one's children and family, domestic work and keep-fit exercises." Reduced work time, they added, "made it easier to coordinate work and family life." Finally, they noted, most participants in the experiments were less exhausted and less emotionally drained at the end of the work day.

But there were drawbacks as well. Some employees actually cited a new and *more* unequal division of work in the household, especially those who worked an evening shift. After they spent the morning working at home, some employees arrived at their paid jobs exhausted. One public-health dentist, who now held evening hours for patients, complained, "The more you have [to work at] evening times, the less you spend with family . . . I see my children and family markedly less than I did before."

Also, even though the 6 + 6 scheme was presented as a new form of full-time work, women workers were afraid that it would be used as a back-door approach to extending part-time employment as a common practice. Participants made it clear that they did not want to go down the road of the part-time trap—that is, being classified as "mothers first" who only worked part-time. They worried about being stigmatized for working shorter hours and wanted to feel that they were putting in a fair day's work.

Finally the employees felt that the shorter hours were designed primarily to benefit customers. Therefore, they did not have a sense of ownership over the program. One participant reported that she was explicitly advised to downplay improved family time as a benefit of participating in the experiment: "We could not state, which I thought was stupid, that it is quite important in [the lives of] women . . . who have family . . . to intertwine work and family together nicely. . . . When we applied [to the experiment] it was . . . made clear that we should not emphasize these things. . . . [Instead, we were advised that] customer orientation and employability were [the most] important aims."

Once the state subsidies disappeared, as the overall unemployment rate fell, many municipalities reverted back to the old work schedules and most of the newly hired workers were let go. Without the rationale of job creation, unions (and some employees) were unwilling to accept the small reductions in weekly salary that accompanied reduced hours. Even though both supervisors and employees rated the experiments positively, employers decided that the resulting increases in productivity, efficiency, and availability of services were not sufficient to absorb the increased labor costs.

The experience of women working in public services contrasts with those of a small group of mostly male manufacturing workers who also participated in 6 + 6 schemes. In the private sector, working time was reorganized without any state subsidies. Nor was job creation the motive. Employers pursued 6 + 6 (as well as 6 + 6 + 6 and 4 × 6 schemes) in order to utilize their capital equipment for longer hours without paying overtime. Employees were not asked to take cuts in their weekly paychecks, but employers did speed up the production process and eliminate some holidays. Nätti and Anttila found that, because productivity increases were more dramatic in manufacturing than in services, the new schedules proved relatively cost-free for private sector employers. The same work was accomplished in less time. Unfortunately, researchers have not studied the impact of the shorter shifts on male workers' ability to balance work and family, or to participate in household labor.

LESSONS FOR THE UNITED STATES

In the United States, the last major push for shorter work hours occurred in the 1930s. During the Great Depression, there was a strong movement for a 30-hour work week and many companies experimented with shorter hours. One experiment with the six-hour day was launched by the Kellogg's cereal company. The objective then, like in Europe today, was to share the work in a period of economic decline. At Kellogg's, the shorter work shifts were gradually "feminized"—transformed into "women's" shifts—and lasted until the mid-1970s.

Today, Americans, on average, work longer hours than employees in any other industrialized country. Even in Japan, where long hours are considered normal, average annual hours are lower than in the United States. Both women and men in the United States work long hours. Yet the U.S. government offers little support for child-care or other services that would help American workers to balance work and family. Not surprisingly, there is renewed interest in shortening regular work hours.

As a recent study by the Families and Work Institute in New York confirms, many Americans feel overworked. Although financial considerations are part of the reason why people work longer hours, the expectations of employers, the norms for coworkers, and the structure of work are also reasons for overwork. The Institute found that 44% of U.S. employees work more hours on their primary job than they would like. Almost one in four reports working 50 hours or more per week. Women, more than men, report feeling overworked and overwhelmed by how much work they have to do. In particular, women report that they have to do too many tasks at once, and that they face more interruptions during the work day. Though the range of preferred hours is quite broad, on average, employees say they would like to work about 35 hours per week.

At the same time that U.S. workers would like shorter hours, employers here, just as in Europe, are shifting to a 24/7 economy. The Finnish effort to reconcile shorter working hours with longer operating hours is worth examining. Taking a cue from Finland, we should move toward employment policies that allow both men and women to work shorter hours at a living wage, leaving plenty of time for themselves and their families. In some cases, especially manufacturing, this can be accomplished through local collective bargaining, since productivity gains can offset costs to employers. In some uses, reductions in weekly wages borne by employees could be offset by increased government provision of services such as child care and health care. Unlike in Finland, however, we should make reconciling work and family an explicit goal of shorter work time strategies.

RESOURCES

Timo Anttila, Jouko Nätti, and Mia Väisänen, "The Experiments of Reduced Working Hours in Finland: Impact on Work-Family Interaction and the Importance of the Socio-Cultural Setting," paper, 8th International Symposium on Working Time, Amsterdam, The Netherlands, March 14–16, 2001.

Väisänen and Nätti, "The Household Working Week and Perceived Work-Family Conflict in Finnish Dual-Earning Households," paper, 8th International Symposium on Working Time, Amsterdam, The Netherlands, March 14–16, 2001.

Nätti and Anttila, "Experiments of Reduced Working Hours in Finnish Municipalities," *Journal of Human Resource Costing and Accounting,* Vol. 4 (2), Autumn 1999, pp. 45–61.

Lonnie Golden and Deborah M. Figart, eds., *Working Time: International Trends. Theory and Policy Perspectives,* Routledge, 2000.

Benjamin Kline Hunnicutt, *Kellogg's Six-Hour Day,* Temple University Press, 1996.

Ellen Galinsky, Stacy S. Kim, and James T. Bond, *Feeling Overworked: When Work Becomes Too Much,* Families and Work Institute, 2001.

23

Europeans Just Want to Have Fun

MICHAEL ELLIOTT

In this essay, Michael Elliott compares Europeans with Americans in their attitudes toward work and leisure. He argues that the Europeans have a better work–life balance. One reason for this, he suggests, is that "Americans value stuff—SUVs, 7,000-sq.-ft. houses—more than they value time, while for Europeans it's the opposite."

Walking across Boulevard St. Michel in Paris last week, on the night before Bastille Day, I bumped into an old friend—an American who has lived in the city for 25 years—who told me he was taking up the tango. When I asked him why, he suggested I take a stroll along the Left Bank of the Seine, opposite Ile St. Louis, and so of course I did.

It was one big party. A drop-dead-gorgeous crowd was tangoing away in a makeshift, open-air amphitheater. Nearby, a multiethnic group was doing the merengue. Hundreds of others were tucking into picnics by the river as a full moon rose in a cloudless sky. Much later that night, after a perfect fish soup in the Place des Vosges, I walked into the narrow passages of the Marais district and stumbled upon an impromptu block party. Someone had set up a sound system on the sidewalk, and the street was packed with people—straight and gay, young and old, black and white—dancing to salsa.

Europe is enjoying itself. O.K., in late July, it always does. The weekend I was in Paris, an estimated 500,000 kids descended on Berlin for the annual Love Parade, a carnival of techno music, dope and sex. Meanwhile, tens of thousands of families started their treks from the damp north of the Continent to their vacation homes in the warm south. But even when the sun isn't shining, Europeans seem to be throwing themselves into fun and festivity with unprecedented zeal. Each weekend, central London is one great bacchanal. Cities that for reasons of politics or religion were once gloomily repressive—Madrid, say, or Dublin— now rock to the small hours. In Prague the foreign visitors who get talked about are not the earnest young Americans who flocked there in the early 1990s, but British partygoers who have flown in for the cheap beer and pretty girls. The place that British historian Mark Mazower once called the true dark continent—and from whose curdled soul the horrors of fascism and communism sprang—has become *Europa ludens,* a community at play.

Source: Michael Elliott, "Europeans Just Want to Have Fun," *Time* (July 28, 2003), p. 76. © TIME Inc. reprinted by permission.

Funny. This is how the U.S. was supposed to be. In a famous series of essays collected in his 1976 book, *The Cultural Contradictions of Capitalism,* Daniel Bell noted how the decline of the Protestant small-town ethic had unhinged American capitalism from its moral foundation in the intrinsic value of work. By the 1960s, Bell argued, "the cultural justification of capitalism [had] become hedonism, the idea of pleasure as a way of life." This magazine agreed. In a 1969 cover story titled "California: A State of Excitement," Time reported that, as most Americans saw it, "the good, godless, gregarious pursuit of pleasure is what California is all about . . . 'I have seen the future,' says the newly returned visitor to California, 'and it plays.'"

But the American future didn't turn out as we expected. While Europeans cut the hours they spend at the office or factory—in France it is illegal to work more than 35 hours a week—and lengthened their vacations, Americans were concluding that you could be happy only if you work hard and play hard. So they began to stay at their jobs longer than ever and then, in jam-packed weekends at places like the Hamptons on Long Island, invented the uniquely American concept of scheduled joy, filling a day off with one appointment after another, as if it were no different from one at the office. American conservatives, meanwhile, came to believe that Europeans' desire to devote themselves to the pleasures of life and—the shame of it!—six weeks annual vacation was evidence of a lack of seriousness and would, in any event, end in economic tears.

Why do Europeans and Americans differ so much in their attitude toward work and leisure? I can think of two reasons. First, the crowded confines of Western Europe and the expansive space of North America have led to varied consumer preferences. Broadly speaking, Americans value stuff—SUVs, 7,000-sq.-ft. houses—more than they value time, while for Europeans it's the opposite. Second, as Bell predicted, America's sense of itself as a religious nation has revived. At least in the puritanical version of Christianity that has always appealed to Americans, religion comes packaged with the stern message that hard work is good for the soul. Modern Europe has avoided so melancholy a lesson.

Whatever the explanation, the idea of a work-life balance is a staple of European discourse, studied in think tanks, mulled over by policymakers. In the U.S., the term, when it's used at all, is said with the sort of sneer reserved for those who eat quiche. But it might still catch on. When Bill Keller was named executive editor of the New York *Times* last week, he encouraged the staff to do "a little more savoring" of life, spending time with their families or viewing art.

Even better, they could take up the tango.

Section 10

Health Care and Delivery

THE UNITED STATES CONTEXT

USA spends more on HC than any other indust. nation

HC in USA based on ability to pay

The United States spends more for health care, both in total dollars and percentage of gross domestic product, than any other industrialized nation. (The following is taken from Eitzen and Baca Zinn, 2006.) It also has the most technologically sophisticated health care with the best trained practitioners. Why, then, when compared to other advanced industrial societies, does the United States have a relatively high infant mortality rate, the highest percentage of low–birth-weight babies, and rank lower in life expectancy? The answer to this contradiction is that health care in the United States is rationed on the basis of ability to pay; the system is superb for people who can afford it, but it falls woefully short for those who cannot. The U.S. system left approximately 46 million uninsured (17.5 percent of whom worked full-time) in 2003, including 8.4 million children (U.S. Census Bureau, 2004). Another 50 million are underinsured, which leaves them exposed to large financial risks or excludes coverage for certain medical problems.

This has serious consequences, endangering the lives of millions of adults and children on the economic margins. They are more likely to delay need health care, receive less preventive and primary care, have illnesses in more advanced stages, all of which result in higher mortality rates (Miringoff and Miringoff, 1999:93).

The ↑ in uninsured ppl is a result of employers limiting coverage

The problem of inadequate or nonexistent health insurance is increasing. Over the past two and a half decades the proportion of Americans without health insurance has risen from 11 percent in 1976 to 16 percent in 2003. This increase in the uninsured results from our reliance on obtaining insurance through employment. The problem is that fewer employers are providing coverage for their employees or are limiting their coverage in order to increase or maintain their profits. Also, when workers change jobs their previous insurance generally is not portable. Of course, workers who are laid off lose their health insurance. Economist Robert Kuttner argues that the United States must change its health care system, in line with what other industrialized nations have:

> The only way to cut through this mess is, of course, to have universal health insurance. All insurance is a kind of cross-subsidy. The young, who on average need little care, subsidize the old. The well subsidize the sick.
>
> With a universal system, there is no private insurance industry spending billions of dollars trying to target the well and avoid the sick, because everyone is in the same system. There is no worry about "portability" when you change jobs, because everyone is in the same system. And there are no problems choosing your preferred doctor or hospital, because everyone is in the same system. (Kuttner, 1998:27)

152

REFERENCES_____

Eitzen, D. Stanley, and Maxine Baca Zinn. 2006. *Social Problems,* 10th ed. Boston: Allyn & Bacon.

Kuttner, Robert. 1998. "Toward Universal Coverage." *Washington Post National Weekly Edition* (July 20):27.

Miringoff, Marc, and Marque-Luisa Miringoff. 1999. *The Social Health of the Nation: How America Is Really Doing.* New York: Oxford University Press.

U.S. Census Bureau. 2004. "Income, Poverty, and Health Insurance Coverage in the United States: 2003." *Current Population Reports* (August):60–226.

24

International Health Systems

PHYSICIANS FOR A NATIONAL HEALTH PROGRAM

A study of major health care systems around the world may help Americans find solutions to our current crisis. This article summarizes the single-payer systems of Canada, Denmark, Norway, and Sweden, as well as the national health care service programs of Britain and Spain. Universal health insurance, of the variety found in Germany and France, rounds out this survey of health care system alternatives.

Learning about other health care systems in the world not only expands our knowledge and understanding of them; it also helps us discover new perspectives on how to improve upon our own. Health care systems in the Organization for Economic Cooperation and Development (OECD) countries primarily reflect three types of programs.

• In a single-payer national health insurance system, as demonstrated by Canada, Denmark, Norway, and Sweden, health insurance is publicly administered and most physicians are in private practice.
• Great Britain and Spain are among the OECD countries with national health services, in which salaried physicians predominate and hospitals are publicly owned and operated.
• Highly regulated, universal, multi-payer health insurance systems are illustrated by countries like Germany and France, which have universal health insurance via sickness funds. The sickness funds pay physicians and hospitals uniform rates that are negotiated annually (also known as an "all-payer" system).

AUSTRALIA

Australia's population size of 19 million people is roughly the same as that of Texas. Its infant mortality rate is 5 per 1,000 live births, and life expectancy at birth is 75.9 years for men and 81.5 years for women. In 1941, the beginnings of Australia's universal health care system emerged. Australia spends 8.5% of its GDP on health care, and its 1998 per capita expense was $2,043-US.

The government administers the compulsory national health insurance program (Medicare). National health insurance is funded by a mixture of general tax revenue, a 1.5% levy

Source: Physicians for a National Health Program, 2000. PNHP website publication. www.pnhp.org. Reprinted by permission.

on taxable income (which accounts for 18.5% of federal outlays on health), state revenue, and fees paid by patients. The government funds 68% of health expenditures (45% federal and 23% state) and has control over hospital benefits, pharmaceuticals, and medical services. States are charged with operating public hospitals and regulating all hospitals, nursing homes, and community based general services. Additionally, the states pay for the public hospitals with federal government assistance negotiated via five yearly agreements. Mainly not-for-profit mutual insurers (private insurance) cover the gap between Medicare benefits and schedule fees for inpatient services. Private insurance covers 1/3 of the population and accounts for 11% of health expenditures.

Patients are free to choose their GP. Primary care physicians act as gatekeepers, and physicians are generally reimbursed by a fee-for-service system. The government sets the fee schedules, but physicians are free to charge above the scheduled fee or they may directly bill the government when there is no patient charge. Prescription pharmaceuticals have a patient co-payment, and out-of-pocket payments account for 19% of health expenditures. Physicians in public outpatient hospitals are either salaried or paid on a per-session basis.

AUSTRIA

Austria is home to 7.6 million people, approximately the same number that live in North Carolina. The country has universal access to health care through a compulsory system of social insurance. A system of private insurance also exists. About 8.2% of Austria's GDP is spent on health care, and the 1998 per capita expense was $1,968-US.

Private doctors with contracts to the social insurance funds are paid on a fee-for-service system with expenditure limits based on the case and per doctor per pay period. Hospital physicians are salaried. Approximately 50% of the health expenditures are funded by progressive payroll taxes, 25% are financed by non-specific taxes, and the rest is funded directly out-of-pocket or through private insurance companies. The contributions to the health insurance funds (payroll taxes) are split between employers and employees on a parity basis.

Patients are free to choose their physicians, as long as the physician has a contract with the insurer. Benefits and prices of services are fixed in agreements between representatives of the insured and representatives of the providers. All medical and nursing education is free. The infant mortality rate in Austria is 4.9 per 1,000 live births, and life expectancy at birth is at 74.7 years for men and 80.9 years for women.

BELGIUM

Belgium is home to about 10.2 million people, almost the same number of people who live in the state of Ohio. Its infant mortality rate is 6 per 1,000 live births, and its life expectancy at birth is 74.8 years for men and 81.1 years for women. Today, Belgium spends 8.8% of its GDP on health care, and the 1998 per capita expense was $2,081-US.

The health care system is funded primarily through sickness funds. Belgium's health insurance program operates at four distinct levels: the central government, national associations, federations of local societies, and local mutual aid societies. The general attitude in Belgium is that the pluralism of the health insurance system stimulates each local fund to work hard to attract and satisfy its members.

Patients have their free choice of any doctor. Primary care physicians are paid via fee-for-service, directly from the patient, or partially reimbursed, except with low-income patients who are exempt from pay. They are reimbursed with a negotiated fee, but extra billing is allowed. Specialists are paid via fee-for-service and are not restricted to hospitals.

CANADA

Canada's population size of 30.5 million people is roughly the same as that of California. Its infant mortality rate is 5.5 per 1,000 live births, and its life expectancy at birth is 75.8 years for men and 81.4 years for women. National health insurance had been discussed in Canada at the federal level since 1919, but no real action was taken until 1944. Today, Canada's health system is characterized by single-payer national health insurance, and the federal government requires that insurance cover "all medically necessary services." Canada spends 9.5% of GDP towards health care, and the 1998 per capita expense was $2,312-US.

National health insurance (Medicare) is a public program administered by the provinces and overseen by the federal government. Medicare is funded by general tax revenues. Federal contributions are tied to population and provincial economic conditions, and provinces pay the remainder. Medicare accounts for 72% of health expenditures. In addition, the majority of Canadians have supplemental private insurance coverage through group plans, which extends the range of insured services, such as dental care, rehabilitation, prescription drugs, and private care nursing. The private sector (private insurance and out-of-pocket payments) accounts for 28% of health expenditures.

Most physicians in Canada are in private practice and accept fee-for-service Medicare payment rates set by the government. Provincial medical associations negotiate insured fee-for-service schedules with provincial health ministries. Some physicians set their own rates but are not reimbursed by the public system. Hospitals are mainly non-profit and operate under global institution-specific or regional budgets with some fee-for-service payment. Less than 5% of all Canadian hospitals are privately owned.

FINLAND

Finland has a population size of 5 million people, which is about the same number of people who live in the state of Maryland. Finland has an infant mortality rate of 4.2 per 1,000 live births and its life expectancy at birth is 73.5 years for men and 80.6 years for women. The country spends 6.9% of GDP on health care, and its 1998 per capita expense was $1,502-US. In 1964, national health insurance was enacted in Finland.

The Finnish health system is primarily funded (80%) by general tax revenues collected by the local and national governments. The basic administrative levels in Finland are divided into communes and municipalities. The local authorities in Finland number 445, averaging about 10,000 people each.

GP's practice mostly in health centers. They are salaried, but many are paid fee-for-service for overtime. Hospital physicians, who must be specialists, are salaried.

DENMARK

Denmark, a small country, is home to 5.3 million people—the same number as in the state of Wisconsin. Its infant mortality rate is 4.7 per 1,000 live births, and its life expectancy at birth is 73.7 years for men and 78.6 years for women. Denmark has had a single-payer national health system since 1961. Approximately 8.3% of GDP is spent on health care, and the 1998 per capita expense was $2,133-US.

The Danish health care system is funded by progressive income taxes, and is publicly administered. Hospitals are run by the 14 counties and the City of Copenhagen. Physicians who work with the hospitals receive salaries, which are determined by negotiation between government and doctor's unions. GP's are 40% per capita fee, and 60% fee-for-service. Specialists are mostly fee-for-service. All medical and nursing education is free.

There is strong incentive for patients to choose a GP in their immediate area of residence. GP's will then make referrals to specialists. There are no co-pays for physician or hospital care, but patients do pay a share of drug costs—usually between 25 and 50%. Private insurance, held by approximately 27% of the population, is used mainly for medications and dental expenses.

FRANCE

France has a population close to that of the entire Midwest—60.9 million people. France has an infant mortality rate of 4.7 per 1,000 live births and a life expectancy at birth of 74.6 years for men and 82.2 years for women. The country has had a national health insurance system since 1928, but universal coverage did not occur until 1978. Approximately 9.6% of France's GDP is spent on health care, and its 1998 per capita expense was $2,077-US.

The French health care system is primarily funded by Sickness Insurance Funds (SIF's), which are autonomous, not-for-profit, government-regulated bodies with national headquarters and regional networks. They are financed by compulsory payroll contributions (13% of wage), of employers (70% of contributions) and employees (30% of contributions). SIF's cover 99% of the population and account for 75% of health expenditures. The 3 main SIF's (CNAMTS, MSA, and CANAM) cover about 95% of the population, and the remaining 5% of the insured population are covered under 11 smaller schemes. The remainder of health expenditures is covered by the central government, by patients' out-of-pocket payments, and by Mutual Insurance Funds (MIF's), which provide supplemental and voluntary private insurance to cover cost-sharing arrangements and extra billings. MIF's cover 80% of the population and account for 6% of health expenditures. The major public authority in the French health system is the Ministry of Health. Below this are 21 regional health offices that regulate each of the 95 provinces.

Patients are free to choose their providers and have no limits on the number of services covered. GP's have no formal gatekeeper function. Private physicians are paid on a fee-for-service basis and patients subsequently receive partial or full reimbursement from their health insurance funds. The average charge for an office visit to a GP and a specialist are $18 and $25, respectively. Private hospitals are profit-making and non-profit making, usually with fee-for-service physicians. Public hospitals employ salaried physicians, who make up 1/3 of all GP's in France. All medical and nursing education is free.

[handwritten margin note: All medical + nursing education is free]

GERMANY

Germany is home to approximately 82 million people, nearly 1/3 of the U.S. population. Germany's infant mortality rate is 4.7 per 1,000 live births, and its life expectancy at birth is 74.5 years for men and 80.5 years for women. In 1883, Germany was the first country to establish the foundations of a national health insurance system and has since gradually expanded coverage to over 92% of the population. Today, Germany spends 10.6% of its GDP on health care, and the 1998 per capita expense was $2,424-US.

Everyone in Germany is eligible for health insurance, and individuals above a determined income level have the right to obtain private coverage. The German health care system is predominantly characterized by Sickness Insurance Funds (SIF's), which are funded by compulsory payroll contributions (14% of wage), equally shared by employers and employees. SIF's cover 92% of the population and account for 81% of health expenditures. The rest of the population (the affluent, self-employed, and civil servants) is covered by private insurance, which is based on voluntary, individual contributions. Private insurance accounts for 8% of health expenditures.

GP's have no formal gatekeeper function. Private physicians, over half of which are specialists, are paid on a fee-for-service basis. Representatives of the sickness funds negotiate with the regional associations of physicians to determine aggregate payments. Physicians who work in hospitals are full-time salaried specialists, whose work is entirely devoted to in-patients. All medical and nursing education is free.

JAPAN

Japan has a population of 122 million people, nearly half that of the United States. The infant mortality rate in Japan is 3.6 per 1,000 live births, and life expectancy at birth is at 77.2 years for men and 84 years for women. Approximately 7.6% of GDP is spent on health care, and the 1998 per capita expense was $1,822-US. Japan's current system of universal health care was initiated in 1958.

The Employee's Health Insurance System is financed by compulsory payroll contributions (8% of wage), equally shared by employers and employees, and covers employees and their dependents. The National Health Insurance System covers the self-employed, pensioners, their dependents, and members of the same occupation. The local governments act as insurers, and premiums are calculated on the basis of income, the number of individuals in the insured household, and assets. Premiums account for 57% of health expenditures. The federal government contributes 24% to medical care expenditures and local governments contribute 7%.

About 80% of hospitals and 94% of private clinics are privately owned and operated. While some public not-for-profit hospitals exist, investor-owned for-profit hospitals are prohibited in Japan. Patients are free to choose their ambulatory care physicians, who are reimbursed on the basis of a negotiated, uniform fee-for-service schedule. Physicians have no formal gatekeeper function. Due to the combination of medical and pharmaceutical practices a large part of a physician's income is derived from prescriptions. Hospital physicians have fixed salaries.

NETHERLANDS

The Netherlands has a population of 15.8 million, which is approximately the same number of people who live in the state of Florida. In 1997, 72% of the population had government-assured health insurance coverage. The infant mortality rate is 5.2 per 1,000 live births and life expectancy is at 75.2 years for men and 80.7 years for women. The Netherlands spend 8.6% of its GDP on health care, and the 1998 per capita expense was $2,070-US.

The health care system in the Netherlands is very similar to that in Belgium; health care is primarily financed by employer-employee social insurance. Health care is provided by private not-for-profit institutions, and the compulsory health insurance system is financed through sickness funds. 70% of the population is in the public health care system. 30% of the population (mostly civil servants and high-income groups) has private insurance, because they are not eligible for social health insurance. There are currently plans to convert the entire system to a tax-based one.

Most primary care physicians are in a solo office practice (54%) or practice in small groups. Reimbursement is by capitation for "public patients" (2/3) and via fee-for-service (1/3). Specialists are salaried and are restricted to hospitals.

NEW ZEALAND

New Zealand has a population size close to that of Atlanta, Georgia—3.5 million people. In 1941, it achieved universal coverage and was the first country with a free-market economy to do so. Radical health sector restructuring occurred in 1993, which introduced a set of market-oriented ideas. However, the new system performed poorly and was thus restructured 3 years later. Today, New Zealand spends 8.1% of its GDP on health care and the 1998 per capita expense was $1,424-U.S. The infant mortality rate is 6.8 per 1,000 live births and life expectancy is at 75.2 years for men and 80.4 years for men.

The health system is funded through taxation and administered by a national purchasing agent, the Health Funding Authority (HFA). Health care is provided by 23 hospital provider organizations (Hospital and Health Services), GP's (most of whom are grouped as independent Practitioner Associations, IPA's), and other noncrown providers of child care, disability support services, etc. These parties compete for the provision of health services. Public funding accounts for 76% of health expenditures. Complementary, non-profit, private insurance, on the other hand, covers about 1/3 of the population and accounts for 7% of health expenditures. It is most commonly used to cover cost-sharing requirements, elective surgery in private hospitals, and specialist outpatient consultations. New Zealand's government is a purchaser and provider of health care and retains the responsibility for legislation and general policy matters.

Health care is free for children, and all patients have their free choice of GP. Out-of-pocket payments account for 17% of health expenditures. GP's act as gatekeepers and are independent, self-employed providers. They are paid via fee-for-service, partial government subsidy, and negotiated contracts with HFA through IPA's. The payment system is currently moving from fee-for-service to capitation. Private insurance and out-of-pocket contributions pay the remainder. Hospitals are mostly semiautonomous, government-owned companies that contract with the HFA. Specialists are commonly salaried, but may supplement their salaries through treatment of private patients.

NORWAY

Norway is home to approximately 4.4 million people, about the same number that live in Washington DC. Norway has had a single-payer national health insurance system since

1966. The National Insurance Act guaranteed citizens universal access to all forms of medical care. Norway's health system is funded by progressive income tax, and from block grants from central government, with 8.96 of GDP being spent on health care, and in 1998 the per capita expense was $2,425-US.

Patients are free to choose their own physician and hospital, however, registration with local GP's who act as gatekeeper, will begin in 2001. Patients are responsible for co-pays for some physician visits, approximately $15. Patients are also responsible for co-pays for prescription drugs, up to $216 per year. Once that level of expense has been reached, prescription drugs are covered at 100%. All hospital care is covered at 100%.

Hospital physicians have fixed salaries. GP's have either fixed salaries or fee-for-service agreements. All medical and nursing education is free. The infant mortality rate in Norway is 4 per 1,000 live births, and life expectancy at birth is at 75.5 years for men and 81.3 years for women.

SPAIN

Spain's population size is close to that of Texas and New York combined—about 39.1 million people. The country has had a comprehensive, single-payer national health service since 1978. The Constitution of 1978 explicitly affirms everyone's right to health care. Spain spends 7.1% of its GDP on health care, and its 1998 per capita expense was $1,218-US.

The Spanish health care system is funded by payroll taxes through the National Institute of Health program (INSALUD), which in 1984 was 75% financed by employers and 25% financed by employees. Those with higher incomes have the option of obtaining private medical care. Public hospitals are run by one of the provinces or municipalities. The INSALUD program operates a large network of hospitals and ambulatory care clinics. Hospital physicians are on full-time salaries.

All medical and nursing education is free. The infant mortality rate in Spain is 5 per 1,000 live births, and its life expectancy at birth is 74.8 years for men and 82.2 years for women.

SWEDEN

Sweden has a population close to that of New York City—8.8 million people. The country has an infant mortality rate of 3.6 per 1,000 live births and a life expectancy at birth of 76.9 years for men and 81.9 years for women. Sweden spends 8.4% of its GDP on health care, the 1998 per capita expense was $1,746. Sweden has had its current universal health care system since 1962. Tuition for medical and nursing education is free, and students generally take loans for living expenses of around $9,000-U.S. per year.

The Swedish health care system is financed by both incomes and patient fees. County councils own and operate hospitals, employ physicians and run the majority of general practices and outpatient facilities. Other physicians work in private practice and are paid by the counties on a fee-for-service basis.

Co-pays, which were mandated in 1970, are capped, with limits on how much a person is required to contribute annually. For example, patients over age 16 pay $9 per day for hospitalization. The maximum individual expense for hospital and physician services is approximately $108 per year. The maximum individual expense for prescription drugs is $156 per year. Once these sums are met, care is covered at 100%.

UNITED KINGDOM

Britain has a population size of 57 million, nearly three times the number of people in Texas. The infant mortality rate in the United Kingdom is 5.7 per 1,000 live births, and life expectancy at birth is 74.6 years for men and 79.7 years for women. Britain has had a National Health Service (NHS) since 1948. 6.7% of GDP goes towards health expenditures, and the 1998 per capita expense was $1,461-US.

The British government is a purchaser and provider of health care and retains responsibility for legislation and general policy matters. The government decides on an annual budget for the NHS, which is administered by the NHS executive, regional, and district health authorities. The NHS is funded by general taxation and national insurance contributions and accounts for 88% of health expenditures. Complementary private insurance, which involves both for-profit and not-for-profit insurers, covers 12% of the population and accounts for 4% of health expenditures.

Physicians are paid directly by the government via salary, capitation, and fee-for-service. GP's act as gatekeepers. Private providers set their own fee-for-service rates but are not generally reimbursed by the public system. Specialists may supplement their salary by treating private patients. Hospitals are mainly semi-autonomous, self-governing public trusts that contract with groups of purchasers on a long-term basis.

The British government this year has announced a huge funding increase for the NHS. Specifically, it will receive 6.2% more in funding every year until 2004. Current plans to improve the system over the next five years include hiring 7,500 more specialists, 2,000 GP's and 20,000 nurses; providing 7,000 more acute beds in existing hospitals and building 100 new hospitals by 2010; demanding that GPs see a patient within 48 hours of an appointment; and finally, guaranteeing that patients wait no more than three months for their first outpatient appointment with a specialist and no more than six months after that appointment for an operation.

BIBLIOGRAPHY

Multiple Country References

1. OECD Health Data 2000. Available at www.oecd.org.
2. National health systems of the world, Volume 1: The countries, Roemer, MI, 1991, New York: Oxford University Press.
3. Multinational comparisons of health care: Expenditures, coverage, and outcomes, Anderson, G (with Axel Wiest), Oct. 1998, The Commonwealth Fund.
4. Primary care: Balancing health needs, services, and technology, Starfield, B, 1998, New York: Oxford University Press.

Single Country References

1. Austria: "Questionnaire on the Austrian health system," Widder, Joachim, MD, PhD, Vienna University General Hospital Department of Radiotherapy and Radiobiology, 2000. "Questionnaire on the Austrian health system," Theurl, E, Austria University, Institut fur Finanzwissenschaft der Universitat Innsbruck, A-6020 Innsbruch, 2000.
2. Belgium and the Netherlands: "Belgium and the Netherlands revisited," Van Doorslaer, E & Schut, FT, Journal of Health Politics, Policy and Law, Oct. 2000.
3. Denmark: Health care in Denmark, published by The Ministry of Health, 1997.

162   PART THREE: INSTITUTIONAL PROBLEMS

4. France: "Health care under French national health insurance," Rodwin, VG & Sandier, S, Health Affairs, Fall 1993.

5. Germany: "The German health system: Lessons for reform in the United States," Jackson, JL, Archival of Internal Medicine, 1997.
   "The German health-care system," Wahner-Roedler, DL, Knuth, P & Juchems, RH, Mayo Clinical Proc, 1997.

6. Japan: "Japanese health care: Low cost through regulated fees," Ikegami, N, Health Affairs, Fall 1991.

7. Sweden: "The health care system in Sweden," published by The Swedish Institute, May 1999.
   "The Health and Medical Services Act," promulgated June 30, 1982.

8. United Kingdom: "Britain's health care, and ours," Sidel, VW, Letter to the Editor, *The New York Times,* Feb. 14, 2000.

25

Health Care Facts

TORONTO HEALTH COALITION

This article debunks some common myths about the health care systems in Canada and the United States. The notion that the privatization of health care in Canada will lead to greater efficiencies and cost savings is analyzed and rejected.

Health care spending is not out of control.   As a percentage of the Ontario economy, health care spending has shrunk from 5.7% for 1994–5 (before the Tories) to 5.3% in 2000–1. It has also shrunk as a proportion of provincial revenues from 38.2% in 1994–5 to 35.1% in 2000–1, despite massive tax cuts. As a percentage of operating expenditures it has increased slightly from 35% in 1997–8 to 37.4% in 2000–1 (Ministry of Finance figures).

The financial "crisis" is not real.   The Ontario government has scared the public with figures showing health care as a greatly increasing share of program costs. Although correct, it is misleading because it does not mean health care costs per person have gone up but that the government reduced spending per person in almost all other programs so health care automatically became a bigger share of the pie.

The figures above show the real picture. The so-called crisis is really an attack on Medicare by a cost cutting government egged on by corporations who see big profits to be made in private medicine.

There are problems with health care due to a bungled reform of the system.   Health care in Ontario is under stress, as we know from media stories and our own experiences, with long waits in emergency, a lack of home care, and not enough hospital beds, and family doctors. This sorry state of affairs has come about after a half-implemented and inadequate reform of Ontario health care system by the Tory government that closed hospitals and emergency rooms without putting the necessary other supports in place such as adequate home care.

Fixing the system is not easy now because the problems are not simple for example:

- Nurses don't want to go back into nursing now there are jobs. One reason is that the jobs are too stressful because there are too few nurses left on the job (What a paradox!).
- How can you reopen hospital beds when there are no nurses?

Source: Toronto Health Coalition. 2000–01. THC website publication. http://toronto_health.tripod.com/facts.htm. Reprinted by permission.

Fixing the system is going to need carefully planned and implemented reforms and will take time. It is not clear that more money is needed but if it is then we can afford it.

We can afford Medicare.   Provincial governments committed to privatization and downsizing and right-wing think tanks suggest that we cannot afford to continue to pay for health care out of taxes. The suggested solution is to remove from Medicare more medically necessary procedures which would be paid for privately. But you don't save any money by shifting how something is paid for (unless some people can no longer get necessary treatment)—you only save money if you create a more efficient system.

And the other thing to remember is that all of us are the "we" in the claim that "we" can't afford Medicare. If "we" don't pay for our Medicare through our taxes, the cost doesn't just go away. We still need health care—it's not a luxury item. So that means that if our taxes don't cover the health care we need, we just have to pay for it in another form—like directly through user fees or private insurance. However, unlike the tax system, which is structured to take into account what we can afford to pay based on what we earn, payment through direct fees will not vary depending on what you can afford to pay. Remember THAT the next time somebody tells you that we can't afford to pay for Medicare. We are going to pay for it one way or the other, and in the United States, the single most common cause of personal bankruptcy is health care costs.

Despite what they may say—we are in danger of Americanizing our health care system.

HOW DO THE TWO SYSTEMS COMPARE?

CANADA	*UNITED STATES*
Total health care spending $3,298 per person	Spends equivalent of over $7,000 per person
Public spending on health as percentage of Canada's total public expenditure—15.3%	Public spending on health as percentage of U.S. total public expenditure—18.5%
Private expenditure—28%	Private expenditure—56%
Spending decreased as a percentage of GDP—from a high of 10.2% in the early 1990's to 9.2% in 2000.	Spending continues to increase as a percentage of GDP—14% in 2000, estimated to rise to 16% in the next few years.
All citizens covered	1 in 7 citizens not covered (45 million people) and even more underinsured
Life expectancy—#2 in the world	Life expectancy—#25 in the world
World Health Organization (WHO) Report 2000—Overall attainment ranking #7	World Health Organization (WHO) Report 2000—Overall attainment ranking #15
Health professionals decide who receives care based on medical need	Insurance companies and ability to pay decide access and treatment
Infant Mortality Rate 5.6/1,000	Infant Mortality Rate 7.8/1,000—40% higher than in Canada

life #2
in the
world.

Comparison of the Canadian and United States Health Systems

Source: Prepared by the Council of Canadians.

We are being told that private health care is more efficient. It is not.   The U.S. has the highest level of privately administered health care of any industrialized country. It costs more than double Canada's system per person, serves only six out of seven people at all, and delivers worse results. Private medicine in Canada is not more efficient—knee surgeries in a private health care clinic in Alberta cost more than four times the cost in public facilities and waiting lists for cataract surgery are the longest in centres with the highest proportion of private clinics because having a private system does not increase the number of doctors.

PART FOUR

Problems of People, Resources, and Place

_____Section 11_____

Cities

THE UNITED STATES CONTEXT

There were two dramatic population movements in the United States during the twentieth century: from rural areas and small towns to the cities and then outward from the central cities to the suburbs. The latter represents an exodus by predominantly young and middle-aged upper-middle-class and middle-class whites as well as business and industry to the outer rings of metropolitan areas. This movement of people and jobs to the suburbs has resulted in many urban problems.

First, the central cities are faced with shrinking economic resources for schools, infrastructure, and other essential services (e.g., recreation, libraries, crime control, and fire protection). This is the result of the loss of their tax base to the suburbs. The suburbs, then, can generally afford better schools, parks, and police protection than found in the cities.

Second, the predominantly white flight to the suburbs leaves the central cities with a disproportionate concentration of minorities (including recent immigrants), elderly, and poor people. Thus, suburbanization has meant the geographic separation of the social classes and races.

Third, the move of warehouses, factories, and other businesses to the suburbs has left inner-city residents with fewer job opportunities. The resulting high unemployment and hopelessness has led to a social deterioration of ghetto neighborhoods that were once stable.

Fourth, related to job loss is disinvestment in urban centers as banks, savings and loans, and insurance companies have redlined certain areas in metropolitan areas. (_Redlining_ is the practice of not providing loans or insurance in what are defined as undesirable areas.) These "undesirable areas" are almost always highly concentrated with racial minorities and located in the central cities. This practice, technically outlawed by federal law but commonly used, results in a self-fulfilling prophecy—individuals and businesses in the "undesirable areas" do not receive loans and insurance, which results in failed businesses, business relocation, and further social disruptions, thus "proving" the negative label by banks and insurance companies.

Fifth, policies by the federal government have further caused the deterioration of central cities. Federal aid to cities has declined ever since the Reagan administration, including funds for mass transit, infrastructure maintenance, and grants for subsidized housing.

Finally, the spreading out of metropolitan areas (urban sprawl) has led to: (1) greater reliance on the automobile; (2) environmental problems such as housing and asphalt replacing farmland and wildlife habitats, and air pollution; and (3) highly congested traffic and long commuting times.

26

How Information Technology Fixed London's Traffic Woes

MALCOLM WHEATLEY

In 2003 London initiated a bold plan to combat congestion. To discourage automobile traffic in an 8-square-mile area of central London, cars that entered between 7 a.m. and 6:30 p.m. on weekdays would be photographed and the drivers charged a toll. This plan reduced traffic and pollution and added revenue earmarked to improve public transportation.

In 1903, 10 years before Henry Ford began mass-producing automobiles, traffic traveled through central London at a sedate 12 mph, with horses providing most of the motive power. One hundred years of progress later, the average speed had slowed—yes, that's right, slowed—to just 9 mph. As in other major cities, traffic congestion has negated a century of determined innovation of the internal combustion engine. Figures showed that London's drivers spent around half their time in queues, incurring 2.3 minutes of delay for every kilometer they traveled.

But on Feb. 17, 2003, London began to fight back. The British capital launched an anticongestion scheme, based on tolls, that is attracting attention from all over the world. Unlike American-style tolls, though, there's no sitting in queues waiting to pay. Or transponders.

Instead, 688 cameras at 203 sites scattered across the 8-square-mile anticongestion area photograph the license plates of the 250,000 cars that traverse it each day. Enter the anticongestion area marked by a red C logo painted on signs and streets. Get photographed. And get ready for a one-off charge payable for that day, irrespective of how long the vehicle is in the zone, or how many times it is photographed. At a data center in central London, Automatic Number Plate Recognition technology is then applied to convert the photograph images to license numbers. Motorists who don't pay the toll that day are fined about $130, automatically.

Now, London's traffic scheme is high profile. The mayors of New York City, Paris and Tokyo are all said to be watching with interest. The reason? Fines and tolls combine to give the project a payback period of about a year and a half, and should in total generate an eye-popping $2.2 billion in 10 years—all of which is earmarked for spending to improve

Source: Malcolm Wheatley, "How IT Fixed London's Traffic Woes," *CIO Magazine* (July 15, 2003). Reprinted through the courtesy of CIO. Copyright © 2005 CXO Media Inc.

169

London's public transportation systems. Best of all, according to a report cited in *The Independent* newspaper in March, traffic in the city's center had fallen by 20 percent, improving journey times by 5 percent. Transport for London, the U.K. capital's transit authority, won't report on the scheme's effects until August; but officials say they expect delays caused by congestion to fall by 20 percent to 30 percent, saving drivers 2 million to 3 million hours of frustration every year. And on present form, the authority seems set for a pleasant surprise: It had been expecting traffic to fall by only 10 percent or 15 percent.

In the British public sector, IT projects often fall flat on their faces. And, as these words are written, Britain's tax authorities are defending yet another botched computer-laden initiative—a new tax credit system developed for Britain's Inland Revenued department that has seen millions of working parents receive late payments, causing in some cases severe hardship.

And the omens for London's congestion charging scheme weren't auspicious: a tight implementation timetable, no preexisting model anywhere in the world to follow, the challenge of integrating new technologies—plus a brand-new transit authority working under a brand-new mayor. The inevitable question: In an area littered with IT disasters, why should this one work? The answer: an intriguing blend of clever procurement, vigorous project management, careful design—coupled with savvy and determined political leadership.

If *The West Wing* ever has a traffic congestion charging plotline, expect it to look a little like what you're about to read. . . .

AN UNCHARTED ROAD

From the outset, the risks were obvious. Quite simply, nothing like this had been attempted in a capital city before. Nor did London's streets lend themselves to the toll-charging proposal, explains consultant Derek Turner, former head of street management at Transport for London. Cramped, narrow, convoluted and literally hundreds of years old, they would require cameras to be sited very carefully in order to achieve sufficiently high levels of number recognition accuracy.

Not only that, but the city's leadership was new, part of a process to have London voters directly elect their mayor for the first time in 2000. This led to the ascension of Mayor Ken Livingstone. Coincidentally, Transport for London, the government agency established to upgrade the metropolitan area's public transit systems, also was new and untested, staffed by people drawn from a clutch of predecessor organizations with different policies, practices and cultures.

Of course, various anticongestion schemes had been discussed and mooted over the years. Livingstone was determined that his tenure would see action, rather than yet more talk. A 1998 independent government white paper previously had highlighted two options—a clampdown on workplace parking and a camera-based toll system. Deeming the parking clampdown to be a political bombshell, Livingstone told Transport for London to get on with the camera-based system. The deadline for delivery: Feb. 17, 2003, one year before the next mayoral election.

For Livingstone, the political risk was huge. He could expect any failure to be viciously seized upon.

That was the bad news. But there were some positives too. Undeniably, the scheme was positive with the public. If Livingstone could pull it off, another election victory seemed assured. And why would a toll system prove popular? Quite simply, most people wouldn't be required to pay it. Although 1 million people entered central London by all forms of transport every morning, 85 percent of them did so by public transport. A minority (motorists) would pay to improve the lot of the vast majority.

And there were ways of minimizing the political risks. In retrospect, one of the smartest moves of the whole project was a decision by Transport for London to recognize its own limitations—limitations in terms of experience, IT ability and management time. (Officials such as Turner, don't forget, were very busy. His days were filled with bringing the capital's streets under a single management for the first time.)

TIME TO OUTSOURCE

Accordingly, explains Malcolm Murray-Clark, one of the two directors appointed by Turner to oversee the scheme, Transport for London made the decision to outsource critical elements of the project management of the scheme—first to consultants from Pricewaterhouse-Coopers, and second to consultancy Deloitte & Touche.

Very early on in the project, then, project managers identified the critical technical elements of the scheme and made judgments about the costs and risks of acquiring these as part of a big-bang solution or instead going for a best-of-breed approach. U.K. public-sector IT projects have often favored the big-bang approach: The congestion charging scheme went the other way. Managers divided the project into "packages" that could, if required, be bought and managed separately.

There were five such packages: the camera technology to be used; the image management store where the images would be collected, turned into license numbers and condensed (duplicates would occur when one vehicle was photographed by several cameras); the telecommunications links between the cameras and the image store; the customer services infrastructure, including the ability to pay by phone, Web and mail; and finally, an extensive network of retail outlets, enabling people to pay at shops, kiosks and gas stations.

And even at this early stage, the policy of risk aversion was having an effect. Murray-Clark says one option would have been to lump the customer services infrastructure and the retail side together in a single customer-facing operation. Instead, retail was seen as a big enough challenge to be bought and managed separately. Likewise, the mere existence of the five packages underpinned a determination to go for best-of-breed in each instance—in every case, the package had to be the best available.

PUTTING CONTRACTORS THROUGH THEIR PACES

Shortly after London's 2001 New Year celebrations had ended, Transport for London began inviting tenders for the five packages. The $116.2 million in IT-related contracts made the project large enough to require listing in the European Union's public-sector register, and tenders were open to companies throughout Europe. Again, the consultant-designed procurement strategy came into play: The camera and communications packages could be bid for separately, while the remaining three could receive bids on a combined basis, or individually. "Ideally, we wanted a single provider, but were retaining the ability to mix and match," says Murray-Clark.

While selecting the camera and communications packages was straightforward, the remaining three packages—the bulk of the IT work—proved more problematic. A long-listing process, managed by Deloitte & Touche, brought the original 40 or so bids down to four. "We went through a couple of months talking to all four, and then reduced the bidders to two," says Murray-Clark.

At this point, the procurement strategy dictated another move that in retrospect seems astute. "We told the two bidders that before we could make a decision, we wanted them to undertake a technical design study," he explains. Taking three months, this step would firm up the technical issues underpinning the contracts—issues such as data throughput, how the retail channels would work, how to achieve the best number recognition performance, and what payments might be expected through each payment channel.

From the perspective of the procurement strategy, explains Murray-Clark, the clever thing about the technical design stage was that it added a lot of value without actually holding anything up. "We were moving ahead but still using the competitive element of the bidding process to get the best solution," he says. The move wasn't without cost—the two bidders were each paid for the work—but the theory was that the cost of paying the losing bidder for doing the work would be more than outweighed by the benefits of using its work to improve the overall quality of the project.

And it was this phase of the project that highlighted the fact that from the technical point of view, the greatest challenge was going to be the creation and management of the image store. It had to process a million records each day (picture those 250,000 vehicles moving about the city center all day)—as well as store them for evidentiary purposes for the subsequent prosecution of nonpayers. Meeting the challenge meant carefully evaluating design considerations (such as using the most reliable technology available) and writing software code that would automatically detect which image of a passing vehicle would yield the most accurate number recognition.

From the perspective of The Capita Group, the winning bidder that emerged in December 2001, the process was a confidence booster. "The experience of the technical design study was actually quite a useful one because it created confidence in both us and Transport for London about how the scheme would work, and how long it would take," recalls Simon Pilling, executive director at Capita, who was in charge of the project. "The deadlines were very tight and were politically driven, and it highlighted where the risks were."

Some of those risks were outside Capita's control, of course. (London officials were anticipating some kind of legal challenge to the scheme, and the city beat back a challenge from the Westminster district arguing that it would unfairly impact them.) But for the rest of it, the company was on the firing line. The contract included, explains Murray-Clark, "a very robust set of liquidated damages against the contractor for failure to deliver against the timescale. We set out the [market] stall, they agreed that that was what they would produce, we agreed to the milestones for getting there, and we agreed on the consequences of not getting there."

There was one additional ingredient: third-party oversight for the main contractor. Despite assigning people who as Pilling puts it "had spent a large part of their working lives on large government projects," Transport for London required that Capita agreed on project management methodologies with the consultants from Deloitte & Touche *before* work could commence. "They were the advising consultant, and their job was to report on how it was being performed," explains Pilling.

GETTING IT DONE

The project plan showed that some 300 years of effort would be required—effort that would have to be done in little over a year, if the project was to go live as planned. From the outset, Transport for London, advised by Deloitte, was determined that milestones would be rigorously monitored. "We had a statement of requirements that said, 'This will happen at this point in the process—now demonstrate it,'" says Murray-Clark. "We'd decided early on that testing wasn't something that could be skimped—as problems were identified, they were ranked in order of priority, and fixed."

Capita had bid for three packages (image management, customer payments and the links to retailers), and it won them all. Transport for London, however, preferred to deal with one prime contractor, and so it awarded the company the task of managing the camera and communications parts of the project as well.

Far from complicating the task, selecting one company probably made it easier: Capita had decided at the outset that all the people working on the project—Capita personnel and subcontractors—would be physically located together in a single building in Coventry, in central England. "If you want a project to work well, it makes sense to bring all your team together—putting everybody together cuts out a lot of bureaucracy, time wasted through traveling, and means that the only videoconferencing we were doing was with the client, back in London," observes Pilling.

The views of the subcontractors are hard to elicit. Essentially, Transport for London has banned them from speaking publicly about the charging scheme, a decision that insiders say is unlikely to ever be reversed. "It was a contractual decision that we made early on in the process," says Murray-Clark. "This was an extremely newsworthy project, and we needed to speak clearly and with a single voice."

But the subtext is also clear. Prime Minister Tony Blair has shown a mastery of public relations far ahead of his opponents. Livingstone wanted his administration controlling the spin on this project.

DELIVERY

As the days after Feb. 17 showed, the news was of course good. In fact, it's hard to find a negative aspect to report—with the sole exception that because so many drivers have been deterred from entering central London, revenue may be below expectations. But for a project with the primary objective of reducing traffic rather than raising revenue, that hardly counts as a major failure.

Why did it work out so well? In addition to the attention paid to procurement and project management, Murray-Clark and Pilling point to a few other factors. First, scope creep was vigorously guarded against—with one of the few add-ons, in fact, being the option for motorists to pay tolls through the popular SMS text messaging format. Second, Capita's deliverables were spread out over a manageable timescale, rather than concentrated toward the project's end. And third, notes Turner: "It simply wouldn't have happened without a strong political leadership and will."

Finally, adds Murray-Clark, "The trick was to not use any new technology—all the technology was proven. What had never been done before was to integrate it—and to do it on time and on budget."

27

New Lessons from the Old World:
The European Model for Falling
in Love with Your Hometown

JAY WALLJASPER

Walljasper asks why European cities are devoid of suburban sprawl, so alive in street culture, and mostly lacking in slums. The answer is an active social policy dedicated to maintaining the vitality of cities by reducing pollution, protecting historic neighborhoods, improving public transportation, expanding pedestrian zones, preserving green spaces, installing bike lanes, and enacting guidelines to halt sprawl.

My infatuation with cities began on a college-vacation visit to Montreal, where I was enchanted by picturesque squares, sleek subway trains and the intoxicating urbaneness all around. Sitting up most of the night in sidewalk cafés along rue St. Denis, I marveled at how different this city felt from the places I had known growing up in Illinois. Street life, in the experience of my childhood, was what happened in the few steps between a parking lot and your destination. Montreal showed me that a city could be a place to enjoy in itself, not merely anonymous space that you travel through between home and work and school.

But it was later—appropriately enough, on my honeymoon—that I fell in love with cities. My wife, Julie, and I toured Paris, Venice and Milan along with lesser-known delights like Luxembourg City and Freiburg, Germany. We came home wondering why American cities—most particularly, our hometown of Minneapolis—didn't instill us with the same sense of wonder. At first, we accepted the conventional wisdom that it was because European cities are so much older, with street plans locked in place before the arrival of the automobile. Yet on subsequent trips abroad, we came to realize that there was something more at work. What explains the fact that most European cities gracefully end at some point, giving way to green countryside at their edges, unlike the endless miles of sprawl in America? How is it that public life and street culture feel so much richer? Why do you seldom see slums?

Source: Jay Walljasper, "New Lessons from the Old World: The European Model for Falling in Love with Your Hometown," *E Magazine* 16 (March/April 2005), pp. 27–33. First published in *E/The Environmental Magazine.*

Intrigued by these questions, I have returned to Europe over a number of years seeking answers. In scores of interviews with urban planners, transportation authorities, politicians, activists, and everyday citizens, I learned that a clear set of public policies accounts for the different spirit of European metropolitan centers. It's not just the antiquity of the towns, but also the way people there think about urban life.

In fact, many of the Europeans I talked to worried about the impact of increasing auto traffic and creeping sprawl on the health of their cities. But rather than accepting these changes as the inevitable march of progress, as many Americans do, they were taking action to maintain the vitality of their hometowns. Urban decay was being reversed, pollution reduced, historic neighborhoods protected, transit systems improved, pedestrian zones expanded, green spaces preserved, bike lanes added, pedestrian amenities installed, and development guidelines enacted to head off ugly outbreaks of sprawl.

EUROPEAN EPIPHANIES

Throughout my travels, I was frequently thunderstruck at some sight (a beautiful plaza, comfortable public buses, a street crowded with bicycles) that was amazing to an American, but to Europeans simply a part of day-to-day life. These moments would depress me at first—why can't we do this at home?—and then rouse me. Of course we can! Americans are an enterprising people, restless in pursuit of improving their lives. If Europe's successes in making cities more livable and lovable were more widely known, people would insist on doing something similar here. Maybe even better.

This notion first hit me when I entered the central train station in the Dutch city of The Hague. In America, I marveled, this building would qualify as one of the world's wonders. Not for its ultramodern architecture; we have suburban office parks from Tampa to Tacoma that can match it for glitz. It was the building's basic function that startled me: the large-scale movement of human beings by means other than the automobile. Streetcars wheeled right into the station, unloading and loading throngs of commuters while an underground parking facility accommodated 3,000 bicycles. I consulted the electronic schedule board and counted more than 20 trains an hour departing for destinations all over the Netherlands and Europe—this in a city about the size of Chattanooga, Tennessee.

A transportation network like the Netherlands' would be beyond the wildest dreams of commuters, environmentalists and city lovers across North America. In Amsterdam, for instance, only 20 percent of people's trips around the city are in a car; 36 percent are made on foot, another 31 percent on bikes, and 11 percent on transit. In the Dutch city of Groningen, 47 percent of all urban trips are on bikes, 26 percent on foot, and 23 percent by car.

But that's not good enough for the Dutch. Alarmed by studies showing sizable increases in traffic in the years to come, government officials have worked to boost alternative transportation. Voters in Amsterdam approved an ambitious plan to eliminate most automobiles in a three-square-mile section of the center city, an idea later adopted in a number of other Dutch towns. Increased public funding has been invested in heavy and light rail, and major employers are now required to locate new facilities near transit stops. New housing and commercial developments are not approved without close scrutiny of their impact on traffic congestion.

With studies showing that people are much more willing to walk or take transit when the pedestrian environment is attractive, attention is being given to sprucing up train stations and making nearby neighborhoods more pleasant places to walk. Forward-looking transportation planners advocate expanded home delivery of goods and increased availability of public storage lockers, recognizing that some people stick with their cars because it's difficult to carry and stow belongings when they're biking, walking or riding transit.

CITIES WITH CENTERS

On a trip to Germany, I sat in the ornate town hall of Heidelberg—a small city known widely as the setting of the beer-garden romance *The Student Prince*—while Bert-Olaf Rieck pointed out the window to a public square so picturesque it might have been used as a set for the famous operetta. He explained that it was where he parked his car while he was a linguistics student at the university. Now that he is a city official, it's his job to help clear cars out of the central city and make Heidelberg known for bike riding just as much as beer drinking and dueling.

Rieck recently had been appointed Heidelberg's bicycle commissioner, a new position arising out of the city's determination to reduce auto traffic in its historic streets. That's why Rieck was plucked out of the ranks of a bicycle activist group and installed at city hall. He was busy working on ways to make bicycles the vehicle of choice for at least one-third of all trips (up from 20 percent) around the city—an ambitious goal already achieved by Copenhagen and the German city of Munster. In the Dutch cities of Groningen, Harderwijk, Houten, Veenendaal and Zwolle, bicyclists account for 40 percent or more of urban trips.

To put bikes on par with cars, Rieck planned a major expansion of the city's bike paths. He had already succeeded in adding 1,500 new parking spots for bikes outside the main train station and snatched a lane of traffic from cars on a main thoroughfare. He proudly led Julie and me down this street on bicycles the city had recently purchased for its employees to use on trips around town. For a frequent bike commuter like me, it was nothing short of euphoric to pedal down a busy avenue in the safety of my own lane.

Heidelberg has a way to go to match the accomplishments of another German town, Freiburg, a city of 200,000 in the Black Forest. Freiburg showed the way for many European cities with its early efforts to incorporate environmental and quality-of-life concerns into its transportation planning. In the early 1970s, it made the radical moves of not scrapping its streetcars, as most cities across the continent had been doing, and establishing one of Germany's first pedestrian zones.

The pedestrian district is now the bustling heart of the city, filled with folks strolling between department stores, an open-air market and numerous sidewalk cafés. The city has also built a new network of bicycle lanes and overhauled its streetcars into a modern light rail system. While people hopped into their autos for 60 percent of all vehicle trips around the city in the 1970s, cars accounted for less than half of those trips 20 years later—with bikes increasing from 18 to 27 percent of all trips and light rail moving ahead from 22 to 26 percent.

Freiburg's success provides a firm answer to American naysayers who contend that people will never leave their cars at home and who deny that what happens in densely populated Old World cities is applicable to our own spread-out metropolitan areas. Freiburg is one of Germany's fastest-growing cities with new development stretching across a wide valley. You see packs of bicyclists waiting at red lights in its expanding suburbs and light rail trains gliding past single-family homes on ample lots.

Freiburg also has promoted many other environmental initiatives. It banned pesticides for urban uses and built a biochemical plant to recycle organic wastes from the city's garbage. The city established a hot line to answer citizens' questions about environmental matters, and it now subjects all new development projects to an in-depth environmental review.

What makes this small city so eager to buck business as usual in favor of environmental innovation? The presence of 30,000 university students helps, but most observers point to the citizens' deep regional pride. People cherish the city's historical charm (the center city was painstakingly rebuilt after suffering substantial damage in World War II) and the natural beauty of the Black Forest, which itself is under assault by pollution.

BIKING TO TIVOLI

The Danish capital of Copenhagen is, as Danny Kaye sang in an old movie about Hans Christian Andersen, "wonderful, wonderful." It rivals Paris and Amsterdam for charm, with lively streets, tidy parks, vibrant neighborhoods, cosmopolitan culture, relaxed cafés and cheerful citizens. But Copenhagen's wonderfulness stems not from some happily-ever-after magic but from inspired thinking and hard work in response to real-world urban conditions.

One of the first things a visitor notices about Copenhagen is the bicycles. They're everywhere. You see prim, briefcase-toting business executives on bikes. Fashionable women in formidable high heels on bikes. Old people, schoolkids and parents with toddlers on bikes. Half of all people who work in the central city arrive by bicycle in the summertime, and, despite Copenhagen's chilly, rainy and sometimes icy weather, almost a third do in the winter.

All these bicycles, in addition to a good train system and an extensive network of pedestrian streets, explain why Copenhagen feels like such a pleasant, comfortable place. This is not just the luck of an ancient city unsuited for modern roadways. (Indeed, Copenhagen is no older than most East Coast American cities, having been completely rebuilt after 1807 when the British navy burned it to the ground.) It is the happy result of sensible urban planning with a strong emphasis on making the town attractive to pedestrians.

Ever since a street in the heart of town was first closed off to traffic in 1962, planners have added additional blocks to the lively pedestrian zone each year, eliminated parking spots and turned traffic lanes into bike lanes. Slowly, central Copenhagen has been transformed from a noisy, dirty, exhaust-choked downtown into a pleasant spot where you just naturally want to hang out. Jan Gehl, head of the urban design department at the Royal Danish Academy of Fine Arts, pointed to extensive studies showing that social and recreational use of the city center has tripled over the past 30 years. And he noted that the streets are just as lively when the shops are closed in the evenings and on Sundays: "A good city is like a good party," Gehl explained. "People don't want to leave early."

Copenhagen's initial plans to create a pedestrian zone were met with just as much skepticism as we would hear about similar plans in America today. "We are Danes, not Italians," Gehl recalled the newspapers complaining. "We will not use public space. We will never leave our cars. The city will die if you take out any cars." But the pedestrian zone was popular from the first day, he noted, and downtown business leaders eventually took credit for a plan they once adamantly opposed. One key to the success of Copenhagen's efforts, Gehl said, is that they have been implemented gradually over 40 years. Drastic changes all at once provoke overreactions, he said.

On the national level, Denmark has worked to halt sprawl with legislation that requires nearly all new stores to be built within existing commercial centers of cities, towns or villages.

URBAN DECAY . . . IN EUROPE?

Strolling away from the charming pedestrian streets and wonderfully preserved buildings of central Copenhagen on my first visit, I stumbled upon a sight familiar to urban Americans: a district of rundown apartment buildings, poor families, hookers, and drug and alcohol casualties. Middle-class flight to the suburbs in the 1960s and 1970s combined with cutbacks in blue-collar jobs brought dramatic changes to an area known as Vesterbro, and to other inner-city Copenhagen neighborhoods.

In America, urban decline is generally attributed to people's overwhelming preference for suburban amenities, but Denmark's policy makers bring a broad regional perspective to issues of struggling city neighborhoods. According to Jan Engell, an official in Copenhagen's planning department, the inner city is seen as an incubator where young people and immigrants can live cheaply as they launch their careers. And if many of them choose to move to bigger homes in outlying areas as they prosper and raise families, this is interpreted not as the failure of city life, but as a sign of its success.

This view of the metropolitan region as a single, unified community in which people choose to live in various areas at different times in their lives has led to an enlightened policy in which local tax revenues are shared between wealthier and poorer municipalities. Responsibility for the higher proportion of low-income, immigrant, elderly, mentally ill and chemically dependent people who live in the inner city and require more government services is borne not just by Copenhagen taxpayers but by everyone in the region.

Imagine what a difference it would make if Westchester County or Chicago's North Shore suburbs chipped in some of their local tax proceeds to boost public schools or drug treatment programs in the Bronx or the South Side! This is a key reason, along with higher levels of social benefits in general, why even Copenhagen's shabbiest quarters don't feel nearly as dangerous or as desperate as American ghettos. Vesterbro, despite its sex shops and drug addicts, remained at the time of my first visit a popular place for students, artists and others attracted to the gritty energy of city life.

On later visits to Copenhagen I have seen the effects of an ambitious revitalization effort that aims to improve Vesterbro without driving away the people who live there. The Danish parliament allotted an ample pot of money for the city, working with landlords and in some cases tenants to fix up blocks of century-old apartment buildings.

All these plans are being carried out in close cooperation with community groups, and tenants have the right to opt out of certain improvements they think will jack up their rents. "This is a democracy experiment as much as a social one," said planning official Jan Engell, noting, for example, that the emphasis on installing sophisticated energy and water conservation systems in the buildings came from residents themselves more than from city hall.

The Vesterbro redevelopment is drawing on lessons learned from the nearby Nørrebro neighborhood, where the city's efforts to make Copenhagen more attractive to middle-class families touched off riots during the 1980s. "Residents felt they were being forced out of the neighborhood," Storskov explained. People were outraged when old buildings were bulldozed and 19th-century streets were reconfigured to meet modern specifications. The new apartment buildings are now far less popular than the old ones left standing, Storskov admitted. "That is why we began to renew houses rather than tear them down, even though it costs more."

What's happening in Vesterbro ought to remind Americans that urban revitalization does not have to mean gentrification—and, indeed, that low-income people often know best what works in their own neighborhoods.

PLACES FOR PEOPLE

All across Northern Europe, cities are exploring ways to boost their vitality and livability. Most cities now have bustling pedestrian zones, and bikeways crisscross even the most crowded metropolises. The Norwegian cities of Oslo, Bergen and Trondheim (borrowing an idea from Singapore) levy a toll on all cars entering the city. Oslo used some of this money to reroute a harborside highway through a new tunnel, which gave the city a water-front pedestrian plaza that's become a favorite hangout for local residents. London recently adopted a similar traffic-pricing measure with surprising success.

"Until recently, American cities with their wide lanes and fast traffic were the model for us," said Joachim Schultis, an urban planning professor in Heidelberg. "But all that has now changed."

Being able to get around by strolling, biking or taking a train without always dodging trucks and cars enhances urban life in ways that are hard to imagine until you've experienced them. The more I visited Europe, the more charged up I got about wanting to see innovations like these back home. There's no reason why our cities can't follow suit, transferring themselves from conduits for cars into places for people. But the first step, I instinctively understood, was finding new ways for Americans to look at the places where they live. We need to fall in love with our hometowns.

Americans have always harbored a bit of mistrust toward cities—these crowded, complex and creatively chaotic places. Going all the way back to Thomas Jefferson's exaltation of yeoman farmers as the backbone of democratic culture, country life has been seen as the American ideal. Generations of conservationists and environmentalists have reinforced these views. Tracing their roots back to Henry David Thoreau and John Muir, ecology activists have sought redemption from ecological devastation in the untrammeled lands. Blessed with far more wilderness than any European nation, Americans generally have viewed any landscape shaped by human hands as somehow tainted. That's why protecting wilderness and saving wetlands are more often the focus of environmental organizations than curbing sprawl or revitalizing inner-city neighborhoods.

Yet our unease about cities—we see them as unnatural, unhealthy, almost un-American—has spawned one of the most spectacular environmental disasters in history: sprawl. Over the past 60 years, millions of Americans have forsaken compact neighborhoods for sprawling acreage outside town. Closer connection to nature among the green lawns may have been the dream, but the truth is that suburban living often means countless hours in the car, cruising down endless miles of pavement, passing ceaseless stretches of new subdivisions and strip malls, all of which depend on limitless supplies of land, fossil fuel, lumber and other environmentally precious resources.

In terms of the environment, cities clearly offer the most Earth-friendly lifestyle. A resident of an inner-city neighborhood who takes public transit to work, walks to local businesses, and shares a modest home with family or friends imposes far less damage on the environment than most Americans do. Of course, an urban address does not automatically confer an enhanced ecological consciousness; indeed, city dwellers are capable of merrily plundering the planet the same as anyone else. But city life does at least offer the opportunity to walk, bike or take the bus to your destinations, and to conserve resources by living in a compact neighborhood. Those things are impossible in most suburbs, where autos are the only way to get from point A to point B. Houses are cut off from stores by impassable swaths of pavement. Schools, day-care centers, libraries and workplaces all sit isolated amid a sea of roaring traffic.

The environment is not the only victim of this all-for-the-auto way of designing our communities. Children can't wander down to the park or skip over to the candy store. Sometimes they can't even cross the street to see neighbor kids. To go anywhere, they have to wait for someone to chauffeur them. Old people and the disabled, many of whom can't drive or have trouble walking across wide busy streets, are similarly placed under a sort of house arrest.

James Howard Kunstler, the author of *The Geography of Nowhere: The Rise and Decline of America's Man-Made Landscape,* insists that there is an even deeper way we pay for this folly of poor urban planning. "It matters that our cities are primarily auto storage depots," he says. "It matters that our junior high schools look like insecticide factories. It matters that our libraries look like beverage distribution warehouses."

When so much of what you see on a typical day is so drab, it's hard to care about what happens to these places. I have fallen in love with Paris, Stockholm, Oxford, Florence and Gouda, Netherlands, as well as New York, New Orleans and even Madison, Wisconsin, because they stir something in my soul. It's more than scenic charm; it's a feeling they inspire as I walk around them with my family or soak up their atmosphere just sitting at a café table or on a public bench.

It's been 15 years since I began roaming European cities in search of ideas that we could take advantage of here in America, and I am happy to report that I'm not alone. Many people, it seems, have returned from Barcelona, Sydney, Buenos Aires, Toronto or Portland, Oregon fired up by what they've seen and wanting to do something like it at home. Historic preservation and sidewalk cafés, tapas bars and Irish pubs, bicycle lanes and farmers' markets all owe some of their popularity to inspiration from abroad.

RECAPTURING THE CITIES

A growing legion of citizens is slowly changing the face of America with the message that there are other ways to build our communities besides the all-too-familiar patterns of sprawl. Architect and town planner Andres Duany argues, "Everything you build should be either a neighborhood or a village." He says great cities are nothing more than a series of villages artfully stitched together. These traditional villages and neighborhoods, he says, provide the basics within walking distance—a grocery, cleaners, café, pharmacy, bakery, park, day-care center, schools and perhaps a bookshop, ice cream parlor, movie house and other social amenities. They should also offer a mix of housing types that can accommodate people of all ages and incomes. Ideally, a transit stop sits in the middle of things, and all parts of the neighborhood are within a five-minute walk of the center.

This simple wisdom, which guided the building of towns and cities for all of human history, was forgotten in America during the post-World War II years when it was assumed that all travel would be by auto. Over the past 50 years, our federal, state and local governments have been preoccupied with building new and faster roads. We've spent billions to widen streets and highways in almost every urban neighborhood and rural township. Millions of trees have been chopped down, tens of thousands of houses torn down and communities everywhere ripped apart, all to meet the needs of the ever-escalating volume and speed of traffic.

But now, in place after place across North America, citizens are speaking out, holding meetings, and fighting city hall (and in some cases working with city hall) on the issue of slowing down traffic. They are fed up that the time-honored tradition of taking a walk has become a frustrating, unpleasant and dangerous pastime. They are tired of worrying about the safety of their children, their pets and their elderly and disabled friends. They are determined to restore a sense of peace and community to their neighborhoods by taking the streets back from the automobile.

Speeding traffic sets in motion a vicious cycle in which people who might prefer to walk or bike end up driving out of fear for their safety. Numerous studies have shown that the speed of traffic, much more than the volume, is what poses a threat to pedestrians. One study conducted by the British government found that pedestrians were killed 85 percent of the time when they were hit by cars traveling 40 miles an hour compared to only five percent of the time when vehicles were traveling at 20 miles per hour.

Lowering speed limits is one logical response. Most German cities have posted 30-kilometer-per-hour (19 mph) limits on all residential streets. But many observers note that people pay less attention to speed limits than to the look of a street in determining how fast they drive. Wide, open streets encourage motorists to zoom ahead. Many people herald the new idea of traffic calming as a more effective way of slowing drivers because it's enforced 24 hours a day, not just when a police car is on the scene. Traffic calming was born in the late 1960s in Delft, Netherlands, when a group of neighbors, frustrated with cars roaring in front of their homes, placed furniture and other large objects at strategic spots in the street, which forced motorists to slow down. City officials, called out to clear these illegal obstacles, knew a good thing when they saw one and began installing their own more sophisticated traffic-calming devices. The idea spread across Europe and Australia, and now has come to North America.

Traffic calming encompasses a whole set of street designs that increase safety and aesthetic satisfaction for pedestrians. The aim is twofold: to slow the speed of traffic and to give drivers a visual reminder that they must share the street with people. Speed bumps, narrowed streets, four-way stop signs, brightly painted crosswalks, on-street parking, median strips, bans on right turns at red lights, crosswalks raised a few inches above the roadway, and curbs that extend a ways into intersections all help make the streets safer and more pleasant for pedestrians.

Opponents claim that traffic calming simply shoves speeding traffic onto someone else's street. But numerous studies have shown that traffic calming measures not only reduce speeds but can actually decrease traffic in general as people make fewer auto trips, either by handling a number of errands on one outing or by switching sometimes to biking, walking or taking public transit. Transportation officials in Nuremberg, Germany found in 1989 when they closed a major downtown street that traffic on nearby streets *decreased*— exactly the opposite of what opponents of the plan had warned.

Many American communities are rethinking traffic issues. Eugene, Oregon, which used to require that all streets be at least 28 feet wide, now allows some to be as narrow as 20 feet. Wellesley, Massachusetts, faced with a plan to widen its congested main street, instead chose to narrow it and expand the sidewalks to encourage walking. Even in auto happy Southern California, the cities of San Bernardino, Riverside and Beverly Hills have narrowed major commercial streets.

In neighborhood after neighborhood across my home city of Minneapolis, citizens have risen up with new ideas about how to make it a better place to live. A vocal supporter of street narrowing was elected mayor, unseating an incumbent in large part because of his vigorous urban-livability platform. Many streets around town have been narrowed or now have speed bumps. A series of new bike paths wind around the city and suburbs. A light rail line has opened to great success. New developments, reflecting the best of classic Minneapolis architecture, are popping up all over the metropolitan region. Independent and idiosyncratic coffee shops have blossomed all over town, giving a village feel to many neighborhoods. New investment has flowed into once-rundown parts of the city, bringing a new sense of hope.

But most important of all, the citizens of Minneapolis have a new appreciation for their home. They understand that the city will thrive if it nurtures its special urban qualities and will fall on its face if it merely tries to imitate suburbia by widening streets, developing strip malls, and adding parking lots. Minneapolis has become proud to be a city once again. It is far different from the disheartened town Julie and I came home to from our honeymoon. Minneapolis now feels like a city whose residents care about it. We've fallen back in love with our hometown.

28

Suburbia Stays in the Neighborhood

HAYA EL NASSER

*Parisians have found a solution to the typical urban sprawl found in the
United States: develop self-contained small towns encircling cities rather
than the endless cookie-cutter suburbs found outside most American cities. These dense yet livable neighborhoods scattered around the Paris
countryside are the envy of urban planners everywhere. Keeping a check
on growth is possible in Paris and France due to a strong tax base, central control over development, and a general appreciation of cities and
mass transportation.*

Just outside the dense suburban ring encircling Paris, a scene unfolds that is extraordinary
to most visitors from America's major cities: Development abruptly ends and the French
countryside begins, complete with postcard-perfect farmhouses, green pastures, villages
and rural roads lined by ancient trees.

The French have a kinder, gentler word for this scene of suburban sprawl: *éparpillement,*
or "scattering." It's a subdued but appropriate term to describe outward growth, Parisian-style.
There are no seas of cookie-cutter homes. No endless strings of shopping centers and strip
malls. No parade of two-car garages, basketball hoops and backyard pools.

Suburbs look and feel like cities, crisscrossed by subways, buses and trains. They're
thriving towns with plenty of small shops but few mega-stores or supermarkets. While
McDonald's restaurants are popping up throughout France, in a suburb such as Saint-
Germain-en-Laye, it's the smell of freshly baked baguettes and brioches—not burgers—
that wafts through the cobbled streets.

This typical European urban pattern is the envy of American planners, environmentalists and, increasingly, politicians who worry that suburban sprawl is out of control. In the
USA, where people are abandoning closer-in suburbs for more remote areas, where subdivisions, office parks and shopping centers are eating up farmland, the struggle to rein in
relentless development farther away from cities is intense.

Source: Haya El Nasser. 2000. *USA Today* (January 5), p. 5A. Copyright © 2000, *USA Today.* Reprinted with
permission.

BOTTLING UP GROWTH

Why, an American visitor to Paris might ask, can you see farmland on the edge of the city from atop the Eiffel Tower, but only a sea of buildings spilling over state lines from the Empire State Building? Why does Chicago take up more than five times the area as Paris for a similar population?

Compacting is key. In a major city such as Paris, there is a tight perimeter that bottles up any American-style sprawl. Of the 11 million people in the Paris metropolitan area, about 86% are packed within a tight 15-mile radius of the city. About 2.2 million live in the city, a 41-square-mile area. Another 7 million-plus live in suburbs within a dozen miles from the city limits. By contrast, in the New York metro area, with a population of 20 million, fewer than half live that close in.

In Paris, the "scattering" starts outside the suburban ring around the city. The Paris metropolitan area fills the entire region of Ile-de-France, an area roughly 75 miles by 62 miles. Yet only 1.5 million people, or 14% of the entire metropolitan population, live farther than 15 miles from the city center.

"One minute and a half before the plane lands in Paris, you are over the countryside," says Guy Burgel, head of the urban geography laboratory at the University of Paris in Nanterre, just outside Paris. "But in the U.S., even if you're landing in Columbus, Ohio, you're over suburbia for 15 minutes."

European countries have traditionally contained suburban sprawl because land is precious here—there's less of it. France is twice the size of Colorado but has 15 times as many people, about 60 million compared with about 4 million. The average Parisian family lives in cramped quarters. If a family wants more space, it buys a weekend house in the country.

EUROPE IS NOT IMMUNE

The paradox, says Alex Marshall, an urban design expert and fellow at Harvard University, is that visitors to European cities feel there is more space because growth is controlled more tightly. European cities are not immune from sprawl, especially now that the European Union has increased trade across borders. There is pressure to build more highways. High-speed trains allow people to live farther from work. But the strong anti-sprawl policies are not likely to change overnight because the shape of cities is rooted in decades—even centuries—of social, political, and economic policies.

Central Control

European countries keep a tight grip on development at the national level. In Britain, landowners do not have an automatic right to build. "There is a national planning policy that is administered at the local level, but development rights have effectively been nationalized," says David Shaw, senior lecturer at the University of Liverpool's department of civic design.

In 1965, when French demographers projected that Paris' metro population would rise from 9 million to 15 million in about 30 years, the government built five *villes nouvelles,* or new cities. They're all on the edge of the innermost suburban ring, further tightening the urbanized area around Paris. The government "has complete control over the development around Paris," Burgel says. As it turns out, population grew by only 2 million because of lower birth rates, the surge of women in the workplace and stricter immigration policies. The new cities each have about 200,000 people instead of the projected 1 million.

And when France decided to build a 75,000-seat stadium, it considered—briefly—a more rural area about 35 miles away from Paris. Instead, it was built in an old industrial suburb less than 10 miles outside the city. "Why didn't we build it out there?" Burgel asks. "Because there's no population there, no life there and there was no mass transit." It was also a way to revitalize a run-down area.

High Taxes

Europe tends to tax sales more than earnings. The tax on a new, medium-size car in the Netherlands is about nine times higher than in the USA. "The U.S. tax code, by contrast, favors spending over saving and provides inducements to buy houses" says Pietro Nivola, a senior fellow at the Brookings Institution, a think tank in Washington.

High energy costs force Europeans to live closer to shops and work because they can't afford to drive long distances every day. Because of heavy taxes, a gallon of regular unleaded gasoline costs about $4 in much of Western Europe, compared with $1.28 in the USA, according to *Energy Detente,* an oil-industry newsletter in Camarillo, Calif. Taxes account for 75% of the price in France vs. 30% in the USA.

High taxes on home-heating fuels encourage living in apartments and small houses, instead of a typical American three-bedroom-plus-family-room home on its own plot of land.

Farm Subsidies

The European Union has an extremely protectionist system designed to keep farmers farming. Import quotas block foreign agricultural products until homegrown supplies run out. Farmers can earn more than half their income from price guarantees and subsidies—and are not as tempted as their U.S. counterparts to sell their property.

"If they really got serious about reducing farm subsidies in the European Union, you would see farmers retiring and selling land to developers just like they do here," Nivola says.

Love of Cities

European cities remain the center of employment, culture and power—and most people want to be as close to them as possible. Pierre André, 39, a project manager for France's biggest private bank, Société Générale, lives in an old house in a close-in suburb, Neuilly-Sur-Seine. He drives about 3 miles to work in another suburb, La Défense. He is less than 10 miles from the city and wouldn't have it any other way. "If you live (18–24 miles) away from Paris, you might as well be (180 miles) away," he says.

As in the USA, homes outside Paris are cheaper, and those who want more space have to move. Some of André's less-well-off friends live in *nouvelles* cities such as Saint Quentin en Yvelines, southwest of Paris, where a few American-style subdivisions are popping up. As often as he's visited his friend, André says he still can't recognize his house because it looks like all the others on the block. But even those new subdivisions are close to the city, about 16 miles from the center.

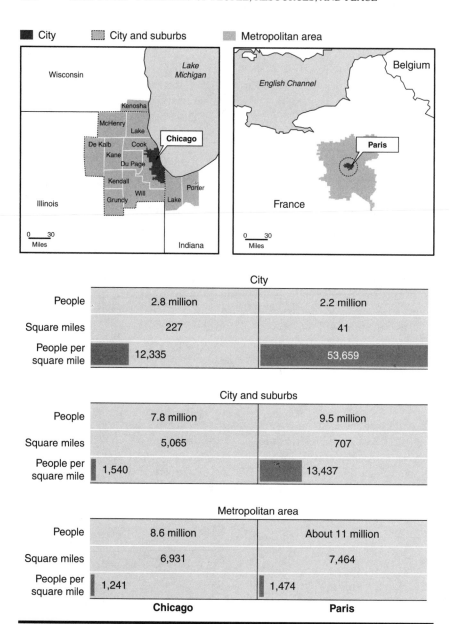

Chicago, Paris Population Densities

Source: U.S. Census Bureau: land area, 1990 data; population, 1997 data; Guy Bergel, Laboratory of Urban Geography at the University of Paris in Nanterre; *World Book Encyclopedia,* 1999; *Europa World Yearbook, 1999.*

Mass Transit

Many European countries pour about half their transportation budgets into public transit, according to Nivola. France spent about $7.7 billion on mass transit and $5 billion on roads in 1999, according to Burgel. This budget year, the United States is spending almost $27.7 billion on highways, or five times as much as for mass transit. Better highways cut driving time and make it easier for workers to live farther from cities.

Culture

Europeans do not move as often as Americans do. The USA has one of the highest mobility rates in the world (about 16% of people move every year). "People (in Europe) don't budge. Even if they're unemployed for one year, two years, three years, they'll stay," Burgel says.

As pressure increases to contain outward growth in the USA, a critical question is whether Americans would really trade their lifestyle and living standard to curb urban sprawl. And with compact European cities wrestling with worsening traffic congestion and mass-transit strikes, just how green are their pastures?

"We can learn lessons about sensible ideas that we might be able to emulate," Nivola says. "But some are not such good ideas, and we should resist them. Do we want a huge, top-heavy central government, extravagant welfare state whose national tax rates are much higher than ours?"

Americans, wary of centralized power, might find that a high price to pay as U.S. planners warm up to a "new urbanism" that looks a lot like Old Europe. "The idea that you can somehow roll back American urban development and convert it back to a European pattern is quixotic," Nivola says.

Section 12

Environment

THE UNITED STATES CONTEXT

The United States has 4.5 percent of the world's population, yet it uses about 25 percent of the world's energy—and in doing so produces 25 percent of the global emissions of carbon dioxide, the major culprit in global warming. In contrast, the European Union accounts for 20 percent of world GDP (Gross Domestic Product), while consuming only 16 percent of the world's energy. "What these figures boil down to is that for every dollar's worth of goods and services the United States produces, it consumes 40 percent more energy than other industrialized nations" (Walter, 2001:1). Moreover, emissions from U.S. power plants alone exceed the total emissions of 146 other nations combined, which represent 75 percent of the world's population (Gergen, 2001).

The United States also produces more garbage than any other nation, on average 4.4 pounds per person per day, most of which is placed in landfills. The European nations, because they are much better at recycling waste, generate only about half the amount of solid waste per capita as the United States.

A critical health danger is related to the production and disposal of toxic wastes (lead, asbestos, detergents, solvents, acids, and ammonia), fertilizers, herbicides, and pesticides that pollute the air, land, and water.

REFERENCES

Gergen, David. 2001. "It's Not Can We, But Will We?" *U.S. News & World Report* (September 24):60.
Walter, Norbert. 2001. "Gobbling Energy and Wasting It, Too." *New York Times* (June 13). Online: www.nytimes.com/2001/106/13/opinion/13WALT.htm.

29

Wind Power Picks Up
as It Crosses the Atlantic

ELLEN HALE

Although the United States pioneered the science of harnessing wind power, these ideas have only been applied in a serious way in Europe. Many European countries now offer tax incentives to utility companies that use the wind as an energy source. As Americans continue to rely on nonrenewable sources, such as oil and coal, European countries are greatly expanding the free and abundant power of the wind.

The relentless winds that blow off the seas and across the British Isles rip umbrellas to shreds and tear trees up by the roots, but now people who live here are finding a silver lining in the gale forces: cheap, clean energy, and lots of it.

Last month, the Irish government approved plans to build the world's largest offshore wind farm in the Irish Sea. In Britain, meanwhile, leases have been granted for 18 other proposed sites for wind farms in waters off the coasts.

Throughout Europe, wind power has turned into a serious source of energy, leaving the USA—the country that pioneered it as a modern technology—in the dust. Amid growing concern about climate change and other environmental problems blamed on the burning of fossil fuels, European governments are encouraging utility companies to harness the wind, especially over the waters where it blows hardest.

"In the United States, most people think wind energy is still smocks-and-sandals stuff—hippie stuff," says Andrew Garrad, an energy consultant in Britain. "Europe is so far ahead. Nearly all countries here have some program—tax incentives, whatever—to encourage wind power. It has become competitive with conventional energy."

'STRATEGIC ADVANTAGE' LOST

Last year, European Union countries produced more than four times as much energy through wind as the USA, and experts predict that within 10 years at least 10% of Europe's electrical energy needs will be supplied by giant wind turbines hooked up to main power grids.

Source: Ellen Hale. 2002. *USA Today* (February 7), p. 10A. Copyright © 2002, USA TODAY. Reprinted with permission.

Europe soaring ahead

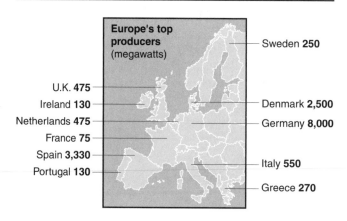

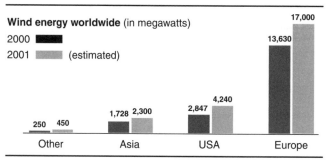

Europe Soaring Ahead

Source: European Wind Energy Association; Garrad Hassun Co.; U.S. Dept. of Energy; United Kingdom Department of Trade and Industry.

Even the technology used to produce power from wind, originally a U.S. development, has moved to Europe: Only one company—Enron, now seeking bankruptcy protection—makes wind turbines in the USA; 90% are now produced in Europe.

"We have frittered away our dominant role in this technology," says Randall Swisher, executive director of the American Wind Energy Association in Washington, D.C. "We had the strategic advantage, and we lost it."

That's not to say Europe has taken the wind out of America's efforts to partially wean itself from oil. Last year was the biggest in history for the U.S. wind energy industry—albeit meager compared with Europe. The fastest growth in wind power in the USA was in Texas, the result of a law passed under the leadership of then-governor George W. Bush. The Texas law requires utility companies to supply 3% of their energy from renewable sources by 2009. Experts consider it the most progressive wind energy law in the United States. It put Bush on the side of many environmentalists—though as president he later angered many by pulling the United States out of the Kyoto protocol, an international treaty on climate change.

Critics say unstable federal policies have suppressed the growth of wind energy in the USA while financial incentives have boosted it here in Europe.

A wind power tax credit enacted by Congress in 1999 expired at the end of last year and has not yet been renewed.

Meanwhile, plans by European turbine manufacturers to open plants in America have been put on hold.

Wind power in the USA comes from turbines planted firmly on gusty stretches of land. Here in Europe, where there's far less open land available, offshore wind farms are burgeoning. Earlier this month, the Irish government gave a company, Airtricity, approval to erect a necklace of 200 giant turbines in the Irish Sea along a 17-mile stretch of the Emerald Isle known as the Arklow Bank. The $570 million project will be capable of providing 520 megawatts of power—enough, officials say, to eventually supply 10% of the country's electrical needs. (One megawatt can power approximately 1,000 homes.)

In Denmark, where 16% of the country's power is already generated by wind power, three wind farms are up and running, one smack dab in Copenhagen harbor and visible to anyone flying in to the capital city. Two more are under construction.

HIGH-TECH ADVANCES

Part of the explosion in wind power is a result of breakthroughs in technology. When the first wind farms were constructed two decades ago in the USA, mostly in California, the turbines were toylike: 30 feet in diameter, noisy and not that efficient. Today, the turbines are wider than the wingspan of a Boeing 747. Fifteen tons of air whoosh through them each second and they rotate more slowly, which means they are quieter.

Allegations that the turbines suck birds into their wind stream have been disproved. "Fewer [birds] fly into them than fly into windows or cars," says Russell Marsh of the World Wildlife Federation in Britain. "The only concern is that they not be located on a migration route. Otherwise, birds live harmoniously with wind farms. They learn to fly around them."

But the primary factor driving the boom in wind power here is the fear of climate change and rising sea levels and other problems associated with it that many scientists say come from burning oil and coal. Last year, the European Union decreed that within

10 years, 12% of energy should come from clean, renewable sources such as wind power, according to Christian Kjaer, policy officer for the European Wind Energy Association.

There is widespread public support for the energy source—in spite of what many consider to be its unsightliness.

And there is universal backing from major environmental groups. In Britain, it even has the stamp of approval of the Royal Society for the Protection of Birds.

"You can look at these things as monstrous blots on the landscape or as a clean and better future," Garrad says. "Most people here are prepared to put up with them for the sake of the environment."

30

The $6.66-a-Gallon Solution

SIMON ROMERO

Although Norway is the third-largest oil exporter, it has the most expensive gasoline. The high cost of gasoline has positive effects for the environment: (1) lower per capita consumption of gasoline; (2) lower car ownership rates; (3) more fuel-efficient vehicles; and (4) fewer emissions of greenhouse gases. Also the high taxes included in the cost of gasoline (about $519 per capita annually) produces revenues to support Norway's extensive social benefits.

OSLO, April 23—Car owners in the United States may grumble as the price of gasoline hovers around $2.25 a gallon. Here in Norway, home to perhaps the world's most expensive gasoline, drivers greeted higher pump prices of $6.66 a gallon with little more than a shrug.

Yes, there was a protest from the Norwegian Automobile Association, which said, "Enough is enough."

And a right-wing party in Parliament, the Progress Party, once again called for a cut in gasoline taxes, which account for about 67 percent of the price.

But "those critics are but voices in the wilderness," said Torgald Sorli, a radio announcer with the Norwegian Broadcasting Corporation who often discusses transportation issues. "We Norwegians are resigned to expensive gasoline. There is no political will to change the system."

Norway, the world's third-largest oil exporter, behind Saudi Arabia and Russia, has been made wealthy by oil. Last year alone, oil export revenue surged 19 percent, to $38 billion.

But no other major oil exporter has tried to reel in its own fuel consumption with as much zeal as Norway. These policies have resulted in Norwegians consuming much less oil per capita than Americans—1.9 gallons a day versus almost 3 gallons a day in the United States—and low car ownership rates. On city streets and rural roads, fuel-efficient Volkswagens and Peugeots far outnumber big sport utility vehicles.

[Norway's gasoline policies stand in contrast to those in the United States, where President Bush made cheaper gasoline a priority during his discussion of energy policy at his news conference on Thursday.]

Gasoline, of course, is not the only expensive commodity in Norway, a traditionally frugal and highly taxed nation. At a pub in Oslo, for instance, a pint of beer might cost the equivalent of $12 and an individual frozen pizza $16. But expensive gasoline is rare among large oil-producing countries that often subsidize fuel for their citizens. Gasoline prices in Norway—with a currency, the krone, strong in comparison with the dollar—have climbed 30 percent since 1998, outpacing a 15 percent increase in the consumer price index in that period, the national statistics bureau said.

Having the world's highest gasoline prices is just one strategy to combat greenhouse gases in this redoubt of welfare capitalism and strict environmental laws. Overall energy consumption, especially of electricity, is quite high, however, with Norway blessed with not just oil but ample hydropower resources.

Norway not only taxes its gasoline. Norwegians also pay automobile taxes as high as $395 a year for each vehicle, and in Oslo there is even a "studded-tire" fee of about $160 for vehicles with all-terrain tires that tear up asphalt more quickly in the winter.

Then there are the taxes on new passenger vehicles that can increase the price of imported automobiles. Norway has no auto manufacturing industry aside from an experiment to produce electric cars, and economists have suggested that that has made it easier to limit automobile use in Norway because there is no domestic industry to lobby against such decisions as in neighboring Sweden, home of Saab and Volvo.

Norway designed the duties to make large-engine sport utility vehicles much costlier than compact cars. For instance, a high-end Toyota Land Cruiser that costs $80,000 in the United States might run as much as $100,000 in Norway.

Economists argue that gasoline prices and other auto taxes in Norway are not so expensive when measured against the annual incomes of Norwegians, among the world's highest at about $51,700 a person, or the shorter workweek of about 37.5 hours that is the norm here. (Norwegians also get five weeks of vacation a year.) The government frequently makes such arguments when responding to criticism over high fuel prices.

"We do not want such a system," Per-Kristian Foss, the finance minister, said in a curt response to the calls for lower gasoline taxes this month in Parliament.

Other European countries have also placed high taxes on gasoline, and some like Britain and the Netherlands have gasoline prices that rival or at times surpass Norway's. In Oslo, as in other European capitals, there is ample public transportation, including an express airport train that whisks travelers to the international airport from downtown in 20 minutes. Yet Norway, with a population of just 4.8 million, differs from much of Europe in its breadth, with an extensive network of roads, tunnels and bridges spread over an area slightly larger than New Mexico.

"Rural areas without good public transportation alternatives are hit a little harder," said Knut Sandberg Eriksen, a senior research economist at the Institute of Transport Economics here who estimates the government collects about $2.4 billion in fuel taxes alone each year, or about $519 for every Norwegian. Some of the revenue supports Norway's social benefits.

"Our government has been grateful to use the automobile as a supreme tax object," Mr. Eriksen said. "The car is its milking cow."

Perhaps as a result of such policies, Norway has lower levels of car ownership than other European countries, with 427 cars per 1,000 people in 2003 compared with more than

500 cars per 1,000 people in both France and Germany, according to the Economist Intelligence Unit. The United States has more than 700 cars per 1,000 people.

The average age of a passenger car in Norway is 18 years when it is scrapped, though this might be changing in a strong economy with the lowest interest rates in 50 years. Registrations of new passenger cars last year climbed 20 percent from 2003. But the frugality of some Norwegians, even in rural areas, suggests older cars will remain at many households.

"Personally I have no need for a new vehicle; I'm proud to hold on to my own for as long as I can," said Johannes Rode, 69, a retired art and music teacher and owner of a 29-year-old red Volkswagen Beetle in Ramberg, a coastal town in northern Norway. "To do otherwise would be wasteful and play into the oil industry's hands."

Caution about oil's risks is common in Norway. The government created the Petroleum Fund more than a decade ago as a repository for most of the royalties it receives from oil production. The $165 billion fund, overseen by the central bank, is intended for the day when oil resources in the North Sea start to dry up.

Meanwhile, unlike other large oil producers like Saudi Arabia, Iran or Venezuela, Norway has done little to encourage domestic petroleum consumption. In part because high gasoline prices deter such a luxury, Norway consumes little more than 200,000 barrels a day of oil while exporting nearly its entire production of 8.3 million barrels a day. This confounds some Norwegians.

"Norway is a rich, oil-producing country with no foreign debt," said Egli Otter, a spokesman for the Norwegian Automobile Association, a sister organization to AAA. "We think that Norway, with its enormous and complicated geography and distances, deserves pump prices at an average European level. Motorists find it very difficult to be taxed into these extremes."

Such opinions contrast with the quick defense of high gasoline prices often voiced around Norway, which is celebrating its 100th year of independence from neighboring Sweden and so far has opted out of joining the European Union.

Sverre Lodgaard, director of the Norwegian Institute of International Affairs, said Norway had a responsibility to manage its oil resources soberly because of its support of world-wide limitations on greenhouse-gas emissions.

"We are engaged on this front," Mr. Lodgaard said. "It is difficult for us to view the example of the United States, which is overconsuming to an incredible extent."

The United States, which uses about a quarter of the world's daily oil consumption, had the cheapest gasoline prices of the 27 industrial countries measured by the International Energy Agency in its most recent analysis of fuel prices. Taxes accounted on average for just 20 percent of the price of gasoline in the United States, the agency said.

Even amid Norway's bluster on gasoline prices, however, environmentalists suggest the nation could do more to achieve greater energy efficiency. One sore point is the consumption of electricity, traditionally generated by hydropower but soon to depend more on a fossil fuel, natural gas.

Producing oil for export in Norway requires large amounts of electricity, and homes in the country, with much of its territory above the Arctic Circle, use electricity for heating, creating much higher electricity consumption levels than elsewhere in Europe. It is not uncommon to drive on well-lighted roads even in remote areas.

Filling the Tank

Norway and other European nations discourage gas consumption by taxing heavily at the pump. By contrast, the United States is looking to lower the cost of gasoline.

	Typical Price for a Gallon of Gasoline	Gallons Used Each Day per Person
Norway	$6.66	1.9
Netherlands	6.55	2.3
Britain	6.17	1.2
Germany	5.98	1.4
Italy	5.94	1.4
France	5.68	1.4
Singapore	3.50	7.3*
Brazil	3.35	0.5
India	3.29	0.1
Mexico	3.20	0.8
South Africa	3.13	0.4
United States	2.26	2.9
Russia	2.05	0.8
China	1.78	0.2
Nigeria	1.48	0.1
Iran	0.47	0.8

*So high because the economy relies heavily on oil refining, petrochemicals and shipping industries, which use a lot of oil.

Source: Reuters; Energy Information Administration

"There are areas in which we have done O.K.," said Dag Nagoda, a coordinator in the Oslo office of the WWF, formerly known as the World Wildlife Fund. "And there are areas in which we can do better."

PART FIVE

Individual Deviance

Section 13: Crime and Crime Control

Section 14: Drugs

Section 13

Crime and Crime Control

THE UNITED STATES CONTEXT

International comparisons of crime data, while inexact, do provide rough approximations of how crime is patterned geographically. What is known is that among the industrialized nations there is not much difference in burglaries, bicycle thefts, and other property crimes. What is striking, however, is that among these nations, the United States has much higher rates of violent crimes (robberies, assaults, murders, and rapes). "For at least a century and probably longer we have been the most murderous 'developed' society on earth" (Harwood, 1997:27). Criminologists are in general agreement that the extraordinarily high rate of violent crime in the United States is the result of the confluence of at least five major forces. First, countries where there is a wide gap between the rich and poor have the highest levels of violent crime. The United States, as we have noted, has the greatest inequality gap among the industrialized nations.

Second, the greater the proportion of the population living in poverty, the higher the rate of violent crime. Criminologist Elliott Currie says, "[We] know that the links between disadvantage and violence are strongest for the poorest and the most neglected of the poor. . . . [The] people locked into the most permanent forms of economic marginality in the most impoverished and disrupted communities [have] the highest concentrations of serious violent crime" (Currie, 1998:127).

Third, violent crime is worse in those societies with weak "safety nets" for the poor. As Currie puts it: "[The United States] though generally quite wealthy, is also far more unequal and far less committed to including the vulnerable into a common level of social life than any other developed nation" (1998:120).

Fourth, the government's "war on drugs" is partly responsible. By making certain drugs illegal, it drives up their prices, making the manufacture, transport, and sale of illicit drugs lucrative. Organized crime syndicates and gangs, in turn, use violent means to control their territories.

And fifth, the greater the availability of guns in a society, the higher the level of violent crime. Without question, the United States has more guns per capita than any other industrialized nation—an estimated 250 million guns and adding about 4 million more annually in a population of 295 million. In fiscal 2000–2001, there were 73 gun homicides in England and Wales. The United States, with about five times the population, had 8,719 firearm murders (Associated Press, 2003).

The U.S. solution to crime ignores these sources of criminal behavior and instead focuses on imprisoning criminals. In 2003 the various levels of government had incarcerated about 2.2 million people in prisons and jails—nearly one-fourth of the entire prison population in the world. This amounted to an incarceration rate of 685 per 100,000 population. The member nations of the European Union, in sharp contrast, average only 87 prisoners per 100,000 population (Rifkin, 2004:82).

REFERENCES

Associated Press. 2003. "Blain Proposes Minimum of 5 Years for Gun Violence." (January 7).
Currie, Elliott. 1998. *Crime and Punishment in America.* New York: Metropolitan Books.
Harwood, Richard. 1997. "America's Unchecked Epidemic." *Washington Post National Weekly Edition* (December 8):27.
Rifkin, Jeremy. 2004. *The European Dream.* New York: Jeremy P. Tarcher/Penguin.

31

Crime Comparisons between Canada and the United States

THE DAILY

This article compares crime trends in the United States and Canada. While property crime rates are similar between the two countries, Canada reports much lower violent crime rates. This article does not provide any possible explanations as to why these differences exist. However, many analysts argue that the differences in violent crime between the two countries are due to more restrictive gun control laws in Canada and a juvenile justice system in that country that lowers levels of recidivism.

Over the past 20 years, Canada recorded much lower rates of violent crime than the United States did. However, rates for property offences have generally been higher in Canada, according to a comparison of police-reported crime between the two nations.

Crime rates in both countries have followed similar trends during the past two decades. After peaking in 1991, rates for both violent and property crime generally declined throughout the 1990s.

Based on selected offences, the United States has had a much higher rate of reported violent crime than Canada. The homicide rate was three times higher in the United States than it was in Canada, while the American rate for aggravated assault was double the Canadian rate. For robbery, the rate was 65% higher in the United States.

On the other hand, since 1990, Canada has recorded slightly higher rates of property crime, although the rates have gradually been converging during the late 1990s. Canada has higher reported rates than the United States for breaking and entering, motor vehicle theft and arson.

Rates for both violent and property offences also followed similar regional patterns in the two nations, rising from east to west.

Compared to American cities, Canadian cities had lower rates of homicides, aggravated assaults and robberies. However, property crime was more prevalent in Canadian urban centres.

Source: The Daily (December 18, 2001).

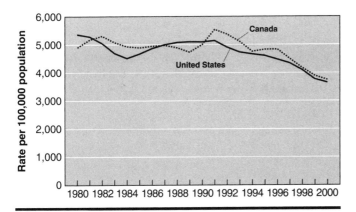

Canadian and U.S. rates of property crime[1] converged in the late 1990s

[1]Property crimes include break and enter, motor vehicle theft, and theft.

VIOLENT CRIME: U.S. RATES HIGHER
FOR HOMICIDE, ASSAULT AND ROBBERY

In 2000, police in the United States reported 5.5 homicides for every 100,000 population—triple the Canadian rate of 1.8. The number of homicides has declined in both countries during the 1990s, particularly south of the border. Two decades ago, the American homicide rate was about four times that of Canada.

About two-thirds of homicides in the United States involved a firearm, compared with one-third in Canada.

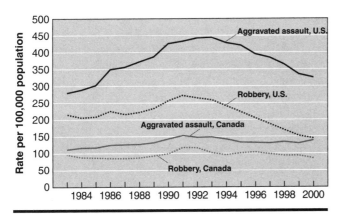

Rates of aggravated assault[1] and robbery higher in the U.S.

[1]For comparison purposes, the Canadian category of aggravated assault includes attempted murder, assault with a weapon and aggravated assault.

Note to Readers

This release is based on analysis in a new report, *Juristat: Crime comparisons between Canada and the United States*, which is available today from the Canadian Centre for Justice Statistics. The data came from the Canadian and American Uniform Crime Reporting (UCR) programs and the Canadian and American Homicide Surveys.

The different number of offences collected in the two UCR programs—106 in Canada and 8 in the United States—prevents direct comparison of the American and Canadian total crime rates. However, it is possible to group comparable offences to indicate overall crime patterns.

This release compares violent crime in the two countries on the basis of homicide, aggravated assault and robbery. Property crime is compared on the basis of breaking and entering, motor vehicle theft, theft and arson. Minor modifications were made for aggravated assault and arson to allow comparisons to be made.

These crime comparisons are based on incidents that come to the attention of police and do not necessarily represent the total volume of crime. Police-reported crime rates are influenced by a number of factors, including the willingness of the public to report crimes to the police, enforcement practices and reporting by police to the UCR programs. As a result, caution must be taken any time comparisons are made.

According to the 2000 International Crime Victimization Survey, which collects comparable Information on victimization across countries, the percentage of victims reporting crimes to the police is similar in Canada and the United States, and has been relatively stable in both countries over time.

To make the American and Canadian categories of aggravated assault comparable, three Canadian offences—attempted murder, assault with a weapon and aggravated assault—were collapsed into one.

In 2000, Americans were far more likely than Canadians to be victims of aggravated assault. The U.S. rate of 324 aggravated assaults for every 100,000 population was more than double the Canadian rate of 143. However, the U.S. rate has been falling since 1994, culminating with a 3% decline in 2000. In contrast, the Canadian rate has remained relatively stable since 1994, but was up 7% in 2000.

The American rate of reported robbery was 65% higher than in Canada in 2000, and the difference was much more pronounced with respect to robberies committed with a firearm. In 2000, firearms were involved in 41% of robberies south of the border, compared with only 16% in Canada. Since 1991, police-reported robbery rates have been declining in both countries. During this period, rates fell 47% in the United States—almost twice the 26% decline in Canada.

PROPERTY CRIME: CANADIAN RATES HIGHER FOR BREAK-INS, MOTOR VEHICLE THEFT AND ARSON

Reported rates for break-ins, motor vehicle theft and arson were all higher in Canada in 2000, whereas the United States reported 11% more thefts.

For most of the 1980s, the Canadian and American rates for breaking and entering were similar. However, between 1989 and 1991, the Canadian rate rose 21%, whereas the

American fell 2%. Since 1991, both nations have reported declines. In 2000, Canada had a nationwide rate of 954 break-ins for every 100,000 population, compared with the American rate of 728.

In 2000, Canadian police reported 521 motor vehicle thefts for every 100,000 population, 26% higher than the rate of 414 in the United States. Canada's rate has surpassed the U.S. level for the past five years.

This difference was primarily due to the fact that Canadians were twice as likely as Americans to experience thefts of trucks, minivans or sports utility vehicles. The rate of stolen cars is virtually the same between the two countries.

While shoplifting and "other thefts," such as pick-pocketing, were greater in the United States, Canadian police reported higher rates of bicycle theft. Since 1991, both countries have experienced general declines in total thefts.

Canada's arson rate of 45 per 100,000 population in 2000 was 41% higher than the American rate.

URBAN CRIME: U.S. CITIES LEAD IN VIOLENT CRIME

On average, for metropolitan areas with populations over 500,000, American cities had higher rates of homicide, aggravated assault, and robbery than did Canadian cities. This is consistent with the overall national patterns.

Police-reported rates of breaking and entering and motor vehicle theft were higher among Canadian urban centres with populations over 500,000 than among American cities with populations exceeding 500,000.

DRUG OFFENCES: U.S. ARREST RATE
THREE TIMES THAT OF CANADA

Two decades ago, the Canadian and American drug arrest rates were almost equal. In 2000, however, U.S. police arrested 581 persons with drug offences for every 100,000 population—three times higher than the Canadian rate of 177.

	CANADA		UNITED STATES	
	REAL TERMS	*RATE*	*REAL TERMS*	*RATE*
Homicide	542	1.8	15,517	5.5
Aggravated assault	43,933	143	910,744	324
Robbery	27,012	88	407,842	145
Break and enter	293,416	954	2,049,946	728
Motor vehicle theft	160,268	521	1,165,559	414
Other theft	683,997	2,224	6,965,957	2,475
Arson	13,724	45	78,280	32

Crime Rate Comparisons between Canada and the United States

[1]Rates are per 100,000 population.

[2]For comparison purposes, the Canadian category of aggravated assault includes attempted murder, assault with a weapon and aggravated assault.

It should be noted that the difference in these arrest rates may be more a reflection of the level of police enforcement and resources rather than actual behavioural patterns.

Since 1980, the American arrest rate for drug possession, trafficking and production has doubled, whereas the Canadian rate has declined 29%. That large increase in the United States is due to increases in arrests for drug possession. In 2000, U.S. police arrested 454 people for every 100,000 population for drug possession—over four times the rate of 100 in Canada.

32

Deaths Reflect Gun Use in U.S.

MICHAEL BOOTH

The gun-related death and homicide rate of children in the United States is many times higher than that of other industrialized countries. Whereas the United States has few restrictions on guns, other industrialized nations either restrict gun ownership or ban guns entirely. In the wake of shootings like those at Columbine High School, other countries have instituted strict gun regulations that have received extensive popular support.

Painful as it was to hear, while bombs were being defused and memorials were being planned in the Columbine High School community, there was an unmistakable chorus last week of "only in America."

The debate rages in the nation on how to sell, register, store, conceal and regulate guns. But there is agreement, among statistical experts in the United States and observers overseas, that guns make America a nation apart.

The gun-related death rate of U.S. children under the age of 15 is nearly 12 times higher than the combined totals of 25 other wealthy, industrialized nations, according to a major study by the Centers for Disease Control and Prevention in Atlanta.

The homicide rate by all causes for U.S. children is five times that in all those nations combined.

The United Nations compared firearms death rates around the world from 1994 and 1995 and found similar disparity. Of the 1,107 children around the world killed by firearms that year, 86 percent died in the United States.

The numbers for adult deaths from firearms are just as striking. Total firearm deaths in the United States in one year reached 35,957.

Japan had 93.

Of course, the United States has a much larger population than most industrialized nations, but that doesn't go far in explaining the difference. Broken down per capita, the U.S. rate of firearm deaths is more than triple the next closest nation, Canada.

In the year the CDC conducted its exhaustive study, three of four Asian countries surveyed reported no firearm deaths among children.

Source: Michael Booth. 1999. *The Denver Post* (April 25), pp. 1A, 19A. Reprinted by permission of *The Denver Post.*

"I don't think American children are inherently worse, or parents are less good parents. There can't be something unusual about Americans that they are more determined to commit violence," said Rebecca Peters, an Australian lawyer who consults around the world on violence issues.

"Our violence is just more lethal," said Franklin Zimring, a law professor at the University of California at Berkeley who compiles youth crime statistics. "So it must be the availability of the means. It's hard to explain how obviously it looks that way to people in other countries."

Guns were only part of the Columbine assault by teenagers Eric Harris and Dylan Klebold; they also exploded a series of homemade bombs assembled from household items that maimed victims with shrapnel. But they did carry an arsenal of rapid-fire handguns and shotguns. Their heavy weaponry was a factor they had in common with recent school killings in Jonesboro, Ark., Paducah, Ky., and Springfield, Ore.

Colorado State University violence expert Ernie Chavez noted that "in one year alone, Los Angeles County had more murders than Canada. I'd be hard pressed to think of any country not in the midst of a revolution that has more violence and weaponry than us."

Estimates on the number of existing firearms in the United States, including handguns, rifles and shotguns, range between 230 million and 250 million.

Other nations have either had longtime restrictions on gun ownership, ranging from careful licensing and registration to outright bans on handguns, or severely tightened their laws in the wake of tragedies similar to Columbine's.

The United States and its local governments have made incremental changes in basic gunownership rights, but even those have been sharply opposed by many gun owners. There are now severe restrictions in the United States on the sale or purchase of fully automatic weapons, and a national waiting period and background check were instituted in recent years.

Like most states, Colorado has no requirement to register or obtain a license for guns.

Guns laws did not change significantly in the United States in the wake of the terrible string of school shootings in the 1997–98 academic year.

U.S. and international child advocates say it would horrify them if gun laws did not change in the wake of the Columbine shootings.

International colleagues of Chicago pediatrician and violence expert Dr. Katherine Christoffel "can't understand how or why America tolerates the level of gun violence that we do," she said. "People in the rest of the world don't live like this."

The strongest U.S. advocate for the rights of gun ownership, the National Rifle Association, declined this week to debate political and international differences.

"I don't think now is an appropriate time to debate public policy, as the tragedy (in Colorado) continues to unfold," said Bill Powers, an NRA spokesman in Washington.

"Anything beyond continued heartfelt sympathy and prayers for the community is just not fitting. Anything beyond those sorts of feelings of respect are just out of line right now," Powers said.

In Great Britain, the 1996 massacre of 16 elementary school children and their teacher in Dunblane, Scotland, prompted an immediate call for a total ban on handguns. The clamor quickly resulted in a British ban on handguns above .22 caliber, and the turning in of 80 percent of the 200,000 handguns around the country.

	TOTAL FIREARMS DEATHS	FIREARM HOMICIDES	FIREARM SUICIDES	FATAL FIREARMS ACCIDENTS
(1995) United States	35,563	15,835	18,503	1,225
(1994) Australia	536	96	420	20
(1994) Canada	1,189	176	975	38
(1995) Germany	1,197	168	1,004	25
(1995) Japan	93	34	49	10
(1992) Sweden	200	27	169	4
(1994) Spain	396	76	219	101
(1994) United Kingdom	277	72	193	12
(1995) Vietnam	131	85	16	30

FIGURE 32.1   Deaths Due to Firearms
Researchers who have studied gun violence as if it were a disease have noted striking differences between the United States and other countries.
Source: Coalition to Stop Gun Violence. *The Denver Post*/Jonathan Moreno.

After a gunman with automatic rifles killed 35 people in Port Arthur, Tasmania, in 1996, Australia banned all automatic and semiautomatic weapons, including pump-action shotguns. The government bought back 700,000 weapons out of an estimated 4 million in the nation, melted them down and instituted strict licensing laws for the remainder, under which owners must justify in detail their need for a weapon.

Outright bans are politically unthinkable in the United States, even among strong advocates of handgun control.

"But there are two things consistent around the world, outside the U.S.," said Mark Pertschuk, Washington, D.C., legislative director for the Coalition to Stop Gun Violence. "No. 1, they have licensing and registration of firearms. No. 2, they have radically lower levels of death. It's not even a gray area," he said.

"It's not that licensing and registration is a one-step fix-it for all of our gun problems. But that's what characterizes an effective, modern system of firearm regulation."

Even after 15 deaths at one school in Colorado, the spectrum of voices speaking out for change in firearms laws remains extremely narrow. Some of the most schooled researchers in the field studiously avoid political comment.

Jim Mercy is one of the directors of a 10-year study on violence as a disease at the CDC. Researchers have concluded that access to firearms is one of the factors pushing America's violent death rates into the epidemiological warning zone.

But on the chances or the need for stricter U.S. gun control, Mercy says, "I think that's an issue I need to stay away from."

33

Reducing Crime by Harnessing
International Best Practices

IRVIN WALLER AND BRANDON C. WELSH

Unfortunately, the best knowledge available regarding how to prevent crime is seldom used in the United States. Exacerbating this problem is the fact that many Western governments, the United States included, are reducing expenditures and eliminating existing crime prevention programs for political reasons or to save costs. The authors of this article argue that employing the best practices of other countries, such as the family-based intervention programs of the United Kingdom, will prove most cost-effective in the long run by reducing spending on prisons and the need for additional police.

A great deal is now known about what works to prevent crime. Landmark reviews of scientific evidence by Sherman and his colleagues for the National Institute of Justice[1] and by Loeber and Farrington for the Office of Juvenile Justice and Delinquency Prevention[2] demonstrate that a great deal does indeed work and much more is promising.

Since 1994, the International Centre for the Prevention of Crime (ICPC),[3] based in Montreal, Canada, has been harnessing this U.S.-based knowledge and the evidence on what works from other countries to help solve local crime problems. Making crime prevention knowledge available and tailoring preventive actions to local conditions in cities and countries is a powerful tool in the effort to fight crime. Failure to use the best know-how to reduce crime slows human and economic development, particularly in fast-growing cities, which are the economic motors of most countries.

ICPC assists cities and countries in reducing delinquency, violence, and insecurity by investing in people and communities in more affordable and sustainable ways. As the central pillar of its efforts to harness crime prevention best practice globally, ICPC supports a Best Practice Bureau to systematically identify, compile, and disseminate information on successful crime prevention practice. It has designed a best practice program to encourage concrete implementation and has launched its "Towards the Use of Best Practice World Wide" Internet site and report.[4] As well, the Centre operates a comparative crime prevention research program to assess the successes, benefits, and directions of crime prevention cross-nationally.

Source: Irvin Waller and Brandon C. Welsh. 1998. *National Institute of Justice Journal* (October), pp. 26–31.

This article summarizes the work program of ICPC to assist cities and countries in reducing delinquency, violence, and insecurity. It reports on the Centre's approach to the prevention of crime, describes a number of proven and promising crime prevention practices around the world, and presents some of the evidence on the comparative economic advantages of investing in crime prevention.

CRIME PREVENTION AS A PROCESS

Successful crime prevention at the community level begins with a rigorous planning model—a process. It is characterized by a systematic analysis of the crime problem and the conditions that generate it, a review of the services and activities in place to tackle those conditions and ways to improve them, rigorous implementation of the program, and evaluation of the impact of the program on crime and its implementation so that improvements can be made. We view prevention activities that adhere to this model as "problem-solving partnerships"—measures developed as a result of a careful effort to identify causal factors while mobilizing the agencies able to influence those factors.

There is a need for this planning model to include efforts to forecast developments in crime, policing, and the social demography in which these occur. It is also important that these exercises are themselves collaborative so that the agencies that can influence the undesirable trends are involved from the beginning of the process.

Many models exist to help guide these efforts, and some are tailored to specific circumstances, such as high-crime neighborhoods. The European Forum for Urban Security, created by the Council of Europe in 1987 to act as the permanent crime prevention structure for Europe, has articulated the following guidelines for effective crime prevention policy and practice:

- The use of a central coalition to define problems and provide needed resources to address them, prepare action programs and the required staffing needs, and tailor local policy to changing conditions.
- The need for a technical coordinator to oversee and maintain the coalition's problem-solving partnership approach.
- Ongoing surveys of victimization, citizens' views of crime problems, and actions taken to keep the preventive practices up-to-date and targeted at local priorities and needs.[5]

There is also a need for strategies by central-government agencies to foster crime prevention at the local level. Research by ICPC[6] has identified the following core elements as important for the success of a central strategy that will foster effective local crime prevention:

- A central secretariat, with these characteristics:
  - —Staff, reporting to a senior official, with a budget for development.
  - —Capacity to mobilize key partners.
  - —Ability to propose strategies based on an analysis of crime problems and preventive practices.
- Delivery of preventive practices made possible through:
  - —Collaboration with other government departments.
  - —Development of local problem-solving partnerships.
  - —Involvement of citizens.

BEST PRACTICE IN CRIME PREVENTION

Many different types of crime prevention projects in various countries have reduced levels of delinquency and violent crime by tackling the causes—those that are conducive to victimization as well as those that generate criminal behavior—and by forming real partnerships at the local level.

For ICPC, crime prevention involves a range of strategies successfully pioneered in Europe, North America, and elsewhere. They involve initiatives by central and local governments as well as activities of the private sector, city management, urban planning, policing, the judiciary, schools, housing, social services, youth services, women's affairs, public health, universities, and the media. Figure 33.1 illustrates the impact of several examples of successful programs drawn from the three crime prevention strategies described below.

Projects selected for discussion are not limited to those where scientific evaluations have demonstrated a reduction in crime "beyond a reasonable doubt." Instead, we also have included projects where the "balance of probabilities" is that they reduced crime.[7]

FOSTERING BETTER DESIGN

Fostering better design is about the improvement of buildings, products, and communities to make it harder, more risky, or less rewarding for offenders to commit crime. This strategy is better known as situational crime prevention.[8] Two projects described below illustrate the extent to which residential burglary can be reduced through situational crime prevention techniques. Each of these projects evolved from an analysis of the causes of crime in which public and private agencies with the solutions were involved. No significant displacement of the crimes to the surrounding areas was found. However, some diffusion of benefits—unanticipated reductions in nontargeted crimes—occurred in adjacent areas.

In the late 1980s, a project team of city officials, police, social workers, and university researchers undertook to tackle repeat victimization in the Kirkholt housing project in Rochdale, England. Burglary victims were offered assistance in removing coin-operated

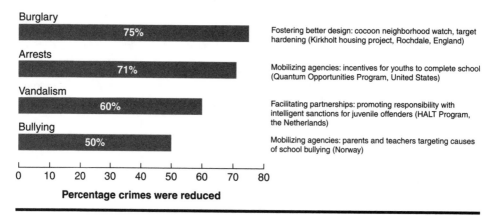

FIGURE 33.1 Problem-Solving Partnerships That Work

Sources: For Kirkholt, see note 9; for Quantum, see note 14; for HALT, see note 15; for Norway, see note 13.

electric and gas meters; in target hardening by upgrading home security with improved locks and bolts; and in establishing a "cocoon" neighborhood watch program in which six or more residents surrounding a victimized dwelling were asked to participate by watching and reporting anything suspicious. Before-after measures showed a 58-percent reduction in burglaries in the first year and a 75-percent reduction by the end of the third.[9]

In 1991, the Dutch safe housing label was initiated by police in the Rotterdam-Leiden-The Hague triangle. The label was introduced nationally in 1996. When housing project developers or housing associations apply for a police secured label, their project and its environment must be approved by the police as meeting standards relating to residents' participation and responsibility, neighborhood management, home watch, and building design. In Rotterdam, a 70-percent reduction in burglaries was observed following the program's first year in a comparison of participating and nonparticipating households.[10]

MOBILIZING AGENCIES

Poverty experienced during formative years, inconsistent and uncaring childrearing techniques, and parental conflict are some of the problems that place young people at increased risk for involvement in delinquency. Efforts to address these key risk factors and prevent child victimization in the home and at school at an early age can produce important short- and long-term downstream benefits in the form of reduced delinquency, later offending, and other related social problems. The crime prevention strategy of mobilizing agencies is about bringing together stakeholders, such as schools, housing, and social services, that have a role to play in addressing these risk factors and enhancing protective factors to improve the lives of children, young people, and their families. The following three programs demonstrate the value of this strategy in preventing delinquency and criminal behavior.

In the late 1970s, a program was initiated in Elmira, New York, to test the efficacy of nurse home visits on mothers' life course development and parental care of children. At the onset of the program, 400 pregnant women who possessed one or more high-risk characteristics (e.g., low socioeconomic status) were randomly assigned to 1 of 4 treatment conditions. The experimental group, which received postnatal home visits up to the child's second birthday, compared with the control group, which did not, showed impressive results across a range of prosocial outcomes, including more than a 75-percent reduction in child abuse and neglect (4 percent versus 19 percent).[11] A 13-year followup postintervention, when the children were 15 years old, confirmed a significant sustained reduction in child abuse and neglect.[12]

In 1983, a comprehensive antibullying program was initiated in 42 elementary schools across Norway. Key components of the program included a booklet for school personnel describing bully/victim problems and how to intervene effectively, information and advice for parents on how to deal with their child if a bully or a victim, and access to an informational video on bullying and its impact for the public. After 2 years, the project had reduced the prevalence of bullying by 50 percent.[13]

The Quantum Opportunities Program, which operated in five U.S. cities (San Antonio, Philadelphia, Milwaukee, Saginaw [Michigan], and Oklahoma City) from 1989 to 1993, offered disadvantaged teenagers afterschool activities for which they received small hourly stipends and a matching amount of funds in a college-fund account. The youths were encouraged to complete school through activities such as computer-assisted instruction, peer tutoring, homework assistance, community service and public event project activities, and development activities such as curriculum on life/family skills and college and job planning. In each city, 50 youths were randomly assigned to either a program group that received the intervention or a control group that did not. After 4 years, the program group achieved a 71-percent reduction in self-reported arrests compared with the control group. Program group members also were less likely to have dropped out of school (23 percent versus 50 percent) and were more likely to have graduated from high school (63 percent versus 42 percent).[14]

FACILITATING PARTNERSHIPS

The crime prevention strategy of facilitating partnerships is about bringing together police, justice services, and those concerned with social development to solve crime problems and promote effective and intelligent sanctions for offenders. In many cases, promoting responsibility is a central feature of programs adopting this strategy. The active ingredient is a focus on increasing the responsibility one holds for one's actions to the victim and the wider society. Two of the three projects reviewed below illustrate the potential crime reductions that can be achieved by this strategy.

In the Netherlands, the HALT Program was created to respond to the problem of youth vandalism. It involves collaboration between police, prosecutors, municipal authorities, victims, and the community to ensure that young offenders repair vandalism damage they have caused and to assist young people in resolving employment, housing, and education problems. After 1 year, the program group, compared with a matched control group, was more likely to have ceased involvement in vandalism (63 percent versus 25 percent)—a 60 percent overall reduction.[15] As a result of the program's success, it has been expanded to more than 40 sites across the country.

In the early 1990s in Scotland, a reeducation program for men convicted of violence against their female partners was started as a condition of a probation order. The program involved weekly group sessions over a period of 6 to 7 months. A quasi-experimental design was used to assess the effectiveness of the program compared with other criminal sanctions (e.g., prison, probation, fines). One year after intervention, female partners of men in the reeducation program (n=27) reported a much lower prevalence (occurrence of at least one incident), 33 percent versus 75 percent, and lower frequency (five or more incidents), 7 percent versus 37 percent, of violence perpetrated by their male partners compared with female partners of men who did not receive the intervention (n=59). This translates into a 56-percent decrease in the prevalence of violence and an 81-percent decrease in frequency.[16]

Throughout France, neighborhood justice "houses" and "offices" have been set up by the Ministry of Justice and local associations to address minor crimes and other legal problems through alternative justice approaches. Staff are trained to provide victim-offender mediation and are legally empowered to deal with cases. It is reported, although not proved, that everywhere they have been set up, they have relieved the courts and settled cases faster.

COST-EFFECTIVENESS OF CRIME PREVENTION

In Europe, North America, and other regions of the world, governments have been forced to find ways to reduce expenditures, restructure departments, and identify investments that will best meet the needs of their citizens. Major reforms have been implemented in areas such as health and education that are vital to citizens. For crime control, the strategic issues are only just beginning to be faced through efforts such as the Comprehensive Spending Review in the United Kingdom, which has reviewed effectiveness arguments in crime reduction and examined the comparative monetary advantages of spending on prisons vis-à-vis family-based intervention programs, for example.[17]

A recent study by The RAND Corporation[18] compared the estimated number of crimes that would be prevented by a $1 million investment in various strategies of intervening at different developmental stages in the lives of at-risk children with the number averted by California's three-strikes law. The study found that more monetary benefits from reduced crime were achieved from spending on parent training and graduation incentive strategies (see Quantum Opportunities Program above) than on the combined strategy of home visits and day care or probation or the three-strikes law.

In 1994, the newly elected government of the Netherlands dedicated an annual budget of 160 million guilders ($100 million) for local crime prevention efforts to tackle the early risk factors for delinquency and later criminal offending. This decision was based largely on scientific research carried out by the Dutch Ministry of Justice.[19] A simulation model using historical crime and crime control trends was developed to forecast the effects of four hypothetical scenarios on government spending on public safety (see Figure 33.2):

- Adding 1,000 extra police officers to a force of 27,620 officers.
- Extrapolating current trends (doing the same).
- Strengthening network criminality prevention—for example, police working with social agencies to address youth crime—to achieve a 10-percent decrease in crime.
- Increasing investment in situational crime prevention by 30 percent.

The situational prevention scenario was predicted to have the strongest effect on reducing criminal justice spending over time and was the most cost-effective. Network criminality

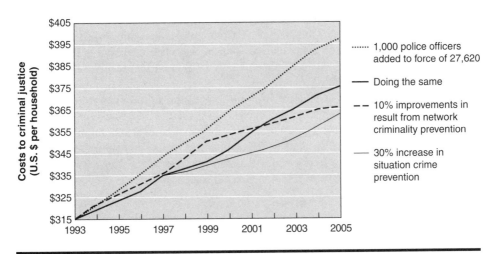

FIGURE 33.2   Crime Policy Scenarios (The Netherlands)

Source: Adapted from van Dijk (1997). See note 19.

prevention was predicted to be the next most effective strategy. The police scenario had the most undesirable impact. Its poor showing had to do with the direct contribution it made to criminal justice spending and its ineffectiveness in dealing with an hypothesized increase in violent crimes—the most expensive category of offenses. Furthermore, after 7 years—by the year 2000—adding more police was estimated to cost the government 100 million guilders (approximately $60 million) more had they done nothing.

MOVING FROM RHETORIC TO EFFECTIVE ACTION

In the last decade, prevention has achieved a prominent position in crime reduction think-ing and practice around the world. Efforts to foster better design, mobilize agencies, and facilitate partnerships have become synonymous with best practice in crime reduction. In many crime-ridden cities and communities where these strategies have been employed, substantial and lasting reductions in delinquency, violence, and insecurity have been achieved; a greater quality of life has been realized; and community and economic growth has flourished.

However, crime prevention remains more rhetoric than action. Governmental invest-ment in crime prevention is extremely low in most industrialized countries—between 2 and 3 percent of criminal justice spending—and is nonexistent in most developing countries and countries in transition.[20] The traditional, reactive approaches to dealing with crime—police, courts, and corrections—continue to dominate national crime policies. Little atten-tion has been paid to the scientific conclusions and the international consensus on what works most effectively to reduce crime.

The International Centre for the Prevention of Crime was set up to help overcome this inaction through its central mission of harnessing international best practice from around the world to solve crime problems. It engages in the exchange of international expertise to promote, for example, the efforts of its U.S.-based partners—the National Crime Prevention Council and the U.S. Conference of Mayors—in working with cities and communities through such well-known and successful projects as the Texas City Action Plan to Prevent Crime and the Comprehensive Communities Program. It offers technical assistance—strategic action-oriented analyses—at the national, local, and political levels to reduce crime more effectively and is a member of the White Paper team for the Minister of Safety and Security in South Africa.

ICPC also harnesses best practice in crime prevention by providing tools to raise awareness of crime prevention's impact. Such tools stress the importance of leadership, the affordability and cost-benefit of crime prevention, and the contribution of prevention strategies and programs to the sustainable development of cities and countries. With these efforts, ICPC is hopeful that effective action in reducing crime will replace the rhetoric that stands in the way of building safer communities and societies.

NOTES

1. Sherman, L. W., D. Gottfredson, D. MacKenzie, J. Eck, P. Reuter, and S. Bushway, *Preventing Crime: What Works, What Doesn't, What's Promising,* Office of Justice Programs Research Report, Washington, DC: U.S. Department of Justice, National Institute of Justice, 1997, NCJ 165366.

2. Loeber, R., and D. P. Farrington, eds., *Serious and Violent Juvenile Offenders: Risk Factors and Successful Interventions,* Thousand Oaks, CA: Sage Publications, Inc., 1998.

3. ICPC is a not-for-profit, nongovernmental organization. It is governed by a board of directors, combining the competencies of cities, prevention experts, the private sector, and specialized institutes from around the world, including the U.S. National Crime Prevention Council and the U.S. Conference of Mayors. It receives support from the governments of Belgium, Canada, France, the Netherlands, the United Kingdom, and the Province of Quebec, which make up an advisory and policy committee.

4. International Centre for the Prevention of Crime, *Towards the Use of Best Practice World Wide,* Montreal, Canada: International Centre for the Prevention of Crime, 1997. The key sections of this report are also available on the Internet at http://www.crime-prevention-intl.org.

5. European Forum for Urban Security, *Urban Security Practices,* Paris, France: European Forum for Urban Security, 1996.

6. Waller, I., B. C. Welsh, and D. Sansfaçon, *Crime Prevention Digest 1997. Successes, Benefits and Directions from Seven Countries,* Montreal, Canada: International Centre for the Prevention of Crime, 1997. This report is also available on the Internet at http://www.crime-prevention-intl. org. On the basis of an ICPC analysis of crime prevention strategies by central governments in seven industrialized countries, including the United States, ICPC regarded the listed elements as core because, among other reasons, government agencies using those elements have shown proven and promising results in preventing crime.

7. To meet the "balance of probabilities" criterion, a project or program must (1) use a problem-solving partnership approach (as defined in this article's section entitled "Crime prevention as a process") and (2) yield results based on at least one of the following: (a) a temporal sequence between the program and the crime or risk outcome clearly observed, or (b) a comparison group present without demonstrated comparability with the treatment group.

8. See Clarke, R. V., ed., *Situational Crime Prevention: Successful Case Studies,* 2d ed., Guilderland, NY: Harrow and Heston, 1997.

9. Forrester, D., S. Frenz, M. O'Connell, and K. Pease, *The Kirkholt Burglary Prevention Project: Phase II,* Crime Prevention Unit Paper, No. 23, London, England: Home Office, 1990.

10. Scherpenisse, R., "The Police Label for Secured Housing: Initial Results in the Netherlands," paper presented at the European Union Conference, "Crime Prevention: Towards A European Level," May 11–14, 1997, Noordwijk, Netherlands, 1997.

11. Olds, D. L., C. R. Henderson, R. Chamberlin, and R. Tatelbaum, "Preventing Child Abuse and Neglect: A Randomized Trial of Nurse Home Visitation, *Pediatrics* 78 (1986): 65–78.

12. Olds, D. L., J. Eckenrode, C. R. Henderson, H. Kitzman, J. Powers, R. Cole, K. Sidora, P. Morris, L. M. Pettitt, and D. Luckey, "Long-Term Effects of Home Visitation on Maternal Life Course and Child Abuse and Neglect: Fifteen-Year Follow-Up of a Randomized Trial," *Journal of the American Medical Association* 278 (1997): 637–643.

13. Olweus, D., "Bully/Victim Problems Among School Children: Basic Facts and Effects of a School Based Intervention Program," in The *Development and Treatment of Childhood Aggression,* ed. D. J. Pepler and K. H. Rubin, Hillsdale, NJ: Lawrence Erlbaum Associates, 1991: 411–448.

14. Hahn, A., *Evaluation of the Quantum Opportunities Program (QOP): Did the Program Work?,* Waltham, MA: Brandeis University, 1994.

15. Kruissink, M., *The HALT Program: Diversion of Juvenile Vandals,* Dutch Penal Law and Policy, The Hague, Netherlands: Research and Documentation Centre, Ministry of Justice, 1990. The control group numbered 90, the program group 179.

16. Dobash, R., R. Dobash, K. Cavanagh, and R. Lewis, *Research Evaluation of Programmes for Violent Men,* Edinburgh, Scotland: Scottish Office Central Research Unit, 1996.

17. Goldblatt, P., and C. Lewis, eds., *Reducing Offending: An Assessment of Research Evidence on Ways of Dealing With Offending Behaviour,* London, England: Home Office Research and Statistics Directorate, 1998.
18. Greenwood, P. W., K. E. Model, C. P. Rydell, and J. Chiesa, *Diverting Children from a Life of Crime: Measuring Costs and Benefits,* Santa Monica, CA: The RAND Corporation, 1996.
19. van Dijk, J. J. M., "Towards a Research-based Crime Reduction Policy: Crime Prevention as a Cost-effective Policy Option," *European Journal on Criminal Policy and Research* 5 (1997): 13 27
20. Waller, Welsh, and Sansfaçon, *Crime Prevention Digest 1997.*

Section 14

Drugs

THE UNITED STATES CONTEXT

The United States has defined some drugs as legal and others as illegal. The contradiction in this policy arises in that the legality of a drug is not correlated with its health consequences. The most dangerous drugs—nicotine and alcohol—are legal even though they are responsible for hundreds of thousands of deaths annually. Alcohol, alone, kills 25 times as many as all illegal drugs combined. Yet it (and tobacco) remain legal and the government wages a costly war against the drugs defined as illegal.

The prohibition against heroin, cocain, marijuana, methamphetamine, and others and the official policies to combat their use are intended to deter crime, but they have the opposite effect. By making drugs illegal and dangerous to produce, transport, and sell, the price is many times greater than if the drugs were legal. Thus, many users turn to crime to sustain their costly habit. Crime is also encouraged as organized crime imports, processes, and distributes the illicit drugs through its networks. This in turn promotes crime as violence between rival groups develops over disputed territorial boundaries. Moreover, the huge amounts of money involved sometimes corrupt police and other government agents. At another level, making drug use illegal creates crime by creating criminals. By labeling and treating these people as criminals, the justice system creates further crime by stigmatizing them, which makes reintegration into society after prison very difficult (about one-third of the prison population are drug offenders). The result, typically, is for the drug users to join together in a deviant drug subculture.

Another irony is that the drug war is intended to reduce the use of illicit drugs by the populace, yet it does not. It turns out that the nations with the most lenient approach (the Netherlands, for example) have *lower* drug use than found in the United States.

34

Does Europe Do It Better? Lessons from Holland, Britain, and Switzerland

ROBERT J. MACCOUN AND PETER REUTER

This article debunks some common myths associated with so-called liberal drug policies in Europe. The authors discuss innovative programs in Europe that use decriminalization, legalization, and drug maintenance to address problems associated with drug use.

Listen to a debate among drug policy advocates and you're likely to hear impassioned claims about the brilliant success (or dismal failure) of more "liberal" approaches in certain European countries. Frequently, however, such claims are based on false assumptions. For example, we are told that marijuana has been legalized in the Netherlands. Or that addicts receive heroin by prescription in Great Britain.

Pruned of erroneous or excessive claims, the experience in Europe points to both the feasibility of successful reform of US drug laws and the drawbacks of radical change. What follows are descriptions of some innovative approaches being tried over there, with judgments of their applicability over here. They fall into three broad categories: eliminating user sanctions (decriminalization), allowing commercial sales (legalization) and medical provision of heroin to addicts (maintenance).

DECRIMINALIZING MARIJUANA: THE CASE OF THE DUTCH COFFEE SHOPS

Dutch cannabis policy and its effects are routinely mischaracterized by both sides in the US drug debate. Much of the confusion hinges on a failure to distinguish between two very different eras in Dutch policy. In compliance with international treaty obligations, Dutch law states unequivocally that cannabis is illegal. Yet in 1976 the Dutch adopted a formal written policy of nonenforcement for violations involving possession or sale of up to thirty grams (five grams since 1995) of cannabis—a sizable quantity, since one gram is sufficient for two joints. Police and prosecutors were forbidden to act against users, and officials adopted

Source: Robert J. MacCoun and Peter Reuter, "Does Europe Do It Better? Lessons from Holland, Britain, and Switzerland." *The Nation* (September 20, 1999), pp. 28–30. Reprinted with permission from the September 20, 1999 issue of *The Nation.* Portions of each week's Nation magazine can be accessed at www.thenation.com.

a set of rules that effectively allowed the technically illicit sale of small amounts in licensed coffee shops and nightclubs. The Dutch implemented this system to avoid excessive punishment of casual users and to weaken the link between the soft and hard drug markets; the coffee shops would allow marijuana users to avoid street dealers, who may also traffic in other drugs. Despite some recent tightenings in response to domestic and international pressure (particularly from the hard-line French), the Dutch have shown little intention of abandoning their course.

In the initial decriminalization phase, which lasted from the mid-seventies to the mid-eighties, marijuana was not very accessible, sold in a few out-of-the-way places. Surveys show no increase in the number of Dutch marijuana smokers from 1976 to about 1984. Likewise, in the United States during the seventies, twelve US states removed criminal penalties for possession of small amounts of marijuana, and studies indicate that this change had at most a very limited effect on the number of users. More recent evidence from South Australia suggests the same.

From the mid-eighties Dutch policy evolved from the simple decriminalization of cannabis to the active commercialization of it. Between 1980 and 1988, the number of coffee shops selling cannabis in Amsterdam increased tenfold; the shops spread to more prominent and accessible locations in the central city and began to promote the drug more openly. Today, somewhere between 1,200 and 1,500 coffee shops (about one per 12,000 inhabitants) sell cannabis products in the Netherlands; much of their business involves tourists. Coffee shops account for perhaps a third of all cannabis purchases among minors and supply most of the adult market.

As commercial access and promotion increased in the eighties, the Netherlands saw rapid growth in the number of cannabis users, an increase not mirrored in other nations. Whereas in 1984 15 percent of 18- to 20-year-olds reported having used marijuana at some point in their life, the figure had more than doubled to 33 percent in 1992, essentially identical to the US figure. That increase might have been coincidental, but it is certainly consistent with other evidence (from alcohol, tobacco and legal gambling markets) that commercial promotion of such activities increases consumption. Since 1992 the Dutch figure has continued to rise, but that growth is paralleled in the United States and most other rich Western nations despite very different drug policies—apparently the result of shifts in global youth culture.

The rise in marijuana use has not led to a worsening of the Dutch heroin problem. Although the Netherlands had an epidemic of heroin use in the early seventies, there has been little growth in the addict population since 1976; indeed, the heroin problem is now largely one of managing the health problems of aging (but still criminally active) addicts. Cocaine use is not particularly high by European standards, and a smaller fraction of marijuana users go on to use cocaine or heroin in the Netherlands than in the United States. Even cannabis commercialization does not seem to increase other drug problems.

TREATING HEROIN ADDICTS IN BRITAIN

The British experience in allowing doctors to prescribe heroin for maintenance has been criticized for more than two decades in the United States. In a 1926 British report, the blue-ribbon Rolleston Committee concluded that "morphine and heroin addiction must be regarded as a manifestation of disease and not as a mere form of vicious indulgence," and hence that "the indefinitely prolonged administration of morphine and heroin" might be necessary for such patients. This perspective—already quite distinct from US views in the twenties—led Britain to adopt, or at least formalize, a system in which physicians could prescribe heroin to addicted patients for maintenance purposes. With a small population of several hundred patients, most of whom became addicted while under medical treatment, the system muddled along for four decades with few problems. Then, in the early sixties, a handful of physicians began to prescribe irresponsibly and a few heroin users began taking the drug purely for recreational purposes, recruiting others like themselves. What followed was a sharp relative increase in heroin addiction in the mid-sixties, though the problem remained small in absolute numbers (about 1,500 known addicts in 1967).

In response to the increase, the Dangerous Drugs Act of 1967 greatly curtailed access to heroin maintenance, limiting long-term prescriptions to a small number of specially licensed drug-treatment specialists. At the same time, oral methadone became available as an alternative maintenance drug. By 1975, just 12 percent of maintained opiate addicts were receiving heroin; today, fewer than 1 percent of maintenance clients receive heroin. Specialists are still allowed to maintain their addicted patients on heroin if they wish; most choose not to do so—in part because the government reimbursement for heroin mainte- nance is low, but also because of a widespread reluctance to take on a role that is difficult to reconcile with traditional norms of medical practice. Thus, one can hardly claim that heroin maintenance was a failure in Britain. When it was the primary mode of treatment, the heroin problem was small. The problem grew larger even as there was a sharp decline in heroin maintenance, for many reasons unrelated to the policy.

'HEROIN-ASSISTED TREATMENT': THE SWISS EXPERIENCE

What the British dropped, the Swiss took up. Although less widely known, the Swiss expe- rience is in fact more informative. By the mid-eighties it was clear that Switzerland had a major heroin problem, compounded by a very high rate of HIV infection. A generally tough policy, with arrest rates approaching those in the United States, was seen as a failure. The first response was from Zurich, which opened a "zone of tolerance" for addicts at the so-called "Needle Park" (the Platzspitz) in 1987. This area, in which police permitted the open buying and selling of small quantities of drugs, attracted many users and sellers, and was regarded by the citizens of Zurich as unsightly and embarrassing. The Platzspitz was closed in 1992.

Then in January 1994 Swiss authorities opened the first heroin maintenance clinics, part of a three-year national trial of heroin maintenance as a supplement to the large metha- done maintenance program that had been operating for more than a decade. The motivation for these trials was complex. They were an obvious next step in combating AIDS, but they also represented an effort to reduce the unsightliness of the drug scene and to forestall a strong legalization movement. The program worked as follows: Each addict could choose the amount he or she wanted and inject it in the clinic under the care of a nurse up to three times a day, seven days a week. The drug could not be taken out of the clinic. Sixteen small clinics were scattered around the country, including one in a prison. Patients had to be over 18, have injected heroin for two years and have failed at least two treatment episodes. In fact, most of them had more than ten years of heroin addiction and many treatment failures. They were among the most troubled heroin addicts with the most chaotic lives.

By the end of the trials, more than 800 patients had received heroin on a regular basis without any leakage into the illicit market. No overdoses were reported among participants while they stayed in the program. A large majority of participants had maintained the regime of daily attendance at the clinic; 69 percent were in treatment eighteen months after admission. This was a high rate relative to those found in methadone programs. About half of the "dropouts" switched to other forms of treatment, some choosing methadone and others abstinence-based therapies. The crime rate among all patients dropped over the course of treatment, use of nonprescribed heroin dipped sharply and unemployment fell from 44 to 20 percent. Cocaine use remained high. The prospect of free, easily obtainable heroin would seem to be wondrously attractive to addicts who spend much of their days hustling for a fix, but initially the trial program had trouble recruiting patients. Some addicts saw it as a recourse for losers who were unable to make their own way on the street. For some participants the discovery that a ready supply of heroin did not make life wonderful led to a new interest in sobriety.

Critics, such as an independent review panel of the World Health Organization (also based in Switzerland), reasonably asked whether the claimed success was a result of the heroin or the many additional services provided to trial participants. And the evaluation relied primarily on the patients' own reports, with few objective measures. Nevertheless, despite the methodological weaknesses, the results of the Swiss trials provide evidence of the feasibility and effectiveness of this approach. In late 1997 the Swiss government approved a large-scale expansion of the program, potentially accommodating 15 percent of the nation's estimated 30,000 heroin addicts.

Americans are loath to learn from other nations. This is but another symptom of "American exceptionalism." Yet European drug-policy experiences have a lot to offer. The Dutch experience with decriminalization provides support for those who want to lift US criminal penalties for marijuana possession. It is hard to identify differences between the United States and the Netherlands that would make marijuana decriminalization more dangerous here than there. Because the Dutch went further with decriminalization than the few states in this country that tried it—lifting even civil penalties—the burden is on US drug hawks to show what this nation could possibly gain from continuing a policy that results in 700,000 marijuana arrests annually. Marijuana is not harmless, but surely it is less damaging than arrest and a possible jail sentence; claims that reduced penalties would "send the wrong message" ring hollow if in fact levels of pot use are unlikely to escalate and use of cocaine and heroin are unaffected.

The Swiss heroin trials are perhaps even more important. American heroin addicts, even though most are over 35, continue to be the source of much crime and disease. A lot would be gained if heroin maintenance would lead, say, the 10 percent who cause the most harm to more stable and socially integrated lives. Swiss addicts may be different from those in the United States, and the trials there are not enough of a basis for implementing heroin maintenance here. But the Swiss experience does provide grounds for thinking about similar tests in the United States.

Much is dysfunctional about other social policies in this country, compared with Europe—the schools are unequal, the rate of violent crime is high and many people are deprived of adequate access to health services. But we are quick to draw broad conclusions from apparent failures of social programs in Europe (for example, that the cost of an elaborate social safety net is prohibitive), while we are all too ready to attribute their successes to some characteristic of their population or traditions that we could not achieve or would not want—a homogeneous population, more conformity, more intrusive government and the like. It's time we rose above such provincialism.

The benefits of Europe's drug policy innovations are by no means decisively demonstrated, not for Europe and surely not for the United States. But the results thus far show the plausibility of a wide range of variations—both inside and at the edges of a prohibition framework—that merit more serious consideration in this country.

35

The Netherlands' Drug Policy

BOB KEIZER

This brief article is from a presentation to the Royal Society of Edinburgh's symposium on Scotland's Drug Problem by the drug policy adviser to the Dutch Ministry of Health. He describes the Dutch drug policies and the reasons these policies are relatively tolerant. The objective of the Dutch drug policy is to prevent or to limit the risks and harm associated with drug use, both to the user and his/her environment. The author states, for example, that by not prosecuting small-scale marijuana dealing and use, the users, who are mainly young people experimenting, are not criminalized and not forced to move in criminal circles, where the risk that they will be pressed to try more dangerous drugs is much greater.

1. INTRODUCTION

In order to understand Dutch drug policy, one first needs to know something about the Netherlands itself. After all, a drug policy needs to be in keeping with the characteristics and culture of the country that produces it. The Netherlands is one of the most densely populated countries in the world. A population of around 16 million lives in an area the size of 41.200 km. Trade and transport have traditionally been key industries in our country, and the Netherlands is universally regarded as the "gateway to Europe." The Dutch have a strong belief in individual freedom and in the division between "church" (in other words, morality) and state. We believe in pragmatism. At the same time, the Netherlands is characterised by a strong sense of responsibility for collective welfare. It has an extremely extensive system of social facilities and health care and education systems that are available to all. The Netherlands has long been a country of great political diversity. Our administrative system is decentralised to the local authorities to a large extent (particularly where drug policy is concerned).

2. THE BASIC PRINCIPLES OF DUTCH DRUG POLICY

These characteristics of our country are reflected in our present drug policy, which was formulated in the mid-seventies. A wide range of addict care facilities is available. Dutch

Source: Bob Keizer, Head of Addiction Policy Division, Ministry of Health, Welfare and Sport, The Netherlands, "The Netherlands' Drug Policy." Introduction presented at drug hearings in 2003.

policy does not moralise, but is based on the assumption that drug use is a fact and must be dealt with as practical as possible. The most important objective of our drug policy is therefore to prevent or to limit the risks and the harm associated with drug use, both to the user himself and to his environment. Because of this, the Ministry of Health is responsible for co-ordinating drug policy. The cornerstone of this policy is the law (the Opium Act), which is based on two key principles. Firstly, it distinguishes between different types of drugs on the basis of their harmfulness (hemp products on the one hand, and drugs that represent an "unacceptable" risk on the other). Secondly, the law differentiates on the basis of the nature of the offence, such as the distinction between possession of small quantities of drugs intended for personal use, and possession intended for dealing purposes. Possession of up to 30 grams of cannabis is a minor offence. Possession of more than 30 grams is a criminal offence. Drug use is not an offence. This approach gives us scope to pursue a balanced policy through our application of criminal law.

Dealing in small quantities of cannabis, through the outlets known as coffee shops, is tolerated under strict conditions. This tolerance is a typically Dutch policy instrument which is based on the power of the Public Prosecutor to refrain from prosecuting offences. This principle is formulated in the law and is called the "expediency principle." The small-scale dealing carried out in the coffee shops is thus an offence from a legal viewpoint, but under certain conditions it is not prosecuted. These conditions are: no advertising, no sales of hard drugs, no nuisance must be caused, no admittance of and sales to minors (under the age of 18), and no sales exceeding 5 grams of cannabis per transaction. The stock of the Coffeeshop should not exceed 500 grams of cannabis.

The idea behind the Netherlands' policy towards the coffee shops is that of harm limitation. This is based on the argument that if we do not prosecute small-scale cannabis dealing and use under certain conditions, the users—who are mainly young people experimenting with the drug—are not criminalized (they do not get a criminal record) and they are not forced to move in criminal circles, where the risk that they will be pressed to try more dangerous drugs such as heroin is much greater.

Many people think that drugs are legally available in the Netherlands, and that we make no effort to combat the supply side of the drug market. Nothing could be further from the truth. There is continual, intensive co-operation between the addict care system, the judicial authorities and the public administrators. With the exception of small-scale cannabis dealing in coffeeshops, tackling all other forms of drug dealing and production has high priority. The police and customs officials regularly seize large hauls of drugs and collaborate closely with other countries in the fight against organised crime. The punishability of drug-related offences is comparable with that in many other countries, and the extent to which we enforce our drug laws is also closely comparable with that in our neighbour countries. The Netherlands has one of the largest prison capacities in Europe, and 25 % of the cells are occupied by violators of our drug laws.

3. RESULTS

We have pursued this policy for over 25 years now. What results has it achieved, measured in terms of its most important objective: harm limitation?

• Cannabis use: As in all other countries the number of regular hemp smokers in the Netherlands has increased in recent years, and the age at which users start has gradually decreased. People who have problems with cannabis use are also making increasing demands on the addict care system during the last few years. There are also signs that cannabis use is stabilising and even is decreasing. However, it is striking that international comparative studies show that both the trend towards increased use and the present scale of use are comparable with those in the countries surrounding the Netherlands, such as Germany, France and Belgium, and certainly lower than those in the United Kingdom and the United States.[1] These statistics suggest that there is almost no connection between the increase in cannabis use and the policy pursued in respect of the users.

• Hard drug addicts: Thanks to a high standard of care and prevention, including the large-scale dispensation of methadone and clean hypodermics, a situation has developed in the Netherlands which is only comparable with that in a handful of other countries. The number of problem addicts is about 3.0 per 1000 inhabitants. This means that the Netherlands is among the countries with the smallest number of problem addicts in the European Union.[2]

• Although we have seen a rise in cannabis use for ten years, the number of problem addicts has been stable over the same period. From this, we can therefore conclude that the "stepping stone" theory has not proved to hold true in our country.

• The population of heroin and crack users in the Netherlands consists of more or less the same group of people, as evidenced by the fact that each year, their average age goes up by almost a year. At the moment, it is roughly 40. Not many young people are taking up heroin or crack. The health damage caused by hard drug use has remained limited. The number of drug deaths[3] and addicts infected with HIV is low. A further consequence of our policy is that a relatively large percentage of the drug users in our country are reasonably well integrated into society.

• Like our neighbor countries, we have noticed an increase in XTC use in recent years. The rate of current use among young people is around 1.4%. Here, however, the use rate has been decreasing significantly recently.

4.   RECENT DEVELOPMENTS AND POINTS FOR DISCUSSION

It will be clear from all of this that, bearing in mind our objective of harm limitation, our policy is reasonably successful. So does this mean that the Netherlands' drug policy is an ideal policy? No, far from it. We are continually confronted with a host of problems, and this means that we are also continually having to modify our policy. Here is a summary of the most significant policy developments and political topics for debate that have arisen in the last few years:

a. Coffee shops

It became clear in the early 'nineties that a number of problems were occurring around the coffee shops. These included problems such as (petty) criminal acts committed by owners and customers, customers hanging around and the comings and goings of the customers' cars, which sometimes caused a nuisance to people living in the neighborhood. The latter was particularly true in the border regions, where more and more foreigners took to visiting the coffee shops to buy cannabis. In response to this, compliance with the conditions was monitored more strictly and the number of coffee shops was also reduced in a number of municipalities. In 1997 the number of coffee shops was estimated at 1179; in 2003 only 754 remained. To reduce drugs tourism, the Dutch authorities also decided to reduce the amount of cannabis that could be sold from 30 grams to 5 grams per transaction.

The reason for doing this was not that we no longer believed in the coffee shop phenomenon, but that the authorities wanted to gain greater control over it. The coffeeshop policy is the primary responsibility of the local administration. The mayors, police chiefs and local politicians of the Netherlands still continue to support the concept. Their argument for doing so is that it is better to control half of the problem than nothing at all. Closing the coffee shops will certainly lead to an increase in dealing on the streets, in private homes and in school playgrounds, which will undoubtedly be accompanied by hard drug sales, while the rate of use among the population will not decline, bearing in mind the figures for use in other countries.

b. Drug dealing and production

In the last few years it has become increasingly clear that some international drug dealing and production activities are being carried out from or through the Netherlands. This mainly applies to the production and transit of XTC and cannabis.

We have been tackling XTC and cannabis dealing and production more intensively in recent years. As a result of this policy, the quantities of drugs seized have increased significantly.

As already remarked, it is a misconception to think that we pursue a tolerant policy towards large-scale drug dealing and production. Nonetheless, the central question is, and remains, this: is large-scale drug dealing and production occurring in the Netherlands because of our policy of tolerance towards users and our coffee shop policy, or is it independent of them?

There is some evidence to support this first view when we look at the 'eighties, a time when we—like many other countries—were not sufficiently alert to the role of organised drug crime. However, this is not true of the 'nineties, as evidenced by the earlier remarks about the efforts of the Dutch police, customs officials and judicial authorities. From the (little) research that has been carried out into the question of whether the Netherlands' drug policy attracts criminals, it appears to be more likely that organised crime simply uses the Netherlands' good infrastructure, the presence of a high-quality chemical industry, the absence of border controls and the massive volume of legal goods flows to conduct its own trade. Every year, Rotterdam transships more than 6 million (!) containers. You need not be a mathematical genius to recognise that even with the strictest detection methods, there is a strong chance that a significant proportion of the trade will not be checked.

c. Nuisance caused by hard drug users

In the early 'nineties the behaviour of heavily addicted drug users began attracting more and more criticism from members of the public. There was a small category of hard drug users who were a constant source of considerable social and judicial nuisance. This took the form of petty crime, disorderly conduct, and making the public feel unsafe. This group comprises roughly 20% of the addict population. The government responded quickly by developing an extensive programme and providing a relatively large budget to fund it. The politicians realised that a drug policy only works if it is supported by the public, and that support was in danger of being lost.

d. Criticism from other countries

Dutch drug policy came in for a good deal of criticism from other countries in recent years. We took this criticism seriously right from the start.

The criticism focused on two main areas. There were well-founded complaints—about trans-border drug trading, for example—but also complaints about the underlying philosophy of the Netherlands' policy. Some countries felt that we had the wrong attitude and that we were setting the wrong example to the world.

In the early 'nineties the bulk of the criticism came from Germany. So we entered into an intensive dialogue with the Germans. The past four years have been characterised by virtually no criticism of the Netherlands' policy. Methadone dispensation has been widespread in Germany, Germany has been setting up experiments with heroin dispensation, and the cannabis policies of the federal states are now comparable with the Dutch policy (although Germany has no coffeeshops).

We have gone through a similar process with France. Various collaborative projects were then started, and Franco-Dutch relations are now excellent again.

Sweden and the US were the next countries to suddenly begin expressing fierce criticism of the Netherlands' drug policy. In this case, the criticism was mainly of a moral nature.

The Netherlands was far from happy with these attacks on our drug policy. We did whatever we could to respond to the criticisms. But the effect of this foreign criticism was not to persuade us to abandon the fundamental principles of our drug policy. Why not?

It was not because we had a sacred belief in our own policy, at any rate. We are well aware of our drug policy's shortcomings and failures. But the main reason why we have not changed tack is our view that, in many respects, the results of our policy are no worse—and in some respects they are better—than the results achieved in comparable countries. Based on the facts and figures, we feel that there are not many desirable alternatives. What is more, in recent years a large number of countries have begun pursuing policies that are more or less comparable with the Dutch approach. If you separate the international debate from the political rhetoric, it is clear that the Netherlands does not have a particularly eccentric policy at all. International opinions at the scientific and practical levels actually differ far less widely than some politicians want people to think. In practice, a rapid process of bottom-up drug policy harmonisation is currently taking place in a number of European countries.

NOTES

1. E.g: last month prevalence pupils 15–16 yrs Netherlands 13%, Ireland 17%, UK 20%, France 22%, USA 17%; General population, recent use: Netherlands 6%, UK 11%, France 8%, USA 11% (NDM, EMCDDA a.o.).
2. Netherlands 3.0, Germany 3.1, France 4.3, Sweden 4.5, UK 9,4, Italy 7.5 (per 1000 inhabitants) (EMCDDA).
3. Acute Drug related deaths per 100.000 inhabitants (2002): Netherlands 0.6, Germany 1.4, Sweden 1.8, (NDM, EMCDDA) For more detailed information: www.trimbos.nl or www.emcdda.org.